Napoleon the Novelist

Naissance de Napoléon.

Napoleon the Novelist

Andy Martin

Polity

The right of Andy Martin to be identified as author of this work has been asserted in accordance with the Copyright, Designs and Patents Act 1988.

First published in 2000 by Polity Press in association with Blackwell Publishers Ltd

Editorial office:
Polity Press
65 Bridge Street
Cambridge CB2 1UR, UK

Marketing and production:
Blackwell Publishers Ltd
108 Cowley Road
Oxford OX4 1JF, UK

Published in the USA by
Blackwell Publishers Inc.
Commerce Place
350 Main Street
Malden, MA 02148, USA

ISBN 0-7456-2535-5
ISBN 0-7456-2536-3 (pbk)

A catalogue record for this book is available from the British Library and has been applied for from the Library of Congress.

Typeset in 11 on 13pt Berling
by Graphicraft Ltd, Hong Kong
Printed in Great Britain
by MPG Books Ltd, Bodmin, Cornwall

This book is printed on acid-free paper.

For Issam

Contents

Acknowledgements

Abdication de Napoléon 1814.

I would like to thank all those people who, by a combination of nagging, bullying, constructive criticism, scorn and sheer indifference, have helped me to finish this book. I am particularly indebted to the professor of French who once ranked 'Napoleon's Novels' right up there with 'Bossuet's Sermons' for its insane lack of sex-appeal. I am also grateful to Addenbrooke's Hospital for putting me *hors de combat* with a knee operation and thereby enabling me to complete the first draft unhindered by the claims of mobility.

Andy Martin
Cambridge, May 2000

The extract from the *Mercure de France* is reproduced by permission of the Syndics of Cambridge University Library. The cartoons from the *Histoire de Napoléon* are reproduced by permission of the Musée Carnavalet (photograph © Photothèque des Musées de la Ville de Paris).

Material from chapter 1 first appeared in *Raritan* (spring 2000), and part of chapter 4 appeared in the Napoleon number of *Modern and Contemporary France* (October 2000).

It may be that universal history is the history of the different intonations given a handful of metaphors.

(Borges)

Achilles exists only by the grace of Homer. Take away the art of writing from this world and you will probably take away its glory.

(Chateaubriand)

I cannot put my pen down.

(Napoleon)

I, Napoleon

Napoléon au mont St-Bernard.

For more than a decade, Stanley Kubrick dreamed of making an epic film of the life of Napoleon, *The Napoleon Symphony*, based on a script by Anthony Burgess, with music by Beethoven. He got as far as hiring the entire army of a medium-sized European country to serve as extras in the battle scenes. The only difference between Napoleon and Kubrick was that Kubrick didn't actually intend to kill anyone. Of course, Kubrick's great plan never quite came to fruition. Nor did Napoleon's.

Sticking one arm inside your jacket and mistaking yourself for Napoleon is still a synonym for madness (even if delusions of grandeur have found other icons to hang their hat on). And yet in the vast lunatic asylum that is the nineteenth century just about everyone from Victor Hugo and Balzac through to Henry James thought of themselves, at one time or another, in one way or another, as Napoleon. Everyone that is, paradoxically enough, except Napoleon himself. Napoleon thought of himself as an extremely successful imaginative writer.

On other occasions, admittedly, he also thought of himself as Jesus Christ, Joan of Arc and Alexander the Great. A certain instability of identity appears to have been integral to his character. *Je est un autre* ('I is another'), in Rimbaud's resonant

phrase, is another classically Napoleonic theme: 'I put an end to
the war in the Vendée by becoming a Catholic; I established
myself in Egypt by becoming a Muslim . . . If I governed a nation
of Jews, I would restore the temple of Solomon.' But what is
indisputably true is that Napoleon began and ended his glorious
career purely as a writer. In the midst of the French Revolution,
Napoleon was grappling with an essay on Happiness which he
hoped would establish him as the new Rousseau. At the end
of his life on Saint Helena, in a prison that became a writers'
colony, he had little choice but to return to his confessions.

Most modern histories of Napoleon are constructed like a
sandwich, with the central section made of radically different
(denser and more nourishing) stuff to the (thin and weight-
less to the point of insignificant) outer layers. But the whole
middle period of Napoleon's life – from the point at which he
takes his rag-tag army over the Alps into Italy, through his
self-proclamation as emperor, right up to the day when he is
captured and sent into exile and a lingering death after Waterloo
– is a natural consequence of his love-affair with language and
literature. During the voyage across the Mediterranean which
would launch his Egyptian expedition, all the while dodging
Nelson's warships, he was still conducting a seminar on the
Discourse on Inequality and arguing about the merits of Homer
versus Ossian. The Empire was less an overflow of revolutionary
zeal than a substitute for the sentimental (but tragic) novel he
sketched out but failed to write. Balzac would say later that he
wanted to do in literature what Napoleon had done in politics.
But, conversely, we may say that Napoleon was at his most
Balzacian in his efforts to rearrange the globe in his own image.
There is, in short, a perfect continuum between Napoleon the
novelist and Napoleon, emperor, liberator and tyrant. Technically, Napoleon only became a dictator at the point at which
he switched from writing to having his thoughts set down by
a team of secretaries. But (as he wrote to Josephine) he could
never quite put down the pen.

This may be the first short book on Napoleon. When Scott
and Hazlitt wrote the first biographies in English of Napoleon
they ran to three or more stout volumes. Modern descendants
still favour the encyclopedic, inclusive, Napoleonic approach.
I have taken a resolutely non-Napoleonic stance on Napoleon

by preferring an aesthetics of omission. But still I can't help being Napoleonic by virtue of obsessing about writing and having an imperfect command of the French language.

Twentieth-century historians have, on the whole, been sophisticated and ironic readers, shrewdly refusing ever to take at face-value anything Napoleon said or wrote. I, on the other hand, have picked up and dusted down the more aesthetic early nineteenth-century view of Napoleon: or, rather, a late eighteenth-century view, echoing Antoine Arnault, who sent a copy of his latest play, *Oscar*, to Napoleon who was busy liberating and looting Italy at the time. Arnault appended the following dedication: 'You, whose youth has been spent playing the games of both Apollo and Mars, like the first of the Caesars; you, with a pen in one hand and a sword in the other, who, perhaps in the midst of your military camp, are writing immortal memoirs: if possible, tear yourself away from them for a few moments and find the time to read my work between victories.' There was no inevitable opposition between pen and sword, active and contemplative. Napoleon invited Arnault to be his collaborator and suggested that they should 'produce a tragedy together'. There never was a dramatic moment of 'choice' (as Jean Tulard has it) between literary and political ambition: Napoleon never gave up one for the other. If I have slightly reversed the priority granted by the last century or so, I am only following in the line of Sainte-Beuve, who naturally assumed that, when all the sound and fury had died down, what was left behind, like an archaeology or geology of the period, was literature: 'words illuminated and irradiated by the memory of action'.

Michelet emphasized the shiftiness of Napoleon, his capacity for self-mythification, defining him as a 'comédien' par excellence. Chateaubriand denounced Napoleon for his 'taste for vulgar literature and habit of writing for newspapers'. Stendhal, with his fondness for reading the Code Napoléon before commencing another novel, paid tribute to the austere poetry of the Bulletins de la Grande Armée. Thiers described Napoleon (not without hyperbole) as 'the greatest writer of the century'. Sainte-Beuve admired his concision, comparing him to Pascal, and added that he was also 'a great critic in his spare time'. But perhaps only Victor Hugo, in lyrical fits of

Napoleonic nostalgia, grasped that the would-be novelist, poet, and journalist (a CV which – with appropriate modifications – could describe Victor Hugo), and the ultimate political and military adventurer were indivisible. The Empire was shaped by a preeminently literary mind. Conversely, no writing is innocent or merely subversive: there is a secret affinity between novelists and Napoleon. And Napoleon and historians. You don't have to want to rule the world to write about Napoleon, but it probably helps.

In 1989, on the bicentenary of the fall of the Bastille, Umberto Eco conducted a survey (in the Italian magazine *Espresso*) which asked, among other questions, 'Who was the greatest hero of the French Revolution?' Danton, Robespierre and even Marat got their share of votes, but the clear winner in the revolutionary hero stakes was: Napoleon. Such are the retrospective rewrites of our collective memory: in fact he distinguished himself by taking little or no part in that immense drama, except to bring the curtain down on it. Supremely ambiguous, half-saviour, half-satan, he continues to fascinate us by his very ambiguity. The colossal rise and his catastrophic fall provide us with a decent working definition of historical tragedy, with the emphasis on hubris. But in order to come to terms with his legacy we need to understand first of all his personal passion for the text. He invited Goethe to Paris to write up his life-story, which might have been called *The Sorrows of Young Napoleon*. But he was not only the stuff of which narratives are made: he 'found the novel in his cradle' (to quote Chateaubriand) and took it with him down to his grave.

When Napoleon went off to battle the French cavalry towed along not just innumerable cannon but a 'portable library' (which he had designed to his own specifications) piled high with a thousand works for entertainment, reflection and improvement. He was particularly attached to theatre and identified strongly with the heroes of Corneille. And in his *oeuvres complètes* he has left behind him some fifty-odd volumes of assorted genres, from the short story and poems through to Enlightenment discourses and grand-scale histories, and not excluding Socratic dialogues.

In his love affairs he was above all a fantasist, less physical than metaphysical, driven by recollections of Rousseau's *La*

Nouvelle Héloïse and Bernardin de Saint-Pierre's *Paul et Virginie*. And there is an element of science fiction in his vision of a seamless, bloodless future of instantaneous and harmonious communications, his synthesis of text, technology and theology. In trying to put Babel back together again, he looked forward to everyone speaking in the same language and thinking rather similar thoughts. At the same time he embraced relativism. A son of the Enlightenment, he was in many ways France's first postmodernist, ironic, sceptical, devious, a self-professed semiotician *avant la lettre*, hooked on the hallucinatory potential of the signifier, an inmate of the hyperreal. Not five minutes after being introduced, Pierre-Louis Roederer recalls, 'we had a long conversation together on pasigraphy [a system of universal writing] and the influence of signs on ideas.' Napoleon remarked that a revolution is 'nothing but an opinion that has acquired some bayonets'. So, similarly, France, Europe, the World, were above all concepts, to be backed up or deconstructed by armies and artillery. But his fundamental lack of a hard empirical sense of reality also led him to tolerate a few million deaths in the pursuit of an idea of happiness.

Although the two words 'Napoleon' and 'empire' have become indissociable, Napoleon practically put the French Empire into reverse: it was actually less extensive at the end of his term than at the beginning. Thus his real contribution on the ground was less than nothing. His more durable impact was at the level of imprinting a certain aesthetics of empire on the French mind (and not just the French). Napoleon's world-view was fashioned out of romantic idealism. But this by no means implies a hazy, alienated, poetic self-consciousness. Curiously, Napoleon does indeed see himself, on his travels – despite being accompanied by masses of French troops – as wandering lonely as a cloud (although 'isolated as an island' would be his preferred metaphor). But his overvaluation of the imaginary and the symbolic, and his undervaluation of the real, are precisely what underlie his ruthlessness. Everything and everyone was, in essence, a fiction, susceptible to rewriting, editing and omission, creation and destruction. And the idea of the unhappy ending – death or suicide or protracted torment – was built into Napoleon's narratives from the beginning.

My children read 'horrible histories' (of rotten Romans, vicious Vikings and the like) which make the bold claim to 'leave all the boring bits out'. Napoleon, similarly, feared *ennui* and abbreviated his own edition of Rousseau's novel. I am naturally anxious, therefore, that in playing down the spectacular and gory aspects of his career, and allowing a lot of the action to take place off stage, I have done nothing but put the boring bits back in and left all the interesting bits out. My hope is that *Napoleon the Novelist* still tells a horrible enough history, even without Beethoven and the thousands of extras.

1

A Prize for Happiness

Napoléon à l'école militaire.

Rousseau was on his way to prison when he became a writer. It was around two in the afternoon.

In the late summer of 1749 Jean-Jacques Rousseau was going to pay one of his regular visits to his friend Denis Diderot, who had been locked up in the château of Vincennes for atheism and libel. He was too broke to pay the coachride, so he walked. But it was a good two leagues (nearly six miles) from the rue de l'Opéra in Paris to Diderot's place of imprisonment, and on this day he was going alone (he often went in the company of Diderot's wife), so he took along some reading matter.

It was a hot day and one easily pictures Rousseau contemplating the rural landscape as he strides along and then pauses, from time to time, in the shade of a tree to rest and leaf through the pages of a book. But in fact the trees at the side of the road had been brutally pruned and afforded little relief from the sun. Surprisingly, Rousseau had picked up the habit of reading as he walked, to prevent himself walking too fast in the heat, he claimed (in the *Confessions*). This gives a completely unexpected snapshot of the archetypal Romantic *promenade solitaire* in the countryside.

'Enough of science and of art,' protested Wordsworth, 'Close up those barren leaves' and head for the woods if you want truth. But if Rousseau goes for a walk in the woods it is only with his head buried in a book. If he bumps into a tree it is because he is not looking where he is going. The odes, the sonnets and the reveries on mountains and rivers and forests and the awe-inspiring wilderness tend to be written, this alternative image of the large-souled Romantic at large implies, in the intervals between chapters or cantos, by way of a short break from reading. Rousseau, for one, was not getting away from literature on his excursion out of Paris. On the contrary, he was taking it with him. The country was an optimal place to read.

And it was while thus proceeding along the road to Vincennes and his destiny, contemplating not nature but that month's issue of the *Mercure de France*, that his life changed for ever. The *Mercure* was an intellectual magazine, carrying news of the court and artistic circles and matters scientific or philosophical (this issue included a short play, a love poem by Voltaire, a song and a dissertation on alchemy). Somewhere on the road from Paris to Vincennes, while flicking through these 'pièces fugitives en vers et en prose', Rousseau came across an announcement that had been placed by the Académie de Dijon, which read (with minor modifications) as follows:

The Académie des Sciences et des Belles-Lettres de Dijon announces to all savants that the Morality Prize for 1750, consisting of a Gold Medal, of the value of 30 pistols, will be awarded to the writer who produces the best solution to the following problem:

Whether the progress in the arts and the sciences has contributed to the improvement or the corruption of manners

Answers in French or Latin. Closing date 1 April 1750. Prize to be awarded at a public meeting of the Académie, Sunday 23 August 1750.

MERCURE
DE FRANCE,
DÉDIÉ AU ROI.
OCTOBRE. 1749.

A PARIS,
ANDRE' CAILLEAU, rue Saint
Jacques, à S André.
La Veuve PISSOT, Quai de Conty,
à la defce te du Pont-Neuf
Chez JEAN DE NULLY, au Palais,
JACQUES BARROIS, Quai
des Augustins, à la ville de Nevers.

M. DCC. XLIX.
Avec Approbation & Privilege du Roi.

MERCURE
DE FRANCE,
DÉDIÉ AU ROI.
OCTOBRE. 1749.
PIECES FUGITIVES,
en Vers & en Profe.

PROGRAMME
De l'Académie des Sciences & Belles-Lettres
de Dijon, pour le Prix de Morale
de 1750.

L'Académie, fondée par M. Hector-Bernard Pouffier, Doyen du Parlement de Bourgogne, annonce à tous les Sçavans, que le Prix de Morale pour l'année 1750, confiftant en une Médaille d'or, de la valeur de trente piftoles, fera adjugé à celui qui aura le mieux réfolu le Problème fuivant.

Si le rétabliffement des Sciences & des Arts à contribué à épurer les mœurs.

Il fera libre à tous ceux qui voudront concourir, d'écrire en François ou en Latin, obfervant que leurs Ouvrages foient lifibles, & que la lecture de chaque Mémoire rempliffe & n'excede point une demie heure.

Les Mémoires francs de port (fans quoi ils ne feront pas retirés) feront adreffés à M. Petit, Secretaire de l'Académie, rue du vieux Marché à Dijon, qui n'en recevra aucun après le premier Avril.

Source: Cambridge University Library

That journey to Diderot's prison proved to be Rousseau's equivalent of Paul's Road to Damascus: it was here that he underwent his definitive conversion. It was on reading the Dijon essay title that, in a moment of quasi-religious revelation, epiphany, enlightenment, *satori*, he 'became an author' (as he remembers it), that he 'saw another universe and [...] became another man'. He had already written contributions to the *Encyclopédie* edited by Diderot (and d'Alembert), but it was only with the challenge to write the Dijon essay – what would become known as his 'First Discourse' – that he was 'suddenly dazzled by a thousand lights'.

So overwhelmed was he by the intoxicating rush of images and ideas and arguments and truths, that he went into a faint and had to collapse under an oak tree for half an hour, after which he found the front of his jacket wet-through with his own tears. Then a 'delirium' took hold of him which continued all the way to Vincennes (decreasing only slightly to a state of sustained 'effervescence' which would last for the next four or five years). He waved a draft of a 'Prosopopoeia to Fabricius' – which he had dashed off in pencil under the tree, eulogizing martial virtues and playing down the idea of progress – in front of Diderot, and Diderot duly urged him to go in for the Dijon prize; Rousseau was made – or 'lost' as he puts it – and the whole of the rest of his life, not just the First Discourse, followed as the inevitable consequence of this one short episode. He would later lament that he had never managed to set down more than a quarter of everything he 'saw and felt' underneath that fruitful tree.

Napoleone Buonaparte, who would evolve into Napoleon Bonaparte, First Consul, Emperor, liberator and tyrant, saw himself as the Rousseau of his generation. He yearned as a young man for the same kind of metamorphosis that his role-model had undergone, the single seismic experience that would brand him forever as a writer. Rousseau was nearly forty when he read that fateful number of the *Mercure*. Napoleon, in more of a hurry, was only twenty when the opportunity of a comparably life-determining moment, uncannily like Rousseau's, presented itself.

Napoleon had (he claimed) read *La Nouvelle Héloïse*, Rousseau's epistolary love-story, around the age of nine and had moved on to the *Discours* some time in his teenage years. Certainly Rousseau was his first and most enduring literary hero (even if it would ultimately be a question of transcending his influence). Both Rousseau and Napoleon were outsider figures: the one from Geneva, the other from Corsica, who had to work harder than the natives to impress their adopted *patrie*. More than Rousseau, Napoleon had a particular sensitivity to what Nietzsche – who in turn adopted Napoleon as one of his heroes – would call 'Eternal Recurrence'. He saw history as, if not repeating itself, at least recycling itself, with small variations: the same elements would re-appear time after time, in diverse permutations, like rhymes in a sonnet.

So it must have been with a feeling of immense certainty, the conviction that fate was finally knocking on his door, that he opened a newspaper in 1790 and read the following:

JOURNAL DE LYON ET DES PROVINCES VOISINES
18 February (No. 7) 1790

EXTRACT FROM THE PROGRAMME
of the Académie des   Sciences, Belles-Lettres et
Arts de Lyon

Raynal Prize of 1791

The Académie proposes, as the subject for the prize do-
nated by the Abbé Raynal, the following question:

'What are the most important truths and feelings to instil
into men for their happiness?'

The prize is 1200 livres and a gold medal. Essays, written in
French or Latin, are to be submitted by 25 August 1791.
The winner to be announced at a public meeting of the
Académie on 29 November 1791.

The dedication to the King had gone, the typeface was plainer,
and the *Journal de Lyon* was not so prestigious as the *Mercure
de France*. But the essentials remained the same.

There is no record that Napoleon soaked his jacket in tears,
but like Rousseau, he was flung into a prolonged delirium,
which perhaps never ceased until his death on Saint Helena.

> The ambition which overturns whole States and individual
> fortunes [he wrote shortly afterwards], that is nourished on
> blood and crimes . . . is, like all disorderly passions, a violent and
> unreflective madness [*un délire violent et irréfléchi*] which ceases
> only with life itself: like a fire that, driven on by a pitiless wind,
> only ends when it has consumed everything.

That fire was Napoleon's thousand lights. He must have felt
himself to be in the presence of an almost religious imperative,
as if God were saying to him, 'Napoleon, this is your chance of
glory – seize it!' This was what he had been born for. Brought
up in Corsica, educated in France, possessed by the spirit of

Rousseau, he had more than enough truths and feelings, happiness and unhappiness, to fill a book, let alone an essay. He was made (or lost).

And Napoleon will surely have been all the more fully convinced that he was in the presence of an irresistible historical conjuncture, a cusp on which the whole of his future career must hang, by the fact that he was on his way to visit a friend in prison at the time. Or so at least it must have appeared to him, anxious as he was to perceive parallels. Napoleon may well have received advance warning of the essay competition from the man behind it, since in this case the friend-in-prison and the originator of the prize were one and the same. Sometime Jesuit, journalist, anti-clerical *philosophe*, occasional sermon ghost-writer, and friend to Rousseau, the Abbé Raynal, Guillaume Thomas François Raynal, was not quite in fact in prison, but in (fairly comfortable) exile. A man of the south who dropped out of the Church and took off to Paris to pursue his literary career, he had been condemned in the *Parlement* and forced out of France on account of his monumental (and collaborative and cheerfully plagiaristic) book, an incendiary history of European colonization in six volumes, *Histoire philosophique et politique des établissements et du commerce des Européens dans les deux Indes*.

Again the parallel with Diderot will not have been lost on Napoleon. Raynal was another contributor to the *Encyclopédie* just as, conversely, Diderot contributed substantially to the *Histoire des deux Indes*. Published in its first edition in 1770, the book was officially suppressed two years later for 'its bold, dangerous, reckless propositions, contrary to good manners and to the principles of religion'. Boldness and recklessness were not lacking in many of Raynal's more inspired and semi-miraculous ideas, such as that ships should be equipped with long feathered wings, dipped in oil, to enable them to hold down the waves in stormy conditions. But even more contentious and deemed liable to sink or at least rock the ship of State was the direct line he drew between European expansion, whether west or east, and despotism and slavery. Every empire, in other words, was immoral, driven by cupidity, shored up by violence and deserving of insurrection. (Raynal took roughly the same line with regard to the Church and his book was duly placed on the Index Librorum Prohibitorum in 1774 for his impiety.) The book seemed to say everything and its exact opposite, but what people remembered were the rousing exhortations to revolt against oppression.

This was probably the most powerful anti-colonial anti-slavery document of the period, echoed by Diderot in his *Supplément au voyage de Bougainville*, blasting the French for corrupting and destroying the paradise of Tahiti. Suppressed or not, it continued to be widely read. One of Raynal's most enthusiastic readers was the young Napoleon, renegade, rebel and fanatically anti-French. Corsica had been colonized by the French, as Napoleon saw it, and he was determined to be the island's liberator. And Raynal provided the intellectual and theoretical ammunition for his crusade.

It was not until 1780 that Raynal rashly allowed an edition of the *Histoire des deux Indes* to appear that carried his name and, moreover, a portrait of the writer, looking down his long nose and frowning severely upon all tyrannies. A warrant for his arrest was issued in May of the following year, the book ('impious, blasphemous, seditious, tending to incite peoples to rise up against sovereign authority and to overturn the fundamental principles of civil order', according to the Avocat général) was publicly burnt by the royal executioner and Raynal fled the country, travelling through Belgium, Holland, Prussia and Switzerland. In 1785 he was allowed back, but only on condition that he remained in the south, well away from Paris. He found refuge in Marseille, where he was so popular – widely known as 'the apostle of freedom' – that he was elected deputy of the city in the spring of 1789, aged 76 (a post he declined, however, to take up).

At the tender age of seventeen, Napoleon wrote Raynal a letter, which his brother Joseph was commissioned to deliver by hand, in which he presents himself as a potential protégé to Raynal's guru and patron. Napoleon is a 'novice historian': 'I am not yet eighteen, but I am already a writer; this is an age at which one must learn.' In his *cahiers* of the period we find Napoleon scribbling down page after page of quotations and précis from the first three volumes of the *Histoire des deux Indes* (alongside a short dissertation on the subject of artillery).

Raynal encouraged his young acolyte, 'impressed by the breadth of his knowledge'. Raynal was widely idolized and treated his disciples with even-handed benevolence and a good measure of flattery. In the case of Napoleon, he probably appreciated his brazen solicitations, which repeated his own assiduous cultivation (forty years previously) of Parisian literary circles: 'every beginner', Napoleon wrote to him, 'must attach himself to an established celebrity.' A quarter of a century later, Marseille would hail the French defeat at Waterloo as a victory, having long hated the Empire for its damaging effect on maritime commerce. But in the summer of 1789 Marseille and the south smiled on Napoleon and his writerly ambitions. *En route* to Corsica, he visited his mentor to 'importune him with admiration' (as he put it) and Raynal approved of his historical projects, assuring him that French literature lacked a good history of Corsica, with a strong anti-French line. Napoleon was invited to join in (or 'was made the ornament of' as the more ornamental Comte de Las Cases has it) a number of animated intellectual lunches, exchanging subversive ideas with Raynal's fellow exiles and other admirers.

He undoubtedly saw himself at this time in the same light: one of the Enlightenment intelligentsia, inevitably in opposition, an expatriate, a dissident and a writer. As a lieutenant in the French army, he had already been in trouble, fined for speaking too much about politics in the mess room, where *omertà* on matters of business was the rule. But he had left his barracks at Auxonne on a long-term sabbatical. From the army's point of view he was practically AWOL for months at a time. Even Las Cases (Napoleon's biographer in the *Mémorial de Sainte-Hélène*) admits that his frequent protracted absences aroused 'extreme jealousy' among his comrades-in-arms. Once they had tried to throw him in the Saône river (they lifted him up over their heads but then backed down). Another time a duel with a fellow officer was arranged. In Auxonne, he was the regiment intellectual, the class swot, a Cyrano among Christophes. But here in Marseille, *chez* Raynal, surrounded by intellectuals and exiles and trouble-makers, he felt perfectly at home.

There is a remarkable absence (for the eighteenth century) of *bons mots* and wit and paradox in the *Histoire des deux Indes*. It is as if Raynal is determined to win his case by out-numbering and overwhelming the enemy, by the sheer quantity as much as the quality of argument, borrowing right and left or brazenly stealing, piling up heterogeneous documents and sensational anecdotes (without the concession of quotation marks to these 'involuntary collaborators' as Anatole Feugère nicely called them). Raynal, a frankly ugly man who was instinctively indifferent to loveliness, was similarly oblivious to matters of style and aesthetics. The more content the better: form was irrelevant.

Horace Walpole, the Francophile man of letters and author of the Gothic novel *The Castle of Otranto*, met Raynal in 1765 at a dinner given by the Baron d'Holbach in Paris. He felt so deluged by Raynal's Niagara of questions that he feigned deafness (Raynal was furious when he later discovered the ploy). But not much more than ten years later, in 1777, he was inviting Raynal to a reception at his own home, Strawberry Hill, having become a profound admirer of the *Histoire* (Raynal duly upbraided him for the excessive luxury of his home). Walpole saw it as an admirable but impossible synthesis. His concise summary (in a letter of 1772) of so compendious and contradictory a work might also stand as a fair résumé of that would-be Raynal, Napoleon, and his own many-sided *oeuvre*, all fifty-odd extraordinary volumes of it:

It tells one everything in the world, how to make conquest, invasions, blunders, settlements, bankruptcies, fortunes, etc.; tells you the natural and historical history of all nations; talks commerce, navigation, tea, coffee, china, mines, salt, spices; of the Portuguese, English, French, Dutch, Danes, Spaniards, Arabs, caravans, Persians, Indians, of Louis XIV and the King of Prussia; of rice and women that dance naked; of camels, ginghams, and muslin; of millions of millions of livres, pounds, rupees, and gowries; of iron, cables, and Circassian women; of law and the Mississippi; and against all governments and religions. This and everything else is in the two first volumes. I cannot conceive of what is left for the four others. And it is all so mixed that you learn forty new trades and fifty new histories in a single chapter.

It could have been at one of Raynal's glittering lunches that Napoleon first received advance notice of the Lyon essay competition, even before he read of it. The middle to late eighteenth century was the heyday of literary and scientific competitions (the same edition of the *Mercure* that sent Rousseau into a delirium also carried news of the poetry prize from the Académie française for a work on the subject, 'The Love of the French for their Kings, as consecrated in their public monuments', and another announcement of an essay on 'the nature and formation of hail'; while the *Journal de Lyon* announced seven other prizes for works on such diverse topics as the chemical analysis of wine, how to make leather waterproof, why sap rises and the manufacture of woollen garments). And Raynal was a master essay-setter. In the wake of the notoriety generated by his own book, and following the Dijon model, he had instituted the essay competition at the Académie des Sciences, Belles-Lettres et Arts de Lyon in 1780, promising 1,200 livres to the winner. In that first year he set the question: 'What are the advantages and disadvantages of the discovery of America?' But his 1,200 livres (equivalent to more than a year's salary for Napoleon) remained intact and the same question was set all over again in 1785, and again in 1787 and 1789. But the entrants, around fifty in all, were each and every one rejected as undeserving of the prize: 'a mass of feeble athletes presented themselves,' according to the Académie, 'but eloquent and philosophical orators did not deign to make their voices heard.'

Thus the 1,200 livres remained untouched throughout the eighties. In a sense Raynal answered his own question with a section entitled 'Reflections on the good and the evil effects that the discovery of the New World has had on Europe' at the end of the ninth volume (1780–3) of an expanded edition of his history, where he puts the emphasis very much on the evil:

> Since the audacious expeditions of Columbus and da Gama, there has arisen in the countries of Europe a previously unknown fanaticism: that of making discoveries. We have traversed and continue to traverse all the climates, bestriding the globe from pole to pole, in our quest for new continents to invade, new islands to ravage, new peoples to pillage, subjugate and massacre.

And the like-minded Napoleon echoes the point in his own *Discourse on Happiness*: 'Frenchmen! . . . we have done enough harm to America.'

At the end of the decade, after four fruitless repetitions of the contest, Raynal and his lieutenants toyed with the idea of changing the subject. Maybe it was too difficult. How about the slave trade and the treatment of indigenous peoples? suggested Raynal. But that was seen as too sensitive in Lyon and eventually they settled on the question of happiness and the most important truths and feelings to instil into men in order to produce it: '*Quelles vérités et quels sentiments importe-t-il le plus d'inculquer aux hommes pour leur bonheur?*' This was a less touchy topic on the face of it, but in a sense, it encompassed the previous theme and the rejected alternative: so long as the truths and feelings are the right ones, and the programme of persuasion and inculcation effective, then all the earlier tragedies – the unhappiness – born out of European expansion might be avoided. All those Europeans who were guilty of genocide and expropriation were simply going about with the wrong ideas in their heads. They had just been badly taught, but Raynal and Lyon were optimistic that matters could be rectified. Enlightenment, at the end of the eighteenth century, was surely within their grasp. The 1,200 livres would be a modest reward indeed for the essayist who could thus solve all the essential problems at a stroke, eradicating injustice and suffering, and finally installing the realm of happiness. Perhaps it is not pitching it too strongly to say that this was an essay that was supposed to save the world.

Napoleon felt from the beginning that the prize had his name on it. The good omens were endless. Had not Raynal himself encouraged him to compete? Everything was set fair for a brilliant literary career. Truths and feelings spilled out of him. Raynal is awarded the epigraph (a quasi-quotation from the *Histoire*: 'There will be morality when governments are free') and an apostrophe:

Illustrious Raynal, if in the course of a life dedicated to unmasking the prejudices of the great, you have been constant and immovable in your zeal for suffering and oppressed humanity, deign today, amidst all the applause of the immense numbers who, summoned by you to liberty, duly pay homage to you, deign to smile on the efforts of a zealous disciple whose essays you have often sought to encourage. The question with which

I shall concern myself is worthy of your stamp, but without having the ambition to rival your stature, I have said to myself, like Correggio: *I too am a painter*.

This appears almost transparently like an attempt to curry favour. But there were no rules in the contest against it. And Raynal was not averse to a degree of hero-worship. The substance of the *Discourse on Happiness* lies squarely within the subversive tradition of the *Histoire des deux Indes*: it is an anti-everything book, anti-tyranny and anti-anarchy; anti-sensibility and anti-sense as well. The grandly declamatory style, moreover, is pure Raynal. There is, however, a self-deprecating finale: 'I am certain at least that someone will win this prize and I find consolation in the thought that I have increased, by my struggle, the triumph of the victor.' Napoleon saw writing, from the beginning, in terms of combat and conquest. And, here, defeat: but this apparent modesty was merely conventional and Napoleon was quietly confident that the 1,200 livres were as good as in his pocket. And he certainly needed them: he had had to give up coffee and survive on dry bread, he complained, and one meal a day. Plus he was having to feed his younger brother Louis, who was under his wing in Auxonne. (Given his big brother's ascetic and bookish existence, it is hardly surprising that Louis was soon begging to go home, although he too would later turn his hand to poetry and the novel.)

But Napoleon did not plunge into the essay recklessly and impulsively. On the contrary, he launched himself upon a sustained campaign of research and preparation. He may have discussed the project with his brother Joseph in Corsica during 1790 (while 'strolling along the beach' suggests Arthur Chuquet colourfully) and certainly settled down to the task in the spring and summer of 1791 back on the mainland, in Auxonne in the east and later in Valence in the south of France. As usual, his military duties would have to wait. 'His total record,' notes Norwood Young, 'was two years with the colours, to over three years away.' (Having already arranged an extension of his leave on the grounds that he was suffering from anaemia and that he needed to take the waters at Orezza, he was late returning to his unit, but incredibly still managed to wangle backpay for the whole of the period he was away, on the strength of documents stating that Mediterranean storms had held him back.)

The French Revolution was in full swing, riots small and large were exploding all over the country, the Bastille had already fallen (in July 1789), Louis XIV clung to power by a thread, and in fits and starts France was spiralling towards the Terror, while Napoleon pondered on how best to achieve happiness with all the scholarly enthusiasm of a zealous undergraduate. 'In the midst of this effervescence,' writes Chuquet, 'Napoleon remained greedy for culture, applying himself, as before, to serious studies.' On 19 July 1789, revolutionary fever had even hit Auxonne, the locals rose in revolt, the register of taxes was burned, and the offices of a Farmer-General were destroyed. The men of the La Fère regiment (Napoleon's) stood by and watched and later got drunk.

The Lyon competition was an opportunity that might not occur again and Napoleon didn't intend to throw it away. He went into intellectual training like an Olympic athlete intent on peaking at the right time. First of all, he set about assembling his vocabulary, the raw material, the troops he would muster for his head-on assault on literary glory. In a small room at a table by the window piled high with books and papers, he would work sometimes for up to eighteen hours a day, stopping for his one meagre meal. No wonder he was thin and reedy, with sunken cheeks and an ashen complexion.

During this period the monastic Napoleon never went to a café or socialized:

> I lived like a bear, always alone in my little room, with my books, which were my only friends. And I could acquire these books and buy this happiness only at the cost of extreme deprivation! When, out of sheer abstinence, I had managed to hold back the sum of two ecus out of six livres, I made my way as joyfully as a child to the shop of a bookseller who lived near to the bishop's house. Often I scoured his shelves with a sinful desire; I would covet a book for a long while before my purse allowed me to buy. Such were the pleasures and the debaucheries of my youth!

From 10 April through to 1 August 1791, all through a summer of deprivation and desire, his folio-sized *Cahier d'expressions* filled up with exotic and sonorous words, the rare and the re- condite, scientific and far-flung nomenclature, drawn from the Sanskrit and Inca languages. Napoleon's notebooks became a small tower of Babel.

Ichthyophage ('fish-eater'), *rhizophage* ('root-eater') – both turn up in the *Discourse* – *lama* ('Tibetan pope'), *bibliographie* (both 'art' and 'science'), *paléographie* ('deciphering and re- cognizing the writings of different ages and the variations of the French language'), *assafeta* ('principal chambermaid of the Queen of Spain'), *particularisme* ('personal interest'): his lexico- logical quest is limitless, universal in scope. Napoleon plunders the archives, raiding histories, memoirs, novels (*Alcibiade*, a free rendering into French by Ranquil Lieutaud from Miessner's German), travel-books (*Voyage en Suisse* by Coxe), Voltaire, Bernardin de Saint-Pierre's *De la chaumière indienne*, Ariosto's *Orlando furioso*. Napoleon was the last great auto-didact of the eighteenth century, a soul striving heroically to attain a kind of omniscience. Following in the footsteps of Diderot and Raynal, his *Cahiers* comprise a one-man *Encyclopédie*, an expanded *Histoire des deux Indes*, a chaotic A–Z of learning, a flawed and far-flung dictionary, an epic attempt to encompass at the end of feudalism, in a period of seismic political change, all avail- able knowledge.

In the month of May 1791 alone, in his relentless quest, Napoleon filled separate notebooks with quotations from and commentary on Voltaire (*Essai sur l'histoire générale et sur les moeurs des nations depuis Charlemagne jusqu'à nos jours*), Machiavelli's *History of Florence*, the *Mémoires secrètes* of Duclos, *A Critical History of the Nobility From the Beginning of Monarchy to the Present, Exposing its Prejudices, its Crimes, and Proving that it has been the Scourge of Liberty, Reason, and Human Knowledge and the Constant Enemy of the People and Kings*, published in 1790 by Delaure, and the *Esprit de Gerson* on the doctrines of the Church in France.

Under the heading of 'notes diverses', *Cahier* 19 assimilates *Pecoil, Pezade, Pizarre* and *Pisse-Vache, Autodafé* and *Apogee*, varieties of tree (coconut, fig, banyan, orange, banana), political regimes of East and West, Montezuma, a rainbow of religions and priests (Maronites, rabbis, Copts, effendis, bonzes), glaciers and avalanches (called *Lavanges* in Switzerland), musical instruments (tympanon), houris, cities (Delhi, Benares, 'the Athens of India'), the names of museums and universities, perfumes, jewels, flowers (tulip: 'the leaf is red and the heart black, to express love and despair'), diseases (goitres) and disasters (typhoons), 1,500 Virgins of the Sun, Daedalus and Pyrrhus, Confucius and Zoroaster, Alexander and Amazonian women, Saxons and Florentines, Merlin and the hippogriff, palanquins, *bayadères*, fakirs, pariahs and rajahs, caravanserais and bazaars, chameleons and troglodytes, mandarins, brahmins, cretins: from the Americas to China, the New and the Old Worlds, from the beginning of time to the apocalypse, through magic, medicine and mysticism, there is nothing that is irrelevant to his vast project. Everything exists, pell-mell, in a technicolour continuum.

More than three decades later, Victor Hugo would steal his aesthetic from Napoleon when it came to writing the preface to his early collection of poems, *Les Orientales*, which would be a calling-card of Romanticism: 'Why should there not be a literature – and particularly the work of a poet – which, in its totality, was like one of these beautiful old cities of Spain, for example, wherein you find everything?' Already in Napoleon, as later in *Les Orientales*, you find promenades beneath orange trees along river banks, festive squares, tortuous streets, labyrinths of buildings, noisy markets, cemeteries, tinselled theatres, a scaffold (from which the skeleton is still dangling in the wind), and a Gothic cathedral alongside the mosque, hidden among sycamores and palm trees.

But if everything hangs together in a vast and all-embracing synthesis, then it is clear that politics and language are as one. Napoleon's *Cahier* 19 thus inevitably dwells on the story of Tryzus the tyrant who

> prohibited his subjects from speaking together. The people circumvented his law by substituting gestures for speech. Trysus prohibited gestures too. Then a citizen came forward and stationed himself in the middle of the town square, where he remained immobile and began to cry. Others did the same. When the tyrant heard of this, he rushed to the square to prohibit crying [*prohiber aux yeux de pleurer*] and was promptly put to death.

Tryzus seems to Napoleon to represent his antithesis. Napoleon is the living champion of self-expression; Tryzus is the incarnation of censorship and suffocation. Napoleon is the whole of language and literature: Tryzus is their eradication. But perhaps the sheer monstrosity of encompassing all the knowledge of the world made Napoleon secretly yearn for an end to writing or at least a short-cut. Hence he recorded the idea that 'All truth is contained in the four *beths* written 120,000 years ago [sic] in the Sanskrit tongue.' If only it was as simple as that. It is understandable that he should also have included a word in his lexicography that was perhaps unfamiliar to him even if its sense was not: *Des soucis* ('anxieties').

But if Napoleon was ready and willing to save the world, he also had the more immediate task in mind of saving himself. The *Discourse on Happiness*, amongst other things, gives the answer to the question that Napoleon was asking himself at this time: how do *I* achieve happiness? And one answer is: by writing. At the end of the happiness essay, Napoleon writes, '[in working on this essay] have I not been happier, have I not attained the goal?' [*N'ai-je pas été plus heureux, n'ai-je pas atteint au but?*]. Writing appears as the sovereign solution to a problem. And the problem is the one formulated succinctly by Shakespeare in Hamlet's soliloquy, 'To be or not to be, that is the question.' In some alternate universe, Napoleon is already dead at the age of 21, his short life ended by his own hand. He is a young man episodically possessed, almost overwhelmed, by feelings of melancholy, a heightened poetic sense of the tears in things.

Already at the age of sixteen, on 3 May 1786, Napoleon had composed a short meditation, 'Sur le suicide'. This text starts with the poet wandering lonely as a cloud – 'Always alone in the midst of people' [*toujours seul au milieu des hommes*] – but, unlike Wordsworth or Rousseau, he finds no consolation in nature ('How far men are from nature!') and remains introverted and depressed: 'I return home and turn inward once more to dream [*pour rêver avec moi-même*] and surrender to the full energy of my melancholy [*me livrer à toute la vivacité de ma mélancolie*].' Immediately his thoughts turn to death: 'Since I must die, is it not better to kill myself?' [*Puisque je dois mourir, ne vaut-il pas autant se tuer?*]. Everything seems to him atrocious and distasteful.

In the *Discourse*, he writes, as if in the grip of some all-encompassing angst, that a man is apt to fear 'the void, the terrible solitude of the heart'. His account, in the final paragraph of his draft version, spells out how he sees his own futile existence:

> When, on rising, a man does not know what he will become and drags out his tedious existence through one *quartier* after another; when, contemplating the future, he perceives only a dreadful monotony, with each day resembling every other; when he asks himself: 'Why have I been created?' then he, I believe, is the most wretched of all men. His corporeal machine breaks down, his heart loses that energy which is natural to man. How can he go on with being, this empty heart? How can he live the life of animals with the moral faculties that are peculiar to our nature? Happy he could be did he not possess these faculties! This man is thrown into despair by trifles. The slightest setback seems to him an intolerable calamity . . . In the void of solitude, will not an interior passion say to him: *No, I am not happy!*

A century or so later, the sociologist Emile Durkheim would diagnose this dysfunction as 'Romantic anomie'. And Napoleon himself calls attention to the slide towards 'the infinity of dreams' (the perils of the '*imagination déréglée*'), and anticipates Baudelaire's flowers of evil in headlining '*les anxiétés de l'ennui*': 'when ennui takes possession of a man's heart, sadness and black melancholia follow, and if this state of depression is protracted, then he chooses self-slaughter' [*il se donne la mort*]. This essay about happiness consists, at its core, of a series of elegant variations on death and, more particularly, suicide: 'giving oneself death'; 'opening up one's own entrails', 'to perish by one's own hand'. It is as if Napoleon chose the army as an honourable way of committing hara-kiri (as indeed it was to become in his would-be novel, *Clisson et Eugénie*). He was pulled back from the brink by Raynal's essay competition. But even so he used the *Discourse* as an opportunity to enact his own end, tracing the itinerary of a Rousseauist child of nature through from birth to fatherhood and finally to death.

Napoleon's valedictory speech, bidding farewell to friends and family, is hauntingly reminiscent of the death of Hilton's High Lama (to use a word from Napoleon's lexicon) in *Lost*

Horizons. 'Adieu, my blessing be upon you, and may it stand guard over your union and your happiness.' [*Adieu, recevez ma bénédiction, qu'elle soit le palladium de votre union et de votre bonheur.*] This is a calm, Zen-like voice, voluntarily embracing the dissolution of the body and the empire of the soul, muffling the violent Dionysian passions of youth in cool Apollonian contemplation. Death is '*douce, désirable même,*' a consummation devoutly to be wished. Who would fardels bear? 'There comes a time when life is no more than a burden; a time when everything announces that it is the right moment to die.' The implicit conclusion of the *Discourse* seems to be that there is no happiness until we go down to our graves in peace. Oblivion is the only certain happiness. Even writing is no certain proof against the tug of the void: 'the *savant* . . . studies, discusses, his reason will be contented, but does he not have a heart? Where will he be led by this accumulation of disparate knowledge?' [*Où le conduira cet amas de connaissances diverses?*]. That question, 'Have I not been happier?' begins to look like something more than a purely rhetorical one. The negative is serious. A more accurate title for the essay might have been: 'Discourse on Unhappiness'.

The *Discourse on Happiness*, like many an undergraduate essay, doesn't really answer the question. Happiness is death and truth is . . . Napoleon gets hung up on the question of truth. He intermittently allows that there may once have been a Rousseauist golden age in which truth was automatically spoken and understood. But the very question of 'what truths should be instilled in people' demonstrates that such truths have eluded us. In fact the existence of literature shows that truth has been lost. 'Literate societies ought never to have been animated by anything other than a love of truth and of men.' But the bold opening imperfect subjunctive [*n'eussent jamais dû être animées*], although a testimony to Napoleon's growing command of French grammar, also indicates that truth has become dissipated in the fog of propositions and prejudices: 'there can be no truths where prejudice, of necessity, reigns' [*il n'est point de vérités où règnent par devoir les préjugés*]. This epistemological or anti-epistemological point is linked by Napoleon with the question of power and the structure of society at large: 'There are no men where kings remain sovereign: there is nothing but the oppressed slave and, viler still, the oppressive slave.' A monarchy forbids truth just as it forbids freedom. In this society there is nothing but 'the tragic spectacle of flattery and the most culpable adulation' while the sciences of morality and politics 'have languished in oblivion or have become entangled in the labyrinth of obscurity' [*ont langui dans l'oubli, ou se sont entortillés dans le labyrinthe de l'obscurité*].

Napoleon sees his writing on an analogy with a journey across stormy seas. 'When I undertook to plot a route across a sea notorious for its shipwrecks, I was guided only by the utility of the journey . . . On my course I only ever came across people who had lost their way.' One of those who had gone astray was surely Rousseau. In his preparation for the *Discourse*, Napoleon was careful to reread Rousseau's own discourses. But just as Rousseau walked with his eyes glued to a book, so Napoleon always read with his pen in his hand and spelt out exactly where he diverged from the text in front of him: 'I do not believe a word of that' and 'I don't believe this!' echo through his note-book. Napoleon did not believe in the 'state of nature' for one thing. But neither, for all practical purposes, did Rousseau. And there were deeper congruities between the two writers.

In his Discourse for the Académie de Dijon, Rousseau took the view that the arts and the sciences had corrupted rather than purified our morals. But he took the arts and sciences as synonymous with the totality of society, embodying 'all the contradictions of the social system'. The pre-social individual in all his splendid isolation was not so much a 'noble savage' as neither outstandingly good nor bad. It was the development of society which had sucked us down into the pit of hypocrisy and deceit and crime and servitude. In short, by the second half of the eighteenth century, we had all become more savage than the savages. Although the 'arts and sciences' were in some sense responsible for this, nevertheless you could not simply turn the clock back and dis-invent them and restore some hypothetical degree zero of society. No, what had caused our downfall could also, paradoxically, bring about our recovery. This *Discourse*, for example, could have a beneficial impact on the state of mankind by bringing this truth to our attention, or if not truth then – Rousseau allows – 'what I took to be the truth'.

It is in this sense that Napoleon is following, however critically and cautiously, the path of Rousseau. 'O Rousseau,' he writes in a typically Raynalian apostrophe, 'why did you have to live but sixty years! You should have been immortal' [*tu eusses dû être immortel*, another of his complex 'if-only' grammatical constructions]. He naturally reaffirms the equality of human rights: 'We are born with unequal resources, no doubt, but with equal rights.' But the path to justice lies through those 'truths and feelings' – or what Napoleon takes to be truths – that are to be instilled into men and women for their happiness, thus reversing our long decline. Rousseau was bound to have an ambivalent attitude towards his own medium – an accomplice in our moral degradation and a tool, perhaps the only tool, of our redemption. That which corrupted can also purify. This is why a couple of centuries of readers have found Rousseau so perplexing to read, because he seems to keep changing his tune, at one moment attacking and the next retreating. And Napoleon shares Rousseau's ambivalence towards writing and language, the arts and the sciences, towards in short the whole of civilization, alternately idolizing and demonizing, asserting and negating, sometimes in the same sentence, savagely tearing apart with a view to reforming and repairing. Hence, no doubt, Norwood Young's stern strictures early last century on the clarity of his writing or the lack of it: 'Napoleon, aged eighteen, is still unable to express himself clearly – a defect he never cured. It has been said of Wellington that "there is hardly an ambiguous sentence in the whole series of his dispatches". It was quite the contrary with Napoleon, whose meaning was sometimes as hard to unravel as his handwriting was difficult to decipher.' Hence, again, Frank McGlynn (most recently) can read the *Discourse* as 'quasi-fascistic' while Vincent Cronin's more benevolent interpretation asserts that 'His aim in life is to work for others' happiness.'

Rousseau thought of his writing in terms of music (he earned his living as a music copyist) and gave priority to harmony over melody. And it was plausible, on the same grounds, for Anthony Burgess to write a novel about Napoleon entitled *The Napoleon Symphony*. But perhaps Napoleon should be seen less, as Burgess saw him, in terms of passionate Beethovenian *Sturm und Drang*, than as providing a cool literary counterpart to a Bach organ toccata, in which sometimes quite antithetical melodic lines counterpoint and intersect and cut across one another (even if not in quite so lucid and orderly a fashion). So Napoleon begins his *Discourse* (rather like the book-shy, tree-loving Wordsworthian poet), with a critique of literature, which is linked with the growth of lies, but he ultimately holds out the hope of salvation through intellectual enlightenment (thus, in fact, taking his book with him on his journey). The Revolution itself is seen as the practical outcome of writing and thinking: 'The liberty that has been conquered after twenty months of energy, struggle and the most violent collisions will for ever testify to the glory of the French, of philosophy and of literature' [*la gloire des Français, de la philosophie et des lettres*]. Words, then, can do things. Ideas have made the Revolution. Which explains why, in the midst of the Revolution, Napoleon was more interested in sharpening his mind than in oiling his gun.

After probably a year or more of reflection, and two seasons of concentrated reading and writing, but still feeling that not quite everything had been said, Napoleon finally submitted his *Discourse* to the Académie de Lyon some time in August 1791, the last entry to get under the wire of the 25 August deadline (although one further late submission was accepted). From now on, in the eyes of the Lyon examiners, he would be known as 'No. 15'. Having sent off his prize-winning essay, after this epic of sustained intellectual endeavour, Napoleon awarded himself a long vacation in September to recover from the rigours of the *Discourse*. It would hardly be surprising if, as has been asserted (but also strenuously denied), not a few of his fellow soldiers were ill-disposed towards yet another Napoleonic sabbatical. First he spends months writing his discourse on happiness, and now here he is going on holiday to Corsica!

There are many reasons for the phenomenon that would become known as the Terror. But one of them must surely be the amount of time the King's soldiers (or the Republic's – Napoleon officially pledged a new oath of allegiance to the Constituent Assembly in July 1791) spent on leave at crucial moments. It appears that even the army may have dimly apprehended this when on 8 September the order went out to suspend all leave. But too late. For Napoleon had already disappeared on another of his three-month furloughs. Having written of it for so long, it was only reasonable that he should now be taking off in pursuit of happiness. First theory, then practice (such is the standard Napoleonic order).

Despite Umberto Eco's Europe-wide survey concluding that Napoleon was the single most heroic figure of the French Revolution, the fact is that Napoleon, although present, was largely absent. If he had taken up the sonnet form during his early days in Paris, he could have easily written, as Charles Baudelaire wrote later, during similarly tumultuous times, 'The Riot, storming in vain at my window, Will not make me lift my head up from my desk.' [*L'Emeute, tempêtant vainement à ma vitre, Ne fera pas lever mon front de mon pupitre.*] It would have been a slight exaggeration – as it was in the case of Baudelaire – but only slight. 'When he was working,' recalled Alexandre des Mazis, 'he would close the shutters of his room in order to be more contemplative.'

At most he only ever appeared to be an occasionally sympathetic (but easily dismayed) spectator of the Revolution. He was typically both in situ and uninvolved during one of the most ferocious attacks on the Tuileries (then the official residence of the King) on 10 August 1792, in which so many of the characteristic elements of the Revolution were in place: the National Guard, *bonnets rouges, sans-culottes,* Jacobins, *fédérés* from Brest, Marseillais rebels, pikes in abundance and, providing only a temporary obstacle, the loyal Swiss Guard, who end up hacked to pieces on the flagstones of the palace. Napoleon, this curious anthropologist with notebook in hand, this early existential hero haunted by his own melancholia, remained a largely passive passer-by and spectator:

> It was from this house [his friend Bourrienne's brother's house at the Place du Carrousel in front of the Tuileries] . . . that I was able to see the events of the day unfold in all their gory detail . . . On my way there, in the rue des Petits-Champs, I was waylaid by a bunch of hideous men parading around a head on the end of a pike. Seeing me reasonably well attired and perceiving me as a gentleman, they came up to me and demanded that I should cry out, *'Vive la Nation!'* – which I did, without further ado, as can be imagined.

His only intervention (if his brother Joseph is to be believed) was negative although heroic: dissuading one of the bloodthirsty Marseillais – with whom he claimed the solidarity of the south – from killing a Swiss guard. He confined himself to watching in fascinated revulsion as women went about cutting off trophies from the bodies of the fallen.

It is less that writing provided an escape from the perils of the Revolution, but rather that the Revolution afforded a distraction from his inward soul-wrestling and austere studies and perpetual susceptibility to the lure of an easeful quietus. But more than anything, in the late summer and autumn of 1791, Napoleon's mind was concentrated on the inevitable Rousseau-like ascent to literary glory that awaited the winner of the Lyon prize. The official verdict came in on 29 November. And after that hot feverish summer of composition, winter was looming.

The illustrious five-strong examining panel was made up of Campigneules, Jacquet, Mathon de la Cour, Vasselier and de Savy (none of whom has left any published work behind them). According to Vasselier, 'Number 15 is a very pronounced dream' [*un songe très prononcé*] a view that might not have displeased Napoleon. The view of Campigneules was rather crueller: 'Number 15 will not detain for long the gaze of the Academicians. It is perhaps the work of a man of sentiment; but it is too badly arranged, too disparate, too rambling (*décousu*, literally, 'unstitched') and too badly written to hold the attention.' Frédéric Masson (a strong Bonapartist) finds the judgement, that Napoleon's work was 'worse than mediocre', incomprehensible. But it is true that the *Discourse* is not a tidy, tightly written work, but more an overflow of the cornucopian *cahiers*. It has a beginning, a middle and an end, but (as Godard would say of his films) not necessarily in that order. Number 15 was sunk by virtue of his over-ambition, the striking incoherence and heterogeneity of his thoughts. Coherence was not Napoleon's strongest suit in this text. But, as if in response to that damning verdict, it would become his life's work.

Only one essay – No. 8, by Pierre Daunou – was awarded a '*mention honorable*' and with his revised version of 1793 Daunou was finally crowned with Raynal's prize (Sainte-Beuve later remarked that 'with his pure, polished and ornate style . . .

Daunou deserved to take the prize'). Las Cases, in *Le Mémorial de Sainte-Hélène*, elegy and eulogy, gives a radically revisionist account of the examiners' report. 'This anonymous memoir [i.e. Napoleon's] was highly regarded' and carried off the prize. (Las Cases even gets the title of the essay wrong.) He may have been misled by Napoleon himself, since Barry O'Meara, the Irish doctor on Saint Helena, was also under the impression that Number 15 became the No. 1 of Lyon.

Rather more Machiavellian and not a little sadistic, Talleyrand (Napoleon's foreign minister) used the essay to torment the Emperor. Napoleon had been unwise enough to reminisce about the *Discourse*. Within a week Talleyrand had dug it out of the archives of Lyon and presented the manuscript to the author, congratulating him for winning the gold medal. Napoleon leafed through a few pages and, furious, flung it into the fire. He could not forget the stinging rejection from the pompous fools of the Académie.

August 1792, amid the attacks on the Tuileries, found Napoleon back in Paris and still revising the *Discourse*: 'My work is finished, corrected, copied, but it is not in these circumstances that one seeks publication; moreover I no longer have that small ambition of becoming an author.' In other words, he was refusing to give up on happiness, and denying it at the same time. There was some question of going off to join his regiment, but his main activity at this juncture was astronomy: 'This is a beautiful divertissement and a superb science.' Even as he was endlessly rewriting he was simultaneously threatening to give it all up and take refuge in the stars from the Revolution and the torment and frustration of writing. This is the pattern of ambivalence, a perpetual dance of bewitchment by language and glowering disenchantment, assertion and censorship, that would be repeated throughout his career.

Meanwhile, the Abbé Raynal went right on setting essays, one for the Académie française (another 1,200 livres, this time for the author of a 'literary work'), another for the Académie royale des Inscriptions et Belles-Lettres in Paris on 'What were the measures and precautions taken by the Greeks and the Romans to preserve law and order and the salubrity of their cities; and whether we can derive any advantages from their knowledge regarding this part of administration.' But for this competition, which ran in 1790, 1791 and 1792, not a single entry was forthcoming. Not one for three whole years. Napoleon was uninspired by the idea of law and order: happiness was more his area of specialization. The golden age of the essay competition was over. Napoleon, No. 15, appears as the last in the noble line of the essayists, the discoursers, the literary olympians, who studded the Enlightenment. There would be no more inspirational ads in the *Mercure de France* or the *Journal de Lyon*, igniting lights and fires. There were enough fires already. 'The Academy, judging by the distinct lack of eagerness to participate in these contests that it would be futile to propose any further topics for so long as circumstances remain unfavourable towards literature, and regarding, moreover, its own destruction as inevitable and imminent, has decided not to arrange any further competitions.' There were to be no more essay competitions for the foreseeable future (and perhaps no more Academies either): that route to immortality was now firmly closed.

It was as if in protest against this development that Raynal finally journeyed back to Paris, at the risk of his life and fortune, to lament the course of the anti-essayistic Revolution. Raynal was seen at this time as the only surviving 'Father of the Revolution' and the *Histoire des deux Indes* had probably had a bigger impact on events than Rousseau's *Contrat Social*. But in Marseille, from the summer of 1789 onwards, Raynal had been witness to rioting, troops, the wrecking and looting of the town hall and speeches by Mirabeau. There was 'too much effervescence of mind'. Rather like a penitent pornographer who fears his overly explicit images are having a negative effect on public morals, he thought in terms of cutting or toning down the more fervent, declamatory, rabble-rousing tirades (either by or in the manner of Diderot) in a new edition of the *Histoire des deux Indes*.

When his exile was finally annulled in April 1791, Raynal travelled north, envisaging a new role for himself as arbitrator and mediator between monarch and masses, and ultimately moderator and judge, as if the Revolution were another essay competition to be adjudicated. On 31 May his 'Address to the Assemblée nationale' was read out in the Assemblée itself, deploring the reduction of the King's power, the dispossession of the Church, various acts of violence and pillage and 'popular tyranny'. For the addressees, it must have been like listening to one of the Lyon examiners who, having examined the Revolutionary essay and found it wanting, was delivering his judgement: a Very Pronounced Dream: no gold medal for the Revolution. At the very moment at which his insurrectionary ideology was triumphant, Raynal recoiled. Jacobins actually went about quoting Raynal's exhortations to regicide and revolt; others (notably Talleyrand) blamed him for the Terror. In a sense everyone was citing Raynal except for Raynal himself, who was taking an anti-Raynalian line and complaining that he had been misinterpreted.

If the author was not yet dead, then he deserved to be: such was the immediate response. Of all people, Robespierre had to intervene to save his skin, making the case that the Abbé was obviously an old fool who had gone off his rocker. Not guilty on account of insanity. But Feugère, his more sympathetic biographer, claims Raynal as a subterranean monarchist from the beginning, who happened to have a gift for subversive rhetoric, and quotes supportively from his *Histoire du Parlement d'Angleterre*:

> Anarchy is a thousand times more harmful than despotism. What I am saying seems to me so self-evident that I have never been able to believe that certain men, who are not without intelligence and who describe themselves as philosophers, have yet been unable to perceive the folly of submitting the conduct of kings to the capricious judgement of the multitude . . . It is an inconvenience, I will allow, that the laws should be violated with impunity by the very prince who is charged with protecting them. But if every individual has the right to revolt against sovereign authority, then the government will find itself without a solid anchorage, and policy will be without principle, rebellions legitimate and revolutions perpetual . . . The whole world will become a chaos which it will be impossible to untangle.

Raynal relinquished active politics and essay-setting and withdrew to the countryside and died in 1796. He saw himself as a man of peace: 'Peace would be the ultimate happiness on earth' [*La paix serait le bonheur de la terre*], he wrote, answering in a sentence the question Napoleon had sweated over for so long.

But he had written of almost nothing but war and the consequences of war. The parallel with Napoleon is inescapable: a man of peace who waged incessant war; a rebel who loathed rebellion – Napoleon would remain Raynal's most 'zealous disciple'.

A matter of a few years after writing the *Discourse on Happiness*, Napoleon would carry the *Histoire des deux Indes* with him across the Mediterranean on his Egyptian expedition. During the same voyage, while Nelson led the English hunt for the French ships, Napoleon was peacefully hosting a seminar aboard the *Orient* on Rousseau's *Discourse on the Origins of Inequality*. Perhaps it could be said of him, as it was said of Raynal, that 'his talent was, in his hands, a destructive weapon which places him among those literary scourges whose appearance is invariably accompanied by tremors, upheavals and ruins' [*des secousses, des bouleversements et des ruines*]. Napoleon readily conceded the point. He was on a pilgrimage to the tomb of Rousseau in Ermenonville, standing contemplatively over the grave on a small island, when he turned and said to his companion Stanislas de Girardin that 'Only the future will teach us whether it would not have been better, for the sake of peace on earth, if Rousseau and I had never existed.'

2
Islands and Continents

Napoléon au siège de Toulon

If the Abbé Raynal were writing this, he would probably have framed it as a question and set it as an essay for aspiring writers.

Which of these propositions is true: Every man is an island; or, No man is an island? Submit your answers to the Académie de Lyon by August. First prize 1,200 livres.

The poet John Donne favoured the idea that 'every man is a piece of the continent', although perhaps there was an element of irony or wishful thinking about his meditation on the subject. Napoleon, had he had another shot at a literary prize, would have tended towards the opposite view, that every man was indeed an island by definition; but – such was his very pronounced dream, his disparate, rambling, unstitched discourse – he did his best to bring everyone else on board his personal island. Thus he found himself poised mid-way between the two attitudes of would-be solidarity and actual insularity. On the one hand, he made the most ambitious shot at globalization prior to the Internet; on the other, islands and their irresistible allegory of isolation kept coming back to haunt him.

Napoleon's life can be measured in islands, mapped out from Corsica to Saint Helena, an itinerary punctuated by Martinique (vicariously, in the form of Josephine), Elba and Paris. Napoleon understands Paris as an island within France. He doesn't simply *arrive* in Paris, he *lands* there, by boat, and calls the Left Bank, his first port of call, 'the Latin Country'. In Egypt, the desert is a sea in which the French columns, harassed by Bedouins, 'are like squadrons followed by sharks' and the oasis, paradoxically, becomes an island. From a Napoleonic perspective, the whole world is nothing but islands, a constellation of rocky promontories, barely holding back the engulfing ocean. At the same time, islands are, in the long term, impossible: islands cannot remain insular for long. Islands can be bridged, hooked up together, annexed and assimilated, until there are no more islands. 'Sainte-Hélène, petite île', the prophetic line Napoleon jotted down in his Auxonne notebooks, stands at this stage as an image of his own identity: at the age of eighteen he fully identified with islands, seeing Corsica and himself alike as islands buffeted by tremendous storms and assaulted by the elements on all sides (an image that Abel Gance was to exploit in his immense film about Napoleon in the scene in which the protagonist escapes his pursuers in a tiny yacht on a tumultuous sea). Napoleon lived and died in accordance with the fate of islands. We forget his place of origin and his geography only at the risk of obscuring his whole mentality.

There was an absurd debate during Napoleon's lifetime (and beyond) about his date of birth. Chateaubriand, Napoleon's admirer and memorialist – his mirror, his rival, his adversary – put it about that 'Buonaparté' (he favoured the Italian spelling and pronunciation) had been born on 5 February 1768 and not on 15 August 1769. To us, now, the difference seems irrelevant or ridiculous, but to the French at the turn of the nineteenth century, the idea was potentially scandalous. The distinction was a gulf: it represented the difference between being Italian and being French. On 15 May 1768 Genoa yielded power over Corsica to France. Corsica had been annexed, absorbed politically into the mainland. Born after this date, Napoleon was French; born before, he was Genovese or just plain Corsican, a foreigner, *l'étranger*, the outsider. According to Chateaubriand's anti-Bonapartist line, Napoleon was an Italian who lied about his birth to acquire coveted French nationality. More, everything he did was part of a cunning plan to bring France to its knees. He was intent on annexing France just as France had annexed Corsica. The French Empire was, in fact, Napoleon's empire over the French. It was politics with a vengeance. Vendetta politics.

It is a tempting idea, but the bare and incontrovertible fact is that Napoleon was indeed born, as he maintained, on 15 August 1769, on the anniversary of the Assumption, in Ajaccio on the south-west coast of Corsica, and was therefore, nominally, legally, French. But mere facts should not be allowed to get in the way of a perfectly good theory. Chateaubriand was right to assert his non-Frenchness. Paradoxically, it was precisely his outsider status within France, the fact that – all judicial niceties notwithstanding – he was a jumped-up Johnny foreigner, which gave him both acceptability on all sides and, ultimately, deniability by all. He remained an islander, a non-mainlander, throughout his life. An islander is always everywhere automatically alien, stateless, a wanderer. He was everyone and he was no one.

Whatever date we choose to assign to his birth, and whatever the notional political affiliation of Corsica, the outstanding feature of Napoleon's origins is geographical and phenomenological. From the beginning, Napoleon was surrounded by vast hostile forces. Like Victor Hugo, half a century later in exile on Jersey, Napoleon was at once horrified and seduced by the raw power of nature represented by waves. 'The vast abyss of the seas [*le vaste gouffre des mers*] encircles you,' he wrote in the *Discourse on Happiness*, 'and the hoarse moaning of the waves as they smash into the rocks conjures up for you the idea of how terrible this element can be for the feeble traveller.' There is a strong suggestion that it is the island background – or rather foreground – that is at the root of his depressive nature: 'Go down to the edge of the sea, look at the setting sun majestically plunging into the heart of infinity [*dans le sein de l'infinité*], and melancholy will overmaster you: you will surrender yourself totally to this emotion. No one can escape the melancholy induced by nature.' The sea is inescapable but atrocious: 'the source of misfortune and misery for my country'.

But there is nothing intrinsically melancholic about the sea, it is rather the thought that beyond it there is a greater land, vast enough to escape island status, that induces Napoleonic angst: 'Happy could we have been [had we not thought of sailing across the sea]. We would never have known of the existence of a continent. Oh, blissful ignorance!' [*Oh l'heureuse, l'heureuse ignorance!!!*]. The island alone and intact is paradise. But hell is other places. Napoleon is fleshing out his theory of unhappiness here. He recalls the case of the native Tahitian, Pontaveri, who comes to France with Bougainville and is stricken to the point of paralysis with homesickness [*'Arbre de mon pays! Arbre de mon pays!'*]. Greenlanders are the same in Denmark, he argues. The island confronted, across the seas, by a continent; the individual faced with a huge, more powerful collective: such are the elements of Napoleon's primal vision of our being-in-the-world [*les terres se distinguent principalement en continents et îles*, from *Cahier* 11, on geography]. Masson notes that Napoleon talked of the island as *Le* – rather than *La* – *Corse*, thus identifying himself and it. So he began, and so, exiled to a rock in the South Atlantic, he ended. The island was Napoleon's archetype, his model of existence. From his perspective, Earth was nothing more than an island floating in space; the universe was an island, marooned in nothingness.

From his outpost in Auxonne, he portrayed his birth in heavily symbolic terms that linked him inextricably with the island. In this account, the natal trauma is mirrored in an external military assault: both the child and the island are bathed in a sea of blood, and barely clinging to life:

I was born when the nation was perishing. Thirty thousand Frenchmen spewed up on our coasts, drowning the throne of Freedom in great waves of blood [*noyant le trône de la Liberté dans les flots de sang*]: such was the odious spectacle that first met my eyes. The cries of the dying, the groans of the oppressed, the tears of despair surrounded my cradle from the hour of my birth.

As usual, Napoleon is his own best commentator. Whenever he describes himself in his early writings, he is invariably *environné*, environed or surrounded (by his environment). Or *abandonné*. They amount to the same thing. In his psychogeographic vision of things, the physiological, the psychological and the political are all gathered together in the governing trope of the island under attack from outside. Corsica is a giant cradle. More, it is as if Napoleon is given birth not by a mere organic mother but by the very land itself, washed with water and blood. Conversely, the history of Corsica is construed in terms of Napoleon's personal experience. The man and the island are one.

A man dreams he is standing on dry land. But then the sea breaks through the barriers holding it back, the land is flooded, and the man who thought himself so secure now finds himself suddenly on a tiny island, completely encircled by water, with unknown monsters prowling beneath the surface. Jung takes this as one of his archetypal dreams and reads it as an exemplary image of the conscious mind being overwhelmed by the unconscious. In this interpretation, the solid earth is all conscious, male and determinate; while the ungovernable and fearsome sea represents the darkness of the unconscious: collective, feminine, the very principle and vehicle of indeterminacy.

Nearly all twentieth-century interpretations of Napoleon are, in effect, versions of this dream run in reverse. Napoleon, so this narrative goes, moves from a precarious island origin towards a majestically continental solidity, with an ironic coda. But Napoleon was a man who carried his own personal island around in his pocket. His career contrived to string islands together like pearls on a necklace. And however apparently vast and immovable the terrain he stood on, Napoleon was always capable of summoning up a flood of some kind. He was like a surfer with a board under his arm and one eye out for an incoming swell on the horizon. He was perpetually dancing over the unfathomable deep, carving a path through dream, symbol and myth, and subject to the ultimate law of the wipeout. Norwood Young is one of the few historians to take Napoleon's island history seriously. 'There is throughout [his work and his life] a singular detachment; the young Corsican is observing the world from without, as an islander who has no part or lot with it . . . this was his attitude towards the human race. It was that of a self-centred, insular egotist.'

The *Discourse on Happiness* imagined torrents of emotion or imagination having to be held back, in the individual mind, by the dams of logic and reason ('Le torrent est plus fort: les digues doivent l'être'). Napoleon's early stories often hinge on holding back the tide or the invasive hordes that are synonymous with it (Carthaginians, Romans, Phoenicians, Trojans, Barbarians, etc.). The sea is not so much threatening in itself as it is a conveyor belt for other innumerable forms of threat. The mountains and highlands and inaccessible forests are where you go to take refuge and hide out, if you have any sense, but the beach is where all the drama is, in the zone between land and sea, where conflicting elements fight it out.

In Napoleon's early fiction (for example, *Nouvelle Corse* or 'Corsican Novella'), I am the island and the island is me: 'I first drew breath in Corsica and, at the same time, conceived a violent love for my unfortunate homeland and for its independence.' The island is an Ark, refuge against the flood; but it is also a fragile vessel that can go down, submerged beneath the torrents (the Genovese, the Germans, the French are always a flood or a tide, surging up and overflowing the land, drowning Corsicans in their own blood). The island is a piece of heaven: hence the Englishman's fantasy in the *Corsican Novella*: 'I found myself in a small world which would provide for my continued existence, sheltered from the seductions of mankind, their power games, their ephemeral passions. There seemed to be no reason why I should not live there, if not in happiness, then at least in virtue and tranquillity.' [*A quoi ne tenait-il que je n'y vécusse sinon heureux, du moins sage et tranquille.*] And, at the same time, it is a foretaste of hell.

Corsica, suggests Dorothy Carrington, presented the image of Christ crucified. Although he would later make occasional comparisons of himself with Jesus Christ, Napoleon's early literary models were rather Old Testament than New. Corsica was an Eden that had been corrupted (the idea, that became a cliché in the nineteenth century, that every poet is in search of a lost paradise, might have been derived from Napoleon). And – despite poor marks for Latin at school – it was Virgil's Troy, overrun by Greeks, having to be reconstructed elsewhere by the refugees. And finally there was Daniel Defoe: 'I saw myself as Robinson Crusoe: like him I was king of my island.' [*Je m'égalai plusieurs fois à Robinson Crusoë. Comme lui j'étais roi de mon île*]. Napoleon suffered all his life from a Crusoe complex: he saw himself perpetually marooned, cast away, in trouble.

Napoleon probably wrote his shipwrecked-on-a-desert-island story, *Corsican Novella*, around the same time as the *Discourse on Happiness*, or shortly afterwards, during the leave that took him back to Corsica. This sentence, from near the opening, is an extremely compact literary counterpart to Beethoven's Pastoral Symphony, where glad feelings on a return to the country lead directly into a storm scene: 'There are few locations as picturesque as that of this island, cut off from all land by immense arms of water, surrounded by rocks against which the waves smash furiously' [*rochers contre lesquels les vagues se brisent avec fureur*]. Next come waves of furious Frenchmen washed up on the beach.

We tend to think of Napoleon as irrevocably at war with the English. This is so far from being the case that it would be truer to say that he was in love with them, but found himself repeatedly disappointed and betrayed. The people he instinctively hates are, in fact, the French. 'Frenchmen!' he writes in 'On Suicide', 'Not content with having carried off all that we cherished, you have also corrupted our morals.' The tragic subject of one of his early fictionalized histories is the Earl of Essex. And in *Corsican Novella* the first-person narrator is another Englishman ('one of these virtuous Englishmen who still shelter our fugitive citizens') who fetches up on the small island of Gorgona (a few miles from the coast of Corsica), joins forces with Corsican guerrillas and finds much in common with them. After all, they are all islanders together; the island is their bond. Whereas the French, on the other hand, are 'the natural enemies of free men'. In a letter to General Pascal Paoli, the exiled Corsican leader, he expressed the desire to come to England to visit him. There is a dubious story that Napoleon showed a fellow student at Brienne, the future Lord Wenlock, a letter requesting admission to the British navy, written in 'remarkably good English'. But there is no doubt that Napoleon identified with England and his early ambition to enter the French navy seemed like a second-best option. The desire to go into the navy – contrary to any Corsican tradition (Corsicans were rarely fishermen, let alone seamen, except when press-ganged by the French) – was typical: to challenge head-on the element he most feared. It took his older brother and mother combined to persuade him to go into the artillery after all.

The elderly Corsican exile of the *Novella* gives the Englishman a snapshot history of the island. It seemed to Napoleon that all Corsicans were natural campfire historians, oral memorialists of heroes and battles, generals and genealogies. It was stories or histories (the two are indistinguishable in French) that drove them on to fight, in a quest for vengeance or redress of past grievances, handed down through the generations. If the whole aesthetics of history and the motivation of literature could be summarized in a single word, that word would be: vengeance. The last words of the imaginary Corsican's dying father – who is 'swimming in his own blood' – are: 'My son, avenge me. This is the first law of nature.' [*Mon fils, venge-moi. C'est la première loi de la nature.*] The son in turn recounts the tale of a mother raped and killed, his wife and three brothers hanged, and seven of his own sons similarly slaughtered. And although he personally accounts for a few dozen Frenchmen, nevertheless the clear implication of this (unfinished) tale is that he passes on the baton to his daughter (who is handy with a gun) and the Englishman, who will be romantically united by their common hatred.

There was one further very powerful literary connection with England (or at least Scotland). In 1765, at the age of 24, not long after his first and fateful meeting with Dr Johnson, James Boswell visited Corsica on a journey that would become a book (first published in 1768). In Bastia, in the mountains, his path would have crossed that of Napoleon's father, Carlo. Boswell had just left Paoli, the Corsican leader; Carlo was in search of him. In September 1783, Napoleon, aged fourteen, writes to his father from school in Brienne: 'I implore you to send me Boswell's *History of Corsica*, along with any other histories or memoirs pertaining to this kingdom. You have nothing to fear, I will take care of them and will bring them back with me to Corsica when I come, though it be six years from now.' He writes of his native island as befits an islander, from the outside. He is already cut off from the source, doomed to rely on a Scottish tourist's eye-view of Corsica to feed his rampant nostalgia for the island he has left behind.

Boswell actually called his book *An Account of Corsica, The Journal of a Tour of that Island; and Memoirs of Pascal Paoli*. That unwieldy title corresponds to the two main elements, a history and geography of Corsica, on the one hand; and, on the other, a biography of Paoli. But the two are equated with one another, as if Paoli is the living incarnation of the island. Rhetorically speaking, Paoli is the personification of Corsica, or Corsica is the anthropomorphism of Paoli. Insurrection is synonymous with Corsica, and Paoli is the singular embodiment of the collective struggle for liberty and independence.

Rousseau, the 'wild philosopher', is Boswell's gateway to Corsica (he provides him with a letter of introduction) and the sign under which the journal is written. Rousseau had drawn up a model constitution for Corsica and wrote in his *Social Contract* that 'There is still in Europe a country capable of legislation. It is the island of Corsica. These gallant people have regained and defended their liberty with a courage and perseverance which merit the advice of a wise man on how to conserve it. I have a certain premonition that this one little island will astound Europe.' In Boswell's hands, Corsica becomes something of a Land that Time Forgot, the last refuge of Rousseau's lost world of soulful primitives, under attack by every corrupt society within sailing distance. Corsicans are the last exemplars of the state of nature. Impoverished they may be, 'But I bid them remember,' says Boswell, 'that they were much happier in their present state than in a state of refinement and vice, and that therefore they should beware of luxury.' Corsica was already a synonym and symbol for doughty resistance to foreign oppressors; Boswell turns it into a fortress against decadence too.

These Rousseauist battalions are under the direct command of Paoli, 'the General'. Tall, strong, manly, noble, he speaks French and Italian with equal ease (and tolerable English). It is no coincidence that he is well-versed in the classics, for he is every inch a classical figure, a hero of Homeric proportions, with a dash of Moses thrown in. He is, in short, the picture of purity, virtue and seriousness. He never laughs, Boswell notes (if Napoleon was impressed by this trait, he could not imitate it: he joked and laughed, even on Saint Helena). Paoli himself draws an analogy between Corsicans and Jews: they are the victims of superior, more numerous, more resourceful powers. He 'observed that the Corsicans had no chance of being like the Romans, a great conquering nation, who should extend its

empire over half the globe. Their situation and the modern
political systems, rendered this impossible.'

But this account of Paoli works by virtue of counterpoint:
he is a classic seen by a romantic; he is a man of action observed
by a contemplative. Boswell admires him as in many ways his
opposite: 'With a mind naturally inclined to melancholy, and a
keen desire of inquiry, I had intensely applied myself to metaphysical researches, and reason beyond my depth, on such
subjects as it is not given to man to know . . . I told him that I
had almost become for ever incapable of taking a part in active
life.' So the figure of Paoli is passed on to Napoleon: the living
image of a condition of self-identity towards which he can
only aspire, but clothed from head to toe in metaphor and
allegory, extravagantly over-determined, elusive by virtue of
his transcendent qualities. Napoleon is a would-be Paoli who
would perhaps have been better off as a Boswell.

It is 29 July 1786. More than two years have passed since
Napoleon wrote to his father asking for the Boswell book. But
we find him, aged sixteen, writing another letter, this time to
a Genevan bookseller, to send him the first two volumes of
L'histoire des révolutions de Corse, by the Abbé Germane and
to give him a full bibliography of all his other 'works on the
island of Corsica'. Napoleon's plan was to do a Boswell: to
produce a history of the island that would also be a panegyric
of Paoli. But he was a serious historian who felt compelled to
trawl through all the sources. He wanted his history to be as
compelling and authoritative as Paoli himself was, a verbal cor-
relative to the man. The majority of Napoleon's early writings
form part of his ultimately unfinished Corsican project.

When he wrote to Paoli, on 12 June 1789, explaining his
reasons for wishing to write a history of Corsica ('to call those
who have power over us to the tribunal of public opinion . . .
and expose their secret machinations' [*découvrir leurs sourdes
menées*]) and eliciting Paoli's patronage (just as he had sought
Raynal's), he implicated Paoli in his own birth and in the lives
of his parents: 'If you deign, General, to approve this work in
which you will be the main subject, if you deign to encourage
the efforts of a young man whom you saw born and whose
parents were always on the right side, I will dare to predict a
favourable outcome.'

It seems likely that, just as he recommended marriage to Boswell, so too Paoli actively encouraged Carlo Buonaparte – who was part of his entourage, occasional secretary and some-time bodyguard – to make a stable home with Napoleon's mother, Letizia, and can therefore be seen as, if not directly a godfather, then at least the presiding spirit over Napoleon's birth (Napoleon told General Gourgaud that Paoli could have been his actual father except for the fact that he was impotent). And the evidence is broadly in accord with Napoleon's blood-spattered conception of his island's history. While he was growing up, guerrilla rebels (or peasants deemed guilty of rebellion) were regularly captured and tortured publicly: their bodies would be systematically broken on the 'wheel' and their corpses exhibited at crossroads or along mule tracks through the hills, dangling from trees or still attached to the instrument of their torment and execution. 'All over the island,' Dorothy Carrington writes in *Napoleon and His Parents*, 'the tortured rotting bodies reminded the Corsicans that they were a beaten people.' In response to the mass revolt of 1774 (when Napoleon would have been five), suppression was swift, ruthless and total: hundreds of actual or potential rebels were hunted down and executed, their women were raped, livestock and crops and homes destroyed. Many were shipped off to Toulon and the galleys, inspiring a Final Solution-type plan to deport all Corsican males and ship in able-bodied Frenchmen to replenish the depleted Corsican gene-pool.

Napoleon responded to this profound sense of insularity and oppression by, if not taking up arms against a sea of troubles, then at least taking up the pen. Existence was struggle and writing was resistance – a series of guerrilla raids on the canon and the big guns of French history. Words were actions. This is the historian not as an academic but rather as avenger. Napoleon, even when a writer, perhaps especially when writing, always saw himself as a man of action. His first task was to hold back the tide of lies. The traitors to the nation had put about a false history of Corsica, 'sowing the seed of calumnies' against Paoli in particular, which are then taken up by more gullible wordsmiths: 'Writers, adopting [this propaganda] as truths, then transmit them to posterity. On reading them, my passion was ignited and I resolved to dissipate these mists of misinformation, these children of ignorance.' [*En les lisant, mon ardeur s'est échauffée et j'ai résolu de dissiper ces brouillards, enfants de l'ignorance.*] This is the genealogy of falsehood. Napoleon was born, he asserted, to rectify untruths and 'blacken with the brush of infamy' [*noircir du pinceau de l'infamie*] the reputations of those who have betrayed Corsica.

Paoli was not just a hero, but his role model too. Napoleon, Paoli and Corsica constituted an indissolvable triad. One of the earliest fragments of manuscript known to us – written when Napoleon was only sixteen – is a hymn of praise to Paoli, the archetypal rebel, à la Boswell, on his sixty-first birthday, a stinging denunciation of the French and a defence of the legitimacy of rebellion against all tyrannies. It concludes: 'Thus the Corsicans were able, while conforming to all the laws of justice, to shake off the Genoan yoke, and they can do likewise with that of the French.' [*Ainsi, les Corses ont pu, en suivant toutes les lois de la justice, secouer le joug génois et peuvent en faire autant de celui des Français. Amen.*] Paoli had refused to accept the Treaty of Versailles of 15 May 1768, transferring rights of dominion from Genoa to France. It was a simple and powerful message: France had no more rights over Corsica than Genoa. Only Corsicans should have power over Corsica. It was inevitable that the paramount project of Napoleon's early years should be a definitive history of Corsica. The island was an obsession and a theme. And Paoli was seen not just as the lynchpin of that history: it was he who would help to father the book. Paoli was patron and muse. Without Paoli, Napoleon could never be a historian.

Paoli is everywhere in Napoleon's early writings. He even manages to make an appearance in the *Discourse on Happiness*:

Monsieur Paoli, whose most distinctive characteristic is his solicitude for humanity and his compatriots, who briefly brought back to the Mediterranean the golden age of Sparta and Athens, endowed with the kind of genius that nature bestows upon one man for the benefit of mankind, Monsieur Paoli on his appearance attracted all the attention of Europe on Corsica.

This is very much in the style of Boswell and the last phrase is perhaps an allusion to Boswell's work. Paoli is the incarnation of revolution, but also the strong-man who puts an end to it: 'Matters were in such disarray that only a law-maker invested with great authority and transcendent genius could save the nation' [*un magistrat revêtu d'une grande autorité et d'un génie transcendant, pouvait seul sauver la patrie*].

But if Paoli became Napoleon's idealized father and law-giver, *le père sublime*, then Carlo, his biological father, the man who could have been but failed to be Boswell, was rejected as a traitor to the nation, a man who deserved to be blackened with the brush of infamy. Carlo had been, we should remember, one of Paoli's trusted lieutenants. But when the French annexed the island, in the wake of overwhelming military victory, Carlo was shrewd enough to become Charles. Guerrillas in the hills were fighting on and refusing to give up their arms, but Carlo chose to swear allegiance to Louis XV and become the protégé of the Comte de Marbeuf, commander-in-chief of French forces. For the first time, there is talk of Bonaparte rather than Buonaparte. The great personal drama of Napoleon's childhood is that while Paoli, the hero, remained tautologically Paoli, immovable, unchanging, as solid as a rock, Carlo – no doubt for the best of reasons, with his numerous and growing family, and left behind in 1769 as Paoli sailed for England and safety – appeared fluid, shifty, opportunistic, two-faced. Resistance hero versus collaborator: that was the clear-cut choice as the young Napoleon saw it. Where Carlo was mired in contradiction and ambiguity, Paoli represented a certain clarity and conviction and resolute resistance to the French. Paoli equalled truth with almost mathematical rigour; while his own father was indistinguishable from falsehood.

The French connection was as much linguistic as political and immoral. Carlo, appointed Corsican delegate to the court of Louis XVI in 1778, took Napoleon, then aged nine, with him to Versailles to be presented to the king, before depositing him at school. He was determined that his son should learn French. French was the language of power and the passport to a glittering career at the heart of the *ancien régime*. Carlo/Charles came to signify Frenchness in Napoleon's mind. From Carlo's point of view, French was a minor concession to realpolitik: it was necessary to speak the language of the dominant power. But in thrusting the French language upon the infant

Napoleon, he was committing the linguistic equivalent of child abuse, like making a left-hander write with his right hand. It was bound to generate conflict. From the beginning, the island that was Napoleon was assaulted by external forces beyond his control. The treacherous father and France were indivisible. Technically, the Bonaparte family was Tuscan in origin and had served on the Council of Ancients of Ajaccio (effectively the Corsican aristocracy). And now he was transformed into a member of the French establishment. There is a strong case for believing that Carlo was playing both ends against the middle and was never fully behind the French presence but only flying a flag of convenience. But whatever the rights and wrongs of his evolution, Napoleon perceived him as a turncoat, transferring his loyalties to outsiders, while he, Napoleon, like Paoli, remained faithful to the island.

He may have gone so far as to denounce his father openly, at his school in Brienne, in front of the monks assembled for dinner, for switching his loyalties from Paoli to the French. Certainly, in the face of bullying and abuse at school, when he was not taking refuge in the library, he would bravely, defiantly brandish his Corsican identity and looked forward to joining forces with Paoli or perhaps taking his place in the struggle. Probably the first cartoon caricature of Napoleon, by one of his fellow pupils at Brienne, shows him at the age of fifteen as a giant, preparing to do battle for Paoli, looking very determined, and ineffectually held back by a dwarf-sized hook-nosed teacher, tugging on his pigtail. The caption reads: 'Bonaparte runs, flies to the aid of Paoli, to rescue him from his enemies.' Verbally and to some extent physically, Napoleon ('Napollione' as he pronounced it, leading to the nickname 'la paille au nez') was already fighting at his side.

This youthful bias was probably still a factor in Napoleon's refusal, when First Consul, to honour his father with a monument, proposed by the city of Montpellier, where he was buried. 'Let us not disturb the rest of the dead,' he replied. 'I also lost my grandfather, and my great-grandfather, why do nothing for them? If it was yesterday that I had lost my father, then it would be decent and natural that I should accompany my regrets with some significant mark of respect; but it was twenty years ago and this event is remote from the general public. Let us not speak of it.' There is more than a certain becoming modesty to this refusal, and Napoleon was not automatically averse to monumentality. He dissolves the memory of his father into that of his ancestors (who preceded the French annexation) and there is a strong sense that his death was an event as remote to Napoleon as it was to the masses, and this coolness is emphasized by the double imperfect subjunctive [*eusse perdu . . . j'accompagnasse*]. Moreoever, he was recalling this statement at the end of his life on Saint Helena, as if nothing had ever changed in his attitude. In the end it was Louis, Napoleon's younger brother, who had the body of Carlo exhumed and transported to the park of Saint-Leu in Corsica, where a monument was finally erected. But he had to do it in some secrecy, presenting Napoleon with a *fait accompli*, no doubt fearful of another veto. Napoleon, then aged fifteen, in Paris, received word of Carlo's death in 1785 with a stoicism verging on indifference (or even, suggests Carrington, 'relief') and referred to it later in terms of liberation and good luck.

The young Napoleon's anti-royalist statements seemed to be aimed as much at his own father as at pretenders to the fatherhood of the nation. 'There are very few kings who would not have deserved dethroning' [*Il n'y a que fort peu de rois qui n'eussent pas mérité d'être détrônés*], he wrote pithily in 1788 at Auxonne in his short 'Dissertation on Royal Authority'. The rather domestic revolution Napoleon dreamed of consisted in dethroning his own father and installing Paoli in his place. The death of Carlo, the compromiser and calculator, collaborator and born-again monarchist, seemed to Napoleon to anticipate the passing of the *ancien régime*. As in the case of that other existential hero, Jean-Paul Sartre, the absence of the father was the making of him, *la chance de ma vie*, bestowing freedom and responsibility upon the growing boy and making possible a total commitment to Paoli and his origins.

From the point of view of today's reader, it is hard to distinguish Napoleon's works of history from his fictions. Both stories and histories are typically unfinished. Fragments of the overarching narrative of a lonely island or individual, up against overwhelming odds, recur. The budding historian cites no sources and psychologizes his characters out of all proportion. The narrative is punctuated by apostrophe and soliloquies overloaded with tearful lyricism. Napoleon was the poet of Corsican history (he did in fact write a poem in the epic style, on the subject of a Corsican hero, which was widely admired at the time among patriots). But, as if himself conscious of the potential slide of history into myth, the young Napoleon made every effort to anchor his writing in authentic documentation. The return to Corsica was driven by the lure of archives. In his memoirs Joseph recalls how his studious younger brother arrived back in Corsica, in 1786, his trunk stuffed with books. They compared their readings and their writings, and then Napoleon went off to Bastia in the north to collect materials for his history.

But he was confronted by one major problem (amongst so many) at this stage: he had forgotten his Italian. 'When I arrive back in my home country,' he wrote anxiously in *On Suicide*, 'what face will I wear, what language will I use?' [*Quand j'arriverai dans ma patrie, quelle figure faire, quel langage tenir.*] The paternal plan, to teach him French, had been so successful that the new language had wiped out the old. Or if he could still speak it – however rustily – he could not write it nor reliably read it. And how could he read the archives without Italian? We know that he made heroic (but largely unsuccessful) efforts to relearn it all over again. Back in Corsica, his brother Joseph recalls him struggling to improve his Italian: 'Impatient, as I was, at our inability to speak the language of the country, he took up the subject, but with little success in the first year; it was only during his second leave that, having resolved to write an essay on the revolutions in Corsica, he redoubled his efforts in order to be able to read the original texts in Italian.' Writing (in French) from Auxonne on 28 March 1789, to his uncle Lucien, who was archdeacon of Ajaccio, Napoleon made the rather plaintive remark: 'Why have you not written to me in Italian? I understand perfectly and I can read your writing very well.' Clearly Uncle Lucien for one does not really believe it. And the repetition at the end of the letter – 'Give me your news in Italian, because I understand it very well' – does not exactly inspire confidence either. At the same time, he affirms that he will be writing to his mother in Italian – thus making three rather obsessive assertions in just one letter. But it is all bluster. He makes the admission that 'I am beginning to learn [Italian]', but it is only a beginning.

Italian is identified explicitly as the mother-tongue, but one which paradoxically has to be learned, while French is strictly the father-tongue and is, in some way, inescapable. Here is the root of Napoleon's classically Oedipal rejection – translated into linguistic terms – of the father and idolatry of the mother ('All that I am, all I have been, I owe to the habits of work I received in my childhood and the good principles given to me by my excellent mother'). And this also explains the otherwise perplexing statement, 'I cannot write to maman, this will be for the first time. I will do it in Italian.' [*Je ne puis écrire à maman, ce sera pour la première fois. Je le ferai en italien.*] He cannot write to her properly in French; when he writes to her finally in Italian, it will be as if it were for the very first time. Italian, as he approaches twenty, will at last – so his theory goes – enable him to bond and communicate with his mother. But needless to add, it was always too late. Language would have been the bridge, but it was down.

There is more than a hint of his nostalgia for everything that has been lost in the letter Napoleon wrote to his mother from Seurre, on 15 April 1789, where he – and a detachment of 100 men – had been sent to put down a small local rebellion (although he did next to nothing while there – except write). The letter is, of course, in French. Napoleon had been invited to the house of a wealthy local family for Easter; but he was not looking forward to it. Rather he looked backwards: 'I would far rather be eating ravioli and lasagna in Ajaccio' [*J'aimerais cependant mieux manger le ravioli ou les lasagnes à Ajaccio*]. Napoleon harked back to Italian food in very much the same terms that he harked back to the Italian language. His mouth, his tongue, were doubly deprived: just as he had to overdose on rich French food, he complained, so too he had no choice but to utter heavy, over-elaborate, indigestible French words. To Napoleon's mind, Italian represented the raw and the natural, while French was the cooked, at the highly cultural end of the 'culinary triangle'.

Claude Lévi-Strauss's phrase (derived from Roman Jakobson) is appropriate because Napoleon anticipated a theme from another of his works, *Tristes Tropiques*. In that book Lévi-Strauss laments the passing of an oral culture in the Amazonian jungles. The Nambikwara tribe, in acquiring literacy, also seem to be caught up in all the vices of society, drawn into power games, hierarchies, oligarchies. Those who command the text also possess dominion over the rest of the tribe. Thus the advent of the written in the rainforest coincides with a re-enactment of the Fall of man. Put more politically, writing facilitates the rise of empires. The text is the keystone not so much to civilization but to exploitation and oppression. Language in its written form is just a blunt instrument for hitting people over the head with.

So too, Napoleon's writing contains an elegy for the oral and indigenous ravioli. Italian – or at least the Corsican dialect of Italian – was the primordial spoken language, the mother-tongue. Whereas French was first of all a literature, and only ever spoken by derivation. French was not natural but a con-struct, the epitome of Rousseau's arts and sciences that impov-erish the moral values of a society even as they enrich its culture. Thus there were two conflicting linguistic theories at work in Napoleon. The one gave priority to a utopian Italian and was broadly in tune with Lévi-Strauss's *Tristes Tropiques*, regretting a lost golden age of uncomplicated truth-speaking. The other, the French Napoleon, mocked the very idea of truth. Reality was lost and displaced and dissolved in the age of writing. And perhaps there never was an original truth to be lost in the first place, nothing but a primordial literariness that permeated everything, inexorably, from the very beginning. On one side of the bridge from Corsican Italian to French, truth is something to be found and recorded; on the far side, truth is made, truth is an illusion about which we have forgotten that it is an illusion. But once the bridge is crossed there is no going back. The *Discourse on Happiness* speaks of history as 'this flaming torch of truth', the foundation of the moral sciences, the indispensable guide to good government. But as Norwood Young notes, 'with all his show of accuracy, Napoleon is – incredible as it may seem – indifferent to facts and contemptu-ous of truth . . . his notes on history are warped by prejudice, and cannot be regarded as the work of an honest seeker after truth.' Compulsively creative, Napoleon would always be a poor academic.

'Napoleon never writes; he dictates,' said Roederer, in a hymn of praise to the oral style which was supposed to eradicate

'the ambiguities of written words.' But there was always, inescapably, a degree of artificiality, awkwardness or strangeness
in Napoleon's use of French, whether in his speech or his texts.
Sainte-Beuve thought highly of Napoleon's 'military eloquence'.
But, as Chateaubriand rightly pointed out, he could never be
mistaken for a native Frenchman (or not metropolitan French).
The Corsican-Italian accent, though attenuated, was never eradicated. Arnault recalls how, even much later, Napoleon completely mangled his reading of Ossian (which he wrote and
perhaps pronounced 'Ocean'): 'his tongue frequently became
twisted around words. Sometimes he replaced a T by an S, sometimes an S by a T. Often he . . . murdered the words he was
reading.' The effect was less 'epic' than 'burlesque'.

Napoleon's first official teacher of French in mainland France
gave him a glowing report, but only some time after the event.
In 1779, after presenting him to the king, Carlo delivered the
nine-year-old boy to a college in Autun, placing him under
the wing of the Abbé Chardon, specifically for the purpose of
improving his command of the language. It was a deep immersion experiment, cutting him off from all Italian speakers. By
all accounts he was a gifted student. 'I only had him for three
months', wrote the Abbé. 'During this time he learned enough
French to engage freely in conversation and to write essays and
translations. At the end of the three months, I sent him off
with M. de Champeaux for the military school at Brienne.'
This upbeat report is not, however, totally borne out by subsequent assessments. If we believe Chardon, the job was virtually done. But at Brienne and beyond, French remained at best
a tool, an instrument, a weapon, to be manipulated more or
less successfully for particular purposes.

Napoleon was never inside the language, he never fully possessed it or claimed it as his own. French was and was not his
language. He always approached the language and the literature from outside, as a foreigner. It could be said that Napoleon colonized and annexed the language, actively and rather
aggressively making it his, rather than painlessly absorbing it,
and roughly importing Italianisms ('fraternicide', 'victimer',
'ultimer', 'immétriguer', 'malcontentement', 'insatisfaction').
This may well account for his quasi-dyslexia. Napoleon systematically got his facts wrong as he took down his rather fanatical

notes from his myriad sources. Here is one example, from his reading of Coxe's *Voyage en Suisse*:

Coxe	Napoleon
5 candidates	8
in 1531	1555
in 1273	1270
50 members	60
3 departments	6
3 mountains	2
16th century	10th
4 syndics	1
102 members	120

It is not enough to call this catalogue of transformations 'mistakes' or inaccuracy (as Norwood Young does), nor even dyslexia ('He was one of those persons who could not spell,' notes Young, 'a fatal disqualification in our day for entrance upon the career of an officer and a gentleman'). Rather it appears as if Napoleon was in revolt against the very medium he was using. He had to modify everything, irrespective of truth-value. His handwriting was notoriously illegible and scrappy: 'a bundle of disconnected and indecipherable characters', according to his close collaborator Méneval. 'His words are missing half their letters.' Napoleon conceded the point but he had an explanation: 'The southern blood which flows in my veins moves with the swiftness of the Rhône. Please excuse me if you find it difficult to read my scribble.' His writing was the product of a struggle, of hot-blooded personality – rooted in place – against the collective mind of France, seen as coolly Apollonian. 'His early difficulties with French coloured the whole of his bearing towards language and literature', as Young writes, and beyond that to the world at large.

Napoleon was doing terrible violence to the French language. That was the view of Father Dupuy, his old French teacher at Brienne. He had retired from the school not long after Napoleon left it. But Napoleon remained ambivalently dependent on his advice long afterwards. Acutely sensitive to his own imperfections, he submitted himself to the judgement of Dupuy on matters of style and grammar and spelling, and he went so far as to ask Dupuy to make a decent final copy of one of his texts.

Dupuy was a man of delicate sensibilities in regard to language, an aesthete, a perfectionist, but above all a stylistic moderate, for whom extremism was anathema. It may seem to us almost incredible that, on 15 July 1789, the day after the Fall of the Bastille, Dupuy should be stirring himself from the depths of his retirement in the small town of Laon, a hundred kilometres or so north-east of Paris, to correct Napoleon's style. No doubt Dupuy saw himself as in some way representing the cause of the *ancien régime* in writing or at least trying to polish the literary manners of the *nouveau*. Perhaps he saw Napoleon, in turn, as carrying out an assault on the fortress of French style, a *sans-culotte* among writers. He gave Napoleon some positive words of encouragement ('I found the substance excellent'), but the main part of his letter was given over to serious strictures, reminiscent of the Lyon judges. 'There are several improper words, poorly arranged, repeated one after another, or dissonant, thoughts which appear to me superfluous or too bold, or liable to arrest or hold up the narration, and there are some excisions, some additions and a few revisions to make in certain places.'

The original work that Napoleon submitted to Dupuy is lost, but it can be more or less reconstructed from his old teacher's remarks. The quest for happiness persists: 'Henceforth, O Corsicans, who could prevent you from being happy?' [*Désormais, ô Corses, qui pourrait mettre obstacle à votre bonheur?*] There are elements of the archetypal *Corsican Novella*: an old man, on the brink of death, expounds his history of Corsica. But the valediction is transposed here into a direct address to Necker (father of Madame de Staël and minister of finance to Louis XVI – a post he had been dismissed from on 12 July), seeking his support and compassion. From Dupuy's point of view, the text appeared wildly over-emotive and over-rhetorical. Napoleon was exclamatory, adjectival, metaphorical, melodramatic, hot-headed: there were too many comparisons, knives and tears, and far too much blood: all this was 'prolix and declamatory'. (Another teacher, Louis Domairon, author of *General Principles of Literature*, would describe his style as 'granite, heated up in a volcano'.)

But if Napoleon had little faith in his own judgement, he had even less in that of others. He demurred over many of Dupuy's proposed revisions. Dupuy had 'taken out all the metaphysics' [*ôté toute la métaphysique*] he complained, and diluted the rhetoric. Dupuy replied that, considering that Napoleon's protagonist was addressing himself to Monsieur Necker – minister to the King! – he would have to tone down some of the more inflammatory language, the youthful outbursts to do with oppression, tyranny and robbing Corsicans of their liberty. And how can this be an old man speaking? Dupuy was an old man, he knew how they spoke. This is out of character, obviously only the words of a young man pretending to be an old man. It has to sound older somehow. More discretion is required, a certain coolness. Dupuy, in his sensible way, recommended that the phrase, 'Monarchs came to power; and with them, despotism' [*Les rois régnèrent; avec eux, le despotisme*], should be omitted, 'as a measure of prudence'. Similarly an apostrophe, beginning 'Proud tyrants . . . !', which could be misconstrued. But even after ten years in France, Napoleon was still in no mood to give up his weapons and surrender, and rejected most of Dupuy's corrections out of hand: 'This type of discourse is commonplace today, even among women.' Moderation was not his style. To the master of moderation he counselled, in return, greater extremism. The *Letters on Corsica* written for Raynal between September and November 1789 remain unrepentantly Napoleonic, uninflected by Dupuyisms. Kings still reign and with them, despotism.

Modelling himself on Dupuy, Napoleon went on to offer stylistic advice to his older brother, putting forward a proto-Hemingwayesque aesthetic of virility and economy: 'I've read your text . . . Some of it is good, but overall it is drowning in a sea of superfluity and flowery pedantries' [*Il y a du bon, mais qui est noyé dans un fatras d'inutilités, de fleurs pédantesques.*] Fluidity was a peril, even stylistically, what was needed was a language hard, harsh, and robust, like a landscape. The island of style had to be defended. 'My friend, you have much work to do. Your style is too diffuse, too flaccid. It lacks energy and sinew . . . Another fault is how readily you indulge your taste for the exotic word regardless of its relevance to the sense. If, instead of four pages, your speech [to the Patriotic Club of

Ajaccio] had been only a half as long, it would be excellent.'
Joseph might well have thought that this was a classic case of
the pot calling the kettle black. But there are signs here – in
1791 – of Napoleon carving out a more minimalist style for
himself, shorn of some of its more rhetorical flourishes. (He
was fair enough to admit, in another letter to Joseph, 'Your
speech . . . was thought better of than I feared. It made a good
impression.')

Here, then, is Napoleon's essential linguistic tragedy: he lost
his Italian, but he never properly acquired French ('*Opprimés
à la merci* . . . is not French', Dupuy told him bluntly). He was
rootless, adrift, at sea, floating restlessly between these happy
islands of authenticity and solidity. The contrast with Paoli could
not be more marked. According to Boswell's account, not only
was Paoli equally at home in Italian and French, but he was
capable of speaking to animals and learning their language too.
Paoli was an omnilinguist; Napoleon was not even a mono.

Nevertheless, after the rejection of the *Discourse on Happiness*, we must record one early coup for the young writer,
perhaps in some ways the high point of his literary career. His
Letter to Matteo Buttafuoco (1791) was a small but indisputable
success. Buttafuoco (or Buttafoco) was the enemy of Paoli,
one of the Corsican deputies at the Assembly in Paris, and
unreservedly pro-French, who had written a manifesto con-
demning Paoli as a 'political charlatan' which had been distributed around the island in large numbers. In classic satirical style,
Napoleon's response damns him with praise. Buttafuoco, the
butt of Napoleon's heavy irony, is a direct political descendant
of his father – a convert to the French cause, a false represent-
ative of the Corsican people – and in some ways the *Letter* reads
as a sideways-on indictment of Carlo. The *Letter* was enthusiastically received by the radical 'Club of Ajaccio'. Its presid-
ent, Massera, wrote to the aspiring author: 'Having acquainted
itself with your writing in which, with as much finesse as force
and merit, you unveil the secret machinations of the infamous
Buttafuoco, the Patriotic Club has voted to have your work
published.' This must have seemed like a breakthrough to
Napoleon. His first work in print, officially judged to be 'useful
to the public good'. A few days later, he sailed back to France,
still riding the wave of this rave review.

It must have been in this mood that he sent his work to Paoli, bursting with youthful confidence and pride. But it was hubris before a fall. Although the Letter supported the Paoli position, Paoli – rather ungratefully it must have seemed – professed not to like it, despite all the acclaim. 'I received the pamphlet of your brother,' he wrote to Joseph. 'It would have made a greater impression on me if it had said less and if it had shown less partiality.' Paoli attacked Napoleon, in effect, for supporting him. Paoli sounded, in fact, rather like old Father Dupuy. More discretion, more neutrality. The fiery Napoleonic style was too over-the-top for his taste.

But Napoleon was not to know of Paoli's negative reaction. In the tentative first draft of the history he sent off to Paoli along familiar lines, Napoleon asserted that there was, in fact, no longer any reason to write, Corsica having been saved by the Revolution, which had turned France into a bastion of liberty. 'There is no longer any sea between us' [Il n'est plus de mer qui nous sépare], as he characteristically put it, meaning no more stormy conflict: they were finally as one. 'When there was danger, all that was needed was courage. When my work could have the immediate object of utility, then I believed that my powers would be sufficient. But today I pass on the mission of writing our history to someone who, although perhaps without my dedication, will surely possess greater talents.' Nadia Tomiche (in Napoléon écrivain) is probably right to read this as a characteristic rhetorical manoeuvre, a feint of modesty. We saw the same technique in the Discourse on Happiness, when he deferred at the end to superior writers.

Although the anxiety about his talents was real, Napoleon was nevertheless desperate to continue with the project. Back in France, in March 1791, he wrote once more to Paoli requesting rather more practical support – original documents, letters on contemporary events – to complete his history of Corsica. So Paoli's reply, arriving the following month, must have come as a stiletto in the heart of his ambitions.

Paoli began by dismissing the work on Buttafuoco ('Do not take the trouble to contradict the falsehoods of Buttafuoco; such a man as this cannot enjoy any credit with a people who have always esteemed honour and who have now recovered their liberty. To pronounce his name is to give him pleasure

... His own family is ashamed of him'). And he declined to lend assistance ('I cannot at present open up my archives and seek out my writings'). But the letter of rejection goes far beyond just coolly refusing to help Napoleon. There is an icy discouragement of Napoleon the historian. There is no question of wishing him better luck with another publisher. He who had been the symbolic father to Napoleon was now trying to abort his career before it was properly launched. 'History is not written in youth,' Paoli affirmed. It required maturity, balance, a Dupuyan cooling of the fires. Perhaps he could begin, Paoli recommended, by collecting a few anecdotes. Raynal had cracked champagne bottles over him; but Paoli, hero and role model and surrogate father, had sunk him, or tried to sink him. It was yet another betrayal.

Paoli replied to Napoleon in Italian. At last Napoleon had his wish come true that someone would write to him in Italian. But, by virtue of the very struggle to understand it, Napoleon – who had of course written to Paoli in French – was inevitably being reminded that he was, linguistically, fundamentally ill-equipped to carry through the task of writing Corsican history. Perhaps any history. French: the language of literature, not of history. And how could one heap enough scorn on France while still speaking French? And what was all this paradoxical nonsense about 'no more sea'? Had Napoleon become pro-French? What had happened to the island mentality? Whether or not this was Paoli's intention, the reference to a man whose 'own family is ashamed of him' hinted at something similar in the case of Napoleon: 'he only speaks and writes to persuade people that he is of some consequence.'

There is a parallel here with the case of Jean Genet, poet, homosexual and thief, in the version of his life recorded by Sartre. At the age of ten, without having done anything wrong, the orphan Genet is accused of being a thief. And, bereft of an identity, Genet chooses to adopt the one that is flung in his face. To adopt the accusation. So too Napoleon, à la Genet, accused by his compatriots of French tendencies, adopted Frenchness, without ever being French (just as at school in France, despised for being Corsican by the French, he had stoutly asserted his non-Frenchness). Napoleon was not born French, he became French. He chose Frenchness, it could be said, but it would be truer to say that he was forced to be French. If he was French, it was (as the existentialists would say) in the mode of not-being. Ironically, then, he followed the path of the father he despised and rejected. Napoleon's *Address to the Municipality of Ajaccio*, dating from 1793, demanded that the citizens sign up to the French Republic in a mass pledge of collective loyalty. There was no more sea between France and Corsica.

Napoleon had, in other words, become a traitor to the cause of an independent Corsica. He soon found himself under threat of arrest, and on the run, pursued around the island by the anti-French faction, led by Pozzo di Borgo. Napoleon was spirited away, concealed by sympathetic shepherds and given a boat to make a hasty exit. His mother and younger brothers and sisters, the object of anti-Bonaparte animosity, were like-wise forced to flee on 23 May 1793. The family home in Ajaccio was pillaged and wrecked and would have been put to the torch but for the proximity of Paolista houses. On 1 June 1793, holed up in Bastia, Napoleon wrote his *Position politique et militaire du département de Corse*, which re-cast Paoli as villain rather than hero (*Le Souper de Beaucaire* sim-ilarly attacked Paoli for betraying the Revolution and crushing the friends of liberty). He had sold out to the English, and England had become the principal threat to Corsica. Only France, Corsica's natural ally, could liberate it – from external influence but also from its own internal divisions. In what would become a model case, Corsica needed saving from itself. On 11 June, Napoleon and his family took ship for Toulon and France.

Cast adrift from Italian, unable to anchor in the safe harbour of French, Napoleon was now to all intents and purposes a writer without a language. Despite all the setbacks and distrac-tions, Napoleon never in fact definitively gave up on the dream of his Corsican history. The project lived on, even if doomed to incompletion. On Saint Helena, where history became an obsession, Montholon recalls that Napoleon returned to his first love: 'I would like . . . you to carry out some research for me in the archives on Paoli. I want to write the history of Corsica: I started work on it in my youth, and I often feel my head is full of memories' [*je me sens parfois la tête pleine de souvenirs*]. He would spend whole nights scouring the *Bibliothèque orientale* in search of the Saracen kings of Corsica.

Napoleon was always exiled. Saint Helena, his ultimate island, was his big chance to make it at last as a historian. He could not resist drawing the parallel to the attention of Las Cases: 'The fatherland is still precious to me,' he said. 'Even Saint Helena could be too' [*La patrie est toujours chère. Sainte-Hélène même pourrait l'être à ce prix*]. His mistake, in abdicating, was not to have returned to Corsica, where he would have been safe, he thought. But, says Las Cases, 'he hadn't wanted people to say that he had watched the ship of the whole French people go down while he alone had the art of finding his way to port.' He had to be shipwrecked again, the eternal Crusoe, living out the plot of the *Corsican Novella*.

The metaphoric notion that 'there is no longer any sea between us' became the core of Napoleon's new theory of happiness. Whether they liked it or not, every man *ought* to be 'a piece of the continent'. There were to be no more lonely islands left on the map, cut off and exposed to the elements, drowning in seas of incoherence, suffering from melancholia. Islands, separate entities, were henceforth to be incorporated into the continent until the continent itself had acquired all the original singularity and self-identity of the island. 'A continent is nothing but a very large expanse of earth surrounded by sea', he wrote in his notes on geography (*Cahier* 11). 'The continent is therefore related to the island, which is likewise a land surrounded by waters.' France, and the whole of Europe, and Asia, and the world, were to be modelled on (the idealized) Corsica. If there were to be no more divisive seas, then Napoleon would have to get round to bestriding the Channel (or digging a tunnel under it). If he had had to learn French (however imperfectly), then everyone else could too, including above all the English. Their French would be even worse than his own. But he would make a start on his home territory: the Mediterranean.

3
Mind over Matter

Napoléon en Egypte
aux Pyramides.

In March of 1798 Napoleon sent a hand-written note to his secretary, Bourrienne, specifying the contents of a 'bibliothèque portative' to accompany him on a forth-coming campaign, ranging across history, fiction, geography, science, poetry, politics and religion, embracing Ossian and the Koran and Raynal's *Histoire des deux Indes*. By the time the Egyptian expedition got under way, in May, the portable library had swollen to more than 1,000 volumes. It was so sprawling that Napoleon had to design a dedicated vehicle – a modified cannon-transport – to accommodate it all. Egypt was the scene of a classic Napoleonic evolution: first reading; then writing; and, finally, taking the library into battle.

Napoleon was an orientalist, steeped in tales of pharaohs, Persia, Hannibal, metempsychosis and Osiris, long before he ever sailed east. Egypt existed first of all as a topic to be con-quered and possessed on the page. Napoleon probably started with Plutarch and one of Voltaire's global histories, moved on to Rollin's three-volume *Histoire ancienne*, and eventually homed in on the Abbé Marigny's more specific *History of the Arabs Under the Caliphate*. He took voluminous notes on this book while in his barracks at Auxonne and during his pacifica-tion mission in Seurre. Then he launched upon his own fictional

reconstruction of a fragment from Marigny concerning a masked
and rebellious prophet during the reign of the twenty-second
caliph. Thus 'Le Masque prophète' – which can be translated as
'The Mask of the Prophet' – was born in the middle of 1789.

This short story tells how the regime of Mahadi, a wise
prince, is challenged by the revolt of Hakem, who is ultimately
defeated. The silver mask of the title is sported by Hakem
to prevent his followers – so he claims – being blinded by the
divine light that emanates from his face: in reality, he is blind
and disfigured. In a final stand, rather than submit to superior
numbers, Hakem poisons his own men, dumps the bodies in a
lime pit and immolates himself, in order to make it appear that
the rebel forces have mysteriously been taken up into heaven.
Hakem is an exceptionally successful liar and con-man.

Mahadi, on the other hand, is *'grand, généreux, éclairé,
magnanime'*, an enlightened leader, rational, benevolent, states-
manlike, serenely steering the Arab empire towards prosperity,
peace and progress. He is also an intellectual who is 'attending
to the task of advancing and encouraging the growth of the
sciences when the peace was disturbed by Hakem' [*il s'occupait
à faire fleurir les sciences et en accélérait les progrès lorsque la
tranquillité fut troublée par Hakem*]. Tranquillity and truth hang
together. Thus Hakem's rebellion is not only divisive, it leads
to the rise of emotion, rhetoric and deception on a mass scale.
It is impossible not to read this story, written in the midst of
the Revolution, as in part an allegorical reflection on develop-
ments in France, an oriental transposition of the fall of the
ancien régime. In this light, it is clear that Napoleon's alleged
enthusiasm for the Revolution is muted and nuanced by a strong
sense of its corrupting consequences. Mahadi is also inevitably,
at this period, a precursor of Paoli, Napoleon's idealized leader
figure, so that Baghdad is, in another aspect, Corsica transported
to the East. But *The Mask of the Prophet* is less an episode in
history than an archetypal narrative, hinging on a primordial
conflict between empire, on the one hand, and subversion on
the other, that is quintessentially literary and, at the same time,
political through and through.

'The caliph and his council felt the necessity of suffocating
at birth such a dangerous insurrection' [*Le Calife et les grands
sentirent la nécessité d'étouffer dans sa naissance une insurrection*

si dangereuse], writes Napoleon, and the virtue of the campaign waged by Mahadi – the prince of knowledge and wisdom, against Hakem – trickster and propagandist – is that it is a struggle to overcome not just subversion specifically, but more generally the political and literary tendency towards untruth and ambiguity. Science is pitted against art. But the ending of the tale, 'Such was the end of Hakem, also known as Burkai, whom his followers believe to have been spirited off to heaven with his men' [*Telle fut la fin d'Hakem surnommé Burkaï que ses sectateurs croient avoir été enlevé au ciel avec les siens*] strongly suggests that even if Hakem is dead his legacy remains intact. There is no escaping literature, not even in Egypt. Especially in Egypt.

'We must go to the Orient, all great glory has been acquired there,' Napoleon told Bourrienne. He dreamed first of joining up with Tippo Sahib in India; then of becoming a mercenary under the Sultan in Turkey; but it was Egypt that finally summoned him, offering a gateway to the world. 'Egypt is the country . . . which has most captured the attention of the literary world', as one of his generals, Sulkowski (who would die there) observed in his 'Description of the route from Cairo to Salehhyeh'. Thanks to the complicity of generations of poets and novelists, from Hugo down to Flaubert, the whole campaign has been generally depicted in heroic and glorious terms, although, militarily speaking, it was nothing but a protracted defeat, miraculously spun out and postponed and parleyed up into something disproportionately wonderful; or an extremely oblique flanking attack on Paris itself. But the Egyptian expedition was, from its inception, an overtly literary phenomenon, an exercise in the epic, with a French audience, an intellectual fantasy that acquired some bayonets.

Talleyrand and the Directoire had their own motives (mainly getting rid of Napoleon), but, for Napoleon, Egypt offered a golden opportunity to enact his oriental idea. His statements and letters of the period freely run together elements of Republican dogma, Raynalian liberationism and Volney's axiom about the preeminence of West over East. But presiding over all these themes is one meta-narrative that Napoleon took away with him (along with so many artistic treasures) from Italy: the overarching idea of a renaissance. France, Egypt, the

Orient, the world and above all, himself: all stood in need of rebirth. And the path to this radical metamorphosis lay through the realm of knowledge.

The Commission des Sciences et des Arts was so much Napoleon's own idea that he had to go about Paris (assisted by Arnault) knocking on people's doors to talk them into joining. He was like an encyclopedia salesman, with this small but significant difference: that the customers he was begging to take up his special offer would actually have to write the book (which became the monumental *Description de l'Egypte*). With all the specifics left out, he inevitably spoke in fanciful abstractions – a noble mission, the fulfilment of destiny, serving the cause of enlightenment. Cuvier, Laplace and David, among others, all reluctantly declined the honour. It says a lot for Napoleon's powers of persuasion – and the susceptibility of the French intellectual – that fully 167 savants (all male), astronomers, artists, poets, naturalists, architects, mineralogists, orientalists and one ex-baritone from the Paris Opera, all signed up to the mystery tour to become Napoleon's multi-talented constellation of collaborators. One of them was Jean Lambert Tallien, who had participated in the overthrow of Robespierre in the Convention in 1794 and had been taken under the Napoleonic wing in Italy.

Tallien penned the prospectus to the first edition of *La Décade égyptienne: journal littéraire et d'économie politique* (published in Cairo in September 1798) in which he argued that the Revolution – 'the reign of liberty' – had generated a large number of periodicals and also a lot of newsworthy events to go in them, both a market for and a plentiful supply of sensationalism. The point was to keep up the flow: 'the uninterrupted series of the most extraordinary events'. The Revolution had whipped up a demand for the spectacular, and the Egyptian expedition existed in order to satisfy it. Napoleon was being touted as the most prolific source of new and exciting stories. This is not as wildly introverted as it sounds. All the evidence suggests that, after his exploits in Italy, Napoleon's typically authorial concern was: what happens next? Egypt was devised in order to top Italy.

But Tallien also set out the theme of an intellectual-led renaissance that would be at the core of France-in-Egypt. The tragedy of the Revolution, he argued, was that it had betrayed the arts and the sciences (the great chemist Lavoisier, for example, had famously been led off to the guillotine, with the phrase, 'The Republic has no need of savants', echoing in his ears). Now, however, there was good news: 'a few men, distinguished by their knowledge and their love of literature, have begun to restore to philosophy [*la philosophie* i.e. in late eighteenth-century terms, all artistic and scientific endeavour] the ascendancy which it should never have lost.' The theory of the so-called 'civilizing mission' was that the French had come to Egypt to spread enlightenment. But matters were by no means that simple or that patronizing. France, like Egypt, had sunk into a trough of ignorance and anti-intellectualism from which it was now emerging. France needed renovating almost as badly as Egypt.

Gaspard Monge, the mathematician and author of *The Art of Manufacturing Guns*, appointed head of the Commission des Sciences et des Arts, had already suffered a major attack of second thoughts. Napoleon had despatched him to Rome to acquire printing presses with fonts in French, Greek and Arabic. While there Monge wrote to Napoleon, in March 1798, to say that all the practical matters were in hand, but he felt he should really be getting back to his research in descriptive geometry at the Polytechnique, which he had helped to establish. 'If I were only younger,' Monge writes weakly, 'no proposition could have been more agreeable to me than that of serving under you.' But he had his duties in Paris to attend to, not to mention an ageing wife. 'Allow me to figure among those mere mortals who admire your talents from afar, appreciating everything you do and singing of your glories.' Napoleon wrote back to him by return of post that he was counting on those printing presses and on Monge, 'even if I have to sail up the Tiber with the whole fleet to come and get you' [*dussé-je remonter le Tibre avec l'escadre pour vous prendre*]. Monge, unwilling to have an armada coming after him, took back his second thoughts and agreed to come of his own volition.

Napoleon's portable renaissance – duly led by Monge – finally sailed out of Toulon on 19 May 1798. The fleet was so vast that 'when [people ashore] looked at the horizon,' wrote Nicholas the Turk, 'they could no longer see water, but only

sky and ships [and] they were seized by unimaginable terror.'
On board his flagship, the *Orient*, while playing cat-and-mouse
with Nelson, Napoleon held a three-day seminar on Rousseau
and presided over debates to do with religion, government, the
age of the world and the interpretation of dreams. The *Orient*
– the ship – was a microcosm and model, in its academic aspira-
tions, of the kind of society the Orient – the place – ought to
be. On his way to Egypt, Napoleon stopped off at Malta. Inside
a week, he had overcome the feeble opposition, expropriated
the Knights Hospitallers of the Order of St John, abolished
slavery, brought in freedom of worship and reorganized the
education system, setting up schools with a predominantly
French curriculum and a new academy on the model of the
Polytechnique, with professorships, library, museum, botanical
garden and observatory attached. He had also shrewdly released
hundreds of Muslims from Maltese jails who would serve him
as useful propagandists later on.

The night landing in Alexandria was relatively uneventful,
Napoleon wrote: nineteen men drowned in the rough seas
and 'the full moon shone down brilliantly, revealing as if in
daylight the whitish earth of arid Africa.' But the journey from
Alexandria to Cairo, straight across the fringes of the Sahara,
during the hottest period of the year, in actual daylight, was
a major test of the Commission's mettle and prompted a cool
scientific paper by Monge on the subject of mirages. Once in
Cairo, the Commission set up their headquarters in an ex-
harem, vacated by one of the Mamelukes, the ruling military
elite, from which Napoleon claimed to be liberating Egypt.
Napoleon could not resist echoing Paris: where the Institut
National (founded in 1795 to replace the Académie française)
was on the banks of the Seine, the Institut d'Egypte arose on
the banks of the Nile. During the occupation of Cairo, amidst
sieges, massacres and cannon-fire, young mathematicians from
the Polytechnique actually sat a calculus exam. Apart from conducting ongoing projects, the Institut would meet every five days
(major battles and expeditions excepting) and boasted thirty-
six full members, divided into four sections, Political Economy,
Physics, Mathematics and Literature and the Arts.

There were, of course, technical matters for the Commission
and the Institut to attend to. Napoleon himself suggested such

subjects as: how to improve bread-baking, purifying the Nile, making beer without hops, the fabrication of gunpowder and his pet project – the construction of a canal through to the Gulf of Suez. But there was practically no limit to the scope of inquiry. A sceptical and satirical English cartoon of the period depicts a couple of French academics being attacked by angry crocodiles – one is bitten in the thigh, another in the backside – while the savants deliver treatises on the subjects of 'The Education of Crocodiles' and 'The Rights of the Crocodile'. This is not so far from the truth. Geoffroy Saint-Hilaire, the naturalist, took an interest in the sexual organs of the crocodile in particular. The meetings of the Institut boasted papers on such heterogeneous topics as: the date tree, the true colour of the sea, magic, prostitution, the ostrich, dancing, the painting of fish, different types of sand and the formation of dunes. Parseval-Grandmaison read out his translation of Tasso and verses from his own poems which perhaps evoked the setting of the Institut itself, whose meetings often took place outdoors, with the fragrance of an orange grove wafting in the air: 'In this magical place, our sense of smell, our taste, our ears and our eyes, all are seduced, all are enchanted.' He sang of rivers, love-birds, fountains, fruits, figs and olives, comparing Egypt to a Garden of Eden. Marcel – director of publishing – translated an ode from the original Arabic whose theme was the greatness of Napoleon. The Institut was Napoleon's *Orient* on dry land, a flagship of enlightenment, crewed by intellectual status symbols.

Napoleon – as vice-president and illustrious member of the mathematics section (he had in fact already been elected to the Institut in Paris in 1797, nominated by Laplace) – thus played out the role of the noble Prince Mahadi, great, generous, enlightened, magnanimous, attending to the task of advancing and encouraging the growth of the sciences. He even threatened to deliver a paper to the Institut on some mathematical topic before being dissuaded by Berthollet. The flavour of the *séances* of the Institut can be discerned from the pages of the *Décade égyptienne*, dedicated to recording the Institut's latest findings. The *Décade*'s subtitle, 'Journal littéraire', was glossed in advertisements and its own leader column: 'This journal, to appear every ten days, will be purely literary: there will be no room for news or discussion of a political nature; but everything

that belongs to the realm of the sciences, of the arts or commerce (whether in general or in particular), everything that is
related to civil or criminal legislation, or to moral and religious
institutions, will be eagerly welcomed.' In Napoleonic terms,
the literary embraced everything, excluded nothing, other than
politics. Except that the one thing omitted or repressed was
never more pervasive. Marcel referred – in his paper on an Arab
poet – to the French *'empire littéraire'*. And it is not absurd to
think of Napoleon's empire as literary in character, in the broad
encyclopedic terms of the *Décade*: at once artistic, scientific,
judicial and religious.

There are three classic hypotheses concerning the hierarchy
between hardware (the military, technology, weapons, economic
resources) and software (ideology, literature, discourse, texts,
language) in the Egyptian expedition (and in the development
of empires generally):

1   Tech is everything, the text nothing (Gellner).
2   Tech and the text are accomplices (Said).
3   The text is everything, the tech nothing (Baudrillard).

The first view of history is broadly deterministic and positivist:
given certain original imbalances of power and science, they
were bound to even out, like water passing from the higher
to the lower level. In the second, it makes a difference what
attitude you – and the culture at large – take up towards these
imbalances. And in the third, mere material differences are of
minimal significance beside the immensities of ideas and theories and images. Most recent historians have seen Napoleon
as a hard-nosed pragmatist, rooted in the real, who only paid
lip-service to ideas when it suited him. Edward Said, in
Orientalism, elevated the status of all intellectual software (the
epistémè or 'interdiscursive formation'), making language and
literature part of a giant conspiracy to pervert the world, and
seeing writers and scholars as being in cahoots with power.
But Napoleon was even more emphatically postmodern in his
approach to the East, conferring an almost magical, fetishistic
power on 'arts and sciences' and privileging the imaginary
and the symbolic – the hyperreal – over the real. The Orient,
for Napoleon, was something to be produced, stage-managed,

scripted. He took a full-blown textual approach towards the East. As the anti-materialist William Blake put it, at the end of the eighteenth century, 'The Foundation of Empire is Art and Science . . . Empire follows Art and not vice-versa as Englishmen suppose.'

Later, back in Paris, Napoleon would confide to the lovely and treacherous Madame de Rémusat that 'Egypt was the most wonderful time of my life because it was the most unreal' [*Ce temps que j'ai passé en Egypte a été le plus beau de ma vie, car il en a été le plus idéal*]. 'In Egypt I found myself delivered of all the frustrating constraints of civilization' [*débarrassé du frein d'une civilisation gênante*]. I could dream of all things and I could see the means to execute what I had dreamed.' The premise that ideas took precedence over things was fundamental to the expedition. The Empire was an emanation of mind and Egypt was planned as a monumental demonstration of the triumph of mind over matter. Napoleon actually used the phrase in his campaign memoir, in defining the West in Platonic and Christian terms by reference to 'the superiority of mind over matter, the soul over the body' [*la supériorité de l'esprit sur la matière, de l'âme sur le corps*]. Inculcate the right ideas and feelings, and people will be happy. Write the story first, then get people to believe it. The real is fluid, mutable, elusive and has to be articulated, constructed, defined. The world has to be thought out before it is entitled to exist. Which is why the Egyptian expedition took on the form of a quest for knowledge, an intellectual Holy Grail. We should avoid being too cynical about the grand motivation – at once simulated and real – which was attributed to the undertaking: to expand human consciousness, improve communications and open Egypt up to systematic study. Sainte-Beuve, for one, certainly read it literally. 'It is in such pages [Napoleon's campaign memoir] that one feels how seriously Napoleon sometimes took his mission of civilizing warrior, and that he was not just another sword in this mythical Orient, but a luminous sword.' In one way, the Egyptian expedition was nothing other than an immensely expensive collective research trip, involving a lot of fieldwork, with frequent recourse to the archives.

The historical theory which underlay the whole episode hinged on the leitmotiv of rebirth. The sciences and the arts had originated in the Orient (specifically the Middle East and, even more specifically, Egypt), travelled westwards and were now being restored to their point of origin. Knowledge was born in Egypt, died – or at least became dormant – but was now being triumphantly born again. Napoleon was carrying the torch, which had been lit on the banks of the Nile, and had been carried through Greece and on into Italy and France (having more or less left England untouched), back again. The Revolution had long championed a theory of regeneration and hooked it up with the Orient. In August 1793, a fountain was erected on the Place de la Bastille, in plaster with a bronze veneer, in the form of the figure of Isis from whose fertile breasts sprang the sacred river of life. The pharaohs were reinstated as precursors of the Enlightenment. But it took Napoleon to seize on the theme and develop its epic potential, its immense scope for creation and annihilation and hyperbole.

Napoleon's huge advantage was that he suffered from an impoverished sense of the present. He was incapable of living for the moment; the idea would have made no sense to him. He lived always in the past and the future, never fully inhabiting the present. The present was so fully occupied by the ghosts of the past and premonitions of the future as to leave no room for the present itself. Presence was a trough, a void, beside the plenitude of what had gone before and what was to come. 'There are two systems,' Napoleon said, 'the past and the future: the present is only a painful transition.' [*Il y a deux systèmes, le passé et l'avenir; le présent n'est qu'une transition pénible.*] Egypt fitted in perfectly with this prior psychological and intellectual predisposition.

But there was a positive benefit to be derived from this systematic negation. 'Egypt is useful not only for what it possesses,' wrote the mathematician Fourier in the introduction to the *Description de l'Egypte*, 'but even more so for what it lacks.' Vivant Denon, the painter, colourfully illustrated this line of thought. After seeing Thebes ('Thebes, whose very name fills the imagination with vast memories'), he had come to the conclusion that Greece had invented nothing, having plagiarized everything Egyptian. In a paper delivered to the Institut, he complains of marching across the desert with the army, of his own 'nullité' and the 'rien' of the empty spaces, but then finds a remarkable consolation in the thought that the dazzling sights of Thebes 'can be classified in the mind only by virtue of sustained reflexion, and that if it is necessary to retain one's first impressions, it is only in the absence of that which gave birth to them that one can analyse, criticize, and adopt them.' The annihilation of the present is actually an integral part of the intellectual reconstruction of the East. The key point about Egypt, from Napoleon's point of view, was that – like him – it barely occupied the present: it was only a shadow of its former self, and had to be imagined and projected in its true magnificence.

This set of presuppositions led to the preeminence of two twin genres, archaeology and science fiction (or technological utopianism), in which the remote past and the imminent future overlap and interlock. The whole work of the Commission des Sciences et des Arts and of the Institut d'Egypte can be summarized in two projects, which are secretly one: the search for a lost origin – *A la recherche du temps perdu*, written by Napoleon – and the recreation of the past (*Le Temps retrouvé*). What H. G. Wells would call 'a nostalgia for the future' pervaded the mission. From Napoleon's point of view, conquest was subordinate to and at every point intimately tied into quest. Probably the best known of Napoleon's Egyptian addresses to his troops belongs to the Battle of the Pyramids and reflects his acute sense of the presence of the past: 'From the heights of these Pyramids, forty centuries gaze down on you' [*Soldats, du haut de ces pyramides, quarante siècles vous contemplent*]. Or, again, on the eve of disembarkation: 'the first city that we will encounter was built by Alexander. At every step we will find memories worthy of exciting the emulation of the French.' [*La première ville que nous allons rencontrer a été bâtie par Alexandre. Nous trouverons à chaque pas des souvenirs dignes d'exciter l'émulation des Français.*] And the presence of the future is equally resonant in this toast, worthy of Jules Verne, that Napoleon made to celebrate the anniversary of the founding of the Republic: 'To the year 3000 of the French Republic.' By way of amplification, Monge toasted 'the perfecting of the human mind and the progress of enlightenment' while Berthier looked forward to 'the expulsion of the Mamelukes and the happiness of the people of Egypt'.

In Egypt Napoleon was still putting the finishing touches
to his *Discourse on Happiness*: 'It is my wish that you let the
people of Misr know that it is my wholehearted intention to
provide them with prosperity and happiness; just as the Nile is
the best and most fortunate river, so will the people of Misr be
the happiest of all creation, if the Lord of the worlds wills it.
Farewell.' After fifty years of hypothetical French dominion,
Napoleon would write in one of his 'if-only' digressions in his
campaign journal,

> civilization would have spread into the interior of Africa by
> way of Sennar, Abyssinia, Darfour, Fezzan; several great nations
> would have been called upon to enjoy the benefits of the arts,
> the sciences, the religion of the true God, for it is through Egypt
> that the peoples of the centre of Africa must receive light and
> happiness [*c'est par l'Egypte que les peuples du centre de l'Afrique
> doivent recevoir la lumière et le bonheur*].

Education (by the French) was the key to happiness. Despite
a certain resentment among his soldiers towards the savants,
Napoleon's thinking filtered through the ranks of the army and
the Institut alike (it would be truer to say they were deliberately
propagated: as his fleet approached its destination, Napoleon
made arrangements to have his proclamations printed and distributed 'in order to give them the widest possible publicity').
Among his many collaborators, the *Décade égyptienne* spoke
rapturously of 'time, reason and public education' making any
military intervention redundant and enabling the French to
concentrate on their research. Likewise Monge looked forward
to a happy ending to their efforts. In a jubilant letter to his wife,
after being the first to climb to the top of the Great Pyramid
in Gizeh, he wrote, 'When this country has been rebuilt, re-
planted and thoroughly penetrated over fifty years by the
French, this will be a paradise on earth. The proprietors will
come to winter here and improve their possessions and will
return to Paris in the spring to feed off their revenues.'

In the land of pyramids, symbols of the ability of mind to
dominate and manoeuvre large and heavy chunks of matter,
there was an almost universal preoccupation with architecture.
But nearly all observations on the subject were framed in the

discourse of decadence. Thus Charles Norry, a young architect, provided footnotes to the initial perceptions of Alexandria, a kind of a running commentary on Napoleon's opening statement:

> We came looking for the Alexandria of Alexander, built by the architect Dinochares, we came looking for this city in which were born, in which were formed, so many great men, this library in which the pharaohs assembled an archive of human knowledge; we came looking finally for this city of commerce with its energetic and industrious populace. And what did we find? Nothing but ruins, barbarism, degradation and poverty on every side.

The architectural icon par excellence, which would become a trademark of Romanticism, and the calling card of Chateaubriand in particular, was the ruin. The ruin was, ironically, perfect: it contained the ghost of what had been and a justification for looking forward to what would be again.

The theme of architecture, translated into ecology, was inevitably linked with that of desertification. The desert became the rampant symbol of decadence, the decline from fertility to sterility. 'The immense space that is currently occupied by this ocean of sand was, in ancient times, a fertile and populous region . . . but everything has been buried beneath the inundation of sand.' But Napoleon insisted that the creeping desert was not the fault of nature, only of bad government, and could therefore be turned around. 'Who is responsible for destroying everything, if not the Mamelukes, with their avarice, injustice and tyranny?' It was culture not nature that was to blame. Everything was willed into existence and all conspiracy theories were true. The critique offered of the Mamelukes provides an exact antithesis of the way the French saw themselves. 'The Mamelukes, although they became the sovereigns of this nation, were as incapable of learning from the experience of the past as they were blind to the anticipation of the future, only ever envisaging the present moment.' [*Les Mamlouks, devenus souverains de cette contrée, aussi peu disposés à profiter de l'expérience du passée qu'à user de prévoyance pour l'avenir, n'envisagèrent jamais que le moment présent.*] The Mamelukes, creatures of the desert, were locked – sensually, greedily – into

the present while the French – in their more spiritual free-
floating way – transcended the moment both backwards and
forwards.

Napoleon was fond of identifying himself symbolically
with the Nile, a force of nature, flooding, seeding, fertilizing,
pushing back the desert. Accordingly he presided over a party
in Cairo in August 1798 to celebrate the opening of the flood
gates. The *Courier de l'Egypte*, the French newspaper and partner to the *Décade*, which however did not disdain to speak
explicitly of political events, was there to record the event for
posterity: 'An instant later, the Nile crossed the dam and flooded
into the canal from which it carries fertility into the countryside around Cairo . . . an immense crowd sang the praises of the
Prophet and the French army and cursed the beys and their
tyranny.' The proposed metamorphosis of Egypt reflected the
changing of the seasons: the country had suffered a winter of
discontent but now the advent of Napoleon ushered in spring
and a new flowering of civilization.

There were other transformations. Napoleon, for one, per-
ennially unfixed as to his own identity, was born again as
Sultan El-Kebir ('the Great') and a convert to Islam. He tried
on a turban and a kaftan (Tallien persuaded him that they did
not suit him, however) and promoted himself as the apostle of
Muhammad, sent to restore Islam to its former greatness. He
tried to have his troops undergo a mass conversion, but conceded that the fact that they all drank alcohol and were largely
uncircumcised counted against them. In the end he negotiated
a special dispensation from the rules for them on the understanding that their access to paradise would be proportionately
limited. General Menou personally went through the conversion
ritual in order to marry a Muslim.

Napoleon collaborated closely with the young Orientalist,
Venture de Paradis (doomed to die in Egypt) on proclamations,
in Arabic, for the consumption of the Egyptians. 'I know
everything,' Napoleon announced to the people of Cairo, in his
mystical pseudo-Islamic style, 'I know all your thoughts, even
what you have not said to a soul . . . all resistance is futile.' [*Je
sais tout, même ce que vous n'avez dit à personne . . . tous les
efforts humains ne peuvent rien contre moi.*] Nothing escaped his
omniscience: 'Know also that I am able to reveal what is in every

one of you because by looking at a person I can know everything about him.' Not everyone was convinced. Abdel Rahman
Al-Jabarti, the Egyptian chronicler and a native of Cairo, with
mixed feelings about the French presence, wrote:

> they [the French] wrote many copies of that (a document) and
> sent them to the notables; they posted them at road intersections,
> the beginning of narrow streets and at the doors of mosques.
> Therein they laid down stipulations containing foolish expres-
> sions which required much consideration for their sense to
> be understood, on account of their lack of understanding of the
> rules of Arabic constructions. The outcome of this was trickery
> for the purpose of taking wealth.

But in Cairo Napoleon was confident enough to improvise
orally and took to analysing and glossing the Koran in seminars
arranged for the purpose. 'In the sacred book of the Koran,'
he declared to a group of imams and muftis and *ulema*, 'it
was written that I would come out of the west to destroy
the enemies of Islam . . . in more than twenty passages, what
is taking place has been foreseen, and what will take place
is similarly explained.' His audience nodded deferentially.
'Each one of us,' they replied, 'pays homage to the perfection of your ideas.' If Napoleon's strategy was one of 'high
charlatanism' (as he would later tell Las Cases), then it was
amply reciprocated.

In keeping with Napoleon's own emphasis on the textual, the
archaeological work of the Commission had a strong literary
slant and focused on the collection of hieroglyphs and a search
for the origin of writing. 'Having found among the bas-reliefs
characters in the act of writing', wrote Vivant Denon – an
ex-diplomat, now artist-in-chief – in a paper of August 1799
explicitly marked for the attention of Napoleon, describing his
experiences in the Valley of the Kings,

> I also came across this roll of papyrus, this unique manuscript
> which has already been the object of your curiosity, this frail
> rival to the pyramids, a precious witness to the preservative
> effects of this climate, a monument respected by time, and
> which forty centuries rank as the most ancient of all books [*que
> quarante siècles placent au rang du plus ancien de tous les livres*].

The meaning of these primordial texts is secondary to the fact of their existence. Hieroglyphs would not be fully decoded until the 1820s, by Champollion and Young. But it was during this expedition that the Rosetta Stone was discovered, in July 1799, in the course of constructing defences. Marcel – whose job it was to make printed copies of the stone – grasped from the moment of its discovery the importance of the parallel texts, in Greek, Egyptian demotic and hieroglyphs. This was the linguistic equivalent of the search for the origin of species. Marcel went on to study later texts and concluded that Loqman's fables were the archetype for Aesop's (and La Fontaine's), while oriental despots inspired the rise of allegorical, coded and ironic forms of expression. 'The taste for the allegorical style has been preserved in the Orient in the present day, and ordinary language habitually tolerates metaphorical locutions, figurative and symbolic forms of expression which the severity and care for exactness of our western languages would not dare to adopt.' In these terms, Napoleon's Egyptian style represented a rapprochement of severity and symbolism, East and West.

Just as the intellectual activity of the Egyptians had allegedly declined, so the amount of sexual activity had increased to take its place. Subsequent travellers – such as Flaubert and Nerval – may well have been, above all, sex tourists. But there is a distinctly puritanical note struck by the lonesome scholars of the Institut:

> Boys aged from twelve to fifteen are already very libidinous. They even resort to aphrodisiacs to stimulate themselves, and have no difficulty in finding partners among members of the opposite sex willing to satisfy their needs. It is perhaps for this reason that masturbation, which has taken such a toll among us, appears unfamiliar to them.

Another writer noted that although 'onanism was virtually unknown . . . the vice that runs counter to the designs of nature is very common, particularly among adults. Even Christians are not exempt from this reproach.' Napoleon highlighted reports of homosexual rape [*des détails grotesques et horribles des moeurs de ces hommes du désert*] from the first French soldiers to be taken prisoner. It was no coincidence that the Institut should have taken over a seraglio and stamped the signature of the

French intellectual over the abode of the carnal in anticipation of the grander cultural metamorphosis to come. (On the other hand, one non-scholarly writer, Admiral Perrée, acknowledged unofficially that 'The Beys have left us some pretty Armenian and Georgian women, whom we have taken possession of in the name of the nation.')

The great balloon experiment was at once a high and a low point in the work of the Commission and Institut. It was designed to demonstrate technological preeminence, but perhaps also a certain airiness and spirituality and resistance to mere gravity. The members of the Institut, under the watchful eye of their vice-president, were constantly carrying out scientific experiments, some of them in public, with a view to impressing the Arabs. They were discouraged that so many of the inhabitants of Cairo appeared indifferent to their efforts with static electricity and windmills and other assorted contraptions. Fortunately, they had a trump card up their sleeves, in the shape of a *montgolfière*. The big day for the launching of the hot-air balloon – in the colours of the tricolour – was loudly announced in the pages of the *Courier de l'Egypte*, trumpeted on hoardings around the city and in leaflets distributed at the market and the mosque. A big crowd duly gathered and were, indeed, vastly entertained. Al-Jabarti has left us the sharpest account of what took place on that balmy afternoon in September 1798:

About an hour after the afternoon prayer, the Frenchmen lit the wick and smoke rose up to the cloth and filled it, so that it was inflated like a ball. The smoke sought to rise to the centre of the cloth, but found no escape and bore the craft up with it; those with ropes pulled, helping it until it rose from the ground. They then cut the ropes and it ascended into the air with the wind and travelled for a few delightful moments. Then its frame fell with the wick, followed by the cloth, and a great many copies of the printed leaflet [advertising the experiment] were scattered about. When that happened to it, the French were ashamed of its fall, and the validity of what they had said was not made manifest, viz. that it could go like a ship in the air with calculated precision and that people could sit in it and travel in it to distant lands to discover information and send communications; rather it appeared to be like the kite made by attendants at festivals and weddings.

It should have been like an episode from the pages of Jules Verne, *Cinq semaines en ballon* perhaps, in which the Africans are convinced that the Frenchmen are gods. But the fate of the *montgolfière* was a foretaste of the outcome of the Egyptian expedition.

The mission of generating an essentially intellectual renaissance was bound to run into some unenlightened obstacles. That was written into the plot. 'An unfortunate and barbarous people have constantly opposed [our] research', Sulkowski noted. Some members of the Commission were slain and the Institut itself came under attack during the insurrection in Cairo on 21–2 October 1798, when assorted scholars, poets and painters were obliged to become soldiers under the captaincy of Gaspard Monge. According to Vivant Denon, who generally carried a sabre and a pair of pistols as well as a paintbrush, 'All the academics had taken up arms. We had designated leaders, each one of us had a plan, but nobody felt obliged to obey anyone.' In the city, the muezzins in their minarets were calling the faithful to revolt rather than to prayer. The savants in their ex-harem put up barricades and prepared to repel assaults. But they survived unscathed. A couple of hundred French died and a couple of thousand Arabs, and Napoleon was obliged to conduct a public execution in the market place of those responsible for inciting the mutiny. The *Décade* regretted that 'the seditious movements which broke out in Cairo prevented the Institut from meeting.' And Napoleon soon returned to discussing the 'book of truth' with the very same sheikhs who had led the revolt.

But more catastrophic for the French than either military resistance or ideological dissent was the progressive revenge of matter over mind. The meetings of the Institut and the increasingly irregular pages of the *Décade* exhibited a growing frequency of alarming medical reports. The literary *Décade* even had to apologize for its tendency to sound like the *Lancet*: 'We invite those who might feel that the medical articles have multiplied out of all proportion to consider that it is indispensable to distribute frequent advice in a new climate, particularly when the maladies can become fiercer than the enemy's fire.'

The early contributions from the medics who formed part of the Commission were broadly along historical, theoretical and charitable lines. René-Nicholas Desgenettes, the chief medical officer, veteran of Italy and member of the Institut, argued that the Egyptians were ex-masters of medicine, now fallen into the ways of superstition [*une foule de superstitions ridicules*], but the French could learn something from the remnants of this lost science [*des traces de cette ancienne science*]. The theme of decadence found another abundant source of illustrations: 'given the infinity of blind people and cripples in this part of the country (Damietta), one can reasonably say that the human species has been almost deformed here.' Desgenettes saw the whole of Egypt as a giant hospital (or madhouse) suffering from a lack of trained staff; or as a drug-den grown befuddled and benighted amid clouds of hashish smoke.

But it was the French who rapidly found themselves disabled. The combination of sunlight and desert produced blindness in the troops. After the trek across the desert to Cairo, Desgenettes was soon producing a memoir on 'ophthalmia'. Further papers followed, increasingly desperate in tone, on dysentery, fever and pestilence, on the severity of their effects and on various would-be remedies. In the margins of these essays can be discerned the outlines of a long-running argument between Napoleon and his medical team. One of the doctors, Bruant, who died treating plague victims in Gaza, was cited by Desgenettes from his correspondence: 'In all illnesses, our first duty is to combat the material causes to which they owe their existence' [*la cause matérielle à laquelle elle doit son existence*]. This would seem an almost tautological and redundant point to make, except for a powerful counter-argument to the effect that the most relevant causes were immaterial, of a purely psychological character.

Napoleon believed the sick were, if not actually faking it, largely victims of their own psychosomatic imaginings. If only his soldiers would stop thinking about getting sick, they would never fall prey to these diseases. He wrote breezily to General Berthier to the effect that:

In a country as healthy as Egypt, I do not intend that [your allegedly sick troops, due to be shipped back to France] should mask, by means of feigned illnesses, the real motive behind their reluctance to share our trials and our perils. I would rather take the risk that they grab a share of our glory.

This was a Catch-22 situation for the soldiers: if they wanted to return home, then they couldn't (but they could, provided they didn't want to). More positive thinking was the answer: that and more fighting.

While Desgenettes and his materialist lieutenants like Bruant devoted their time to pinning down material causes (climate, contagion) and coming up with cures (rhubarb, tisanes, opium), Napoleon and his mentalists played down diarrhoea and played up mental health. On the one hand there is talk of hospitals, pharmacies, latrines, diet and incineration, on the other of the health-giving properties of vigorous marching. According to one report intended for the eyes of Napoleon and singing his sort of song:

> The history of warfare contains a wealth of examples of how, to end epidemics which were bringing down whole armies, it was necessary to remove the troops from their barracks and take them on long forced marches, often leading right into the mouth of the enemy. The sudden cessation of our epidemic since the departure of the Second Light Infantry for Manssourah, and its subsequent return to Damietta, already confirm the efficacy of this treatment.

Napoleon heartily approved of these sentiments and shortly afterwards took most of his army off into Syria, rapidly exchanging the Koran for the Bible as he passed through Palestine (readings were given beneath his tent in the evenings). Perhaps this add-on to the Egyptian expedition was an inevitable extension of his oblique strategy of sneaking up on India (the prized British possession), but it was also, certainly, a shot across the bows of the *malades imaginaires*. Regular wars were Napoleon's idea of a welfare state. But Syria was a turning-point in the expedition in more ways than one.

We know that Napoleon's solution to troops too sick to travel was euthanasia, through opium – a treatment that Desgenettes refused to administer. But the uplifting picture by Gros of Napoleon mingling with the plague victims in Jaffa, heedlessly exposing himself to the risk of contracting the disease (and perhaps curing one or two of them by the laying on of hands) is equally plausible (Desgenettes confirms that something like it really took place), once understood as part of the ongoing debate between hardline cause-and-effect physiologists and the more idealist, mentalist school. Napoleon was immune to the plague, the point would seem to be, because he thought healthy thoughts. Conversely, he argued, if you're afraid of contracting the disease, you certainly will: 'It is one of the peculiarities of the plague that it is most dangerous to those who fear it [*elle est plus dangereuse pour les personnes qui la craignent*]; those who allowed themselves to be mastered by their own fear are almost all dead.' He calculated that his own intervention at the plague house had given the army a few months' breathing space.

The incursion into Syria was only a circuitous form of retreat in any case, after the crushing blow of having the French fleet wiped out at Aboukir. And Saint-Jean d'Acre was certainly a fortress too far for Napoleon. 'If only I had taken Acre . . .' is a phrase that came easily to Napoleon's lips: then he would have worn a turban, become emperor of the Orient and returned to Paris via Constantinople. But it is a mistake to suppose that it was the Syrians who were under siege, when it was the French who were already besieged by sickness and physical depletion, subverted by the microbiological. The Acre episode was only a sideshow staged to distract the gaze from the main story. But the military turnaround was also the occasion of a striking shift – almost an inversion – in the dialogue between Napoleon and Desgenettes.

It is possible to read into Desgenettes a degree of irony or possibly of duress, in making a report 'under the eye of the commander-in-chief' (i.e. Napoleon). But it seems likely that, on his return from Syria, when delivering a paper to the Institut, Desgenettes had picked up some Napoleonic habits of mind and turns of phrase. Although he stopped short of actually accusing the sick of malingering, Desgenettes did discern a conspiracy among the doctors: 'the medical administration had acquired a sort of dictatorial authority', he complained, 'doctors were everywhere proclaiming the terrors [of the epidemic], and as a result of imprudently electrifying the susceptible and unregulated imagination of the multitude, they thereby contributed to the development of this scourge that they feared so much.' Desgenettes boldly put forward the full-blown mentalist hypothesis that illnesses sprang forth, fully formed, from the heads – particularly the memories – of doctors: 'their

heads hazily full of the history of the events that took place in
Marseille in 1720, they saw them everywhere reborn.'

Napoleon, on the other hand, had learned from Desgenettes
and drawn on the medical lexicon. He was soon sailing back to
Toulon (in September 1799), to all intents and purposes desert-
ing in the face of the enemy, taking just a handful of his original
Commission with him, and leaving the dregs of his army to
put up whatever resistance they could to the encroaching combined forces of Arabs, Turks, British and Russians. Napoleon's
return smacked more of one of Hakem's confidence tricks than
of the magnanimity of the noble Mahadi. He certainly dumped
the bodies of his plague-ridden soldiers in a lime pit, even if
he did not personally poison them. 'Have a big lime-pit dug',
he ordered, 'and chuck in the dead.' But before sneaking away,
in September 1799, Napoleon fingered Desgenettes as the guilty
man responsible for the debacle in Syria, having failed to inform
him quickly enough of the risk of an epidemic. Desgenettes, in
this new interpretation of events, had been too much of the
mentalist school, and insufficiently attentive to the encroach-
ment of illness. The plague, Napoleon conceded, was yet
another enemy – 'one of the greatest enemies that the army has
to fear' [*l'un des plus grands ennemis que l'armée ait à redouter*]
– and one had to be on constant alert for an attack. Desgenettes,
he argued, had taken his eye off the bacillus.

Always the *bricoleur*, constantly adapting and improvising and
absorbing alternative ideas, Napoleon latched on to the idea
of doctoring. He became a materialist, but only in a mentalist
mode: putting it in Jakobsonian terms, a metaphorical met-
onymist. That is, he saw the symbolic value of medicine, the
allegorical possibilities of the status of doctor. Napoleon pitched
the pretext for his departure in terms of a greater crisis affect-
ing the homeland. While Egypt was being reconstructed, cracks
had started to appear in the French temple of civilization, he
concluded after reading recent newspapers, the English equivalent of the *Courier*, deviously delivered by Sir Sidney Smith.
It was logical: 'he had restored the arts and sciences to their
cradle', but the cycle of decadence had begun to kick in once
more back home, and a further dose of regeneration would
be required in Paris. France, too, was sick and cried out for
treatment. Thus there was, after all, no necessary contradiction

between medicine and politics. Napoleon grasped the opportunity to take on a new role, to be reborn as a healer, just as he and his army had ostensibly become converts to Islam. 'He resolved that very instant to return to Europe,' wrote Las Cases (under the eye of Napoleon), 'and remedy, if there was still time, the ills of the fatherland and save it'. [*Il résolut à l'instant même de passer en Europe, pour remédier, s'il en était temps, aux maux de la patrie et la sauver.*] Such was Napoleon's personal renaissance: he was transformed from professor to doctor.

Desgenettes, in turn, took over the editorship of the *Courier* and the presidency of the Institut. In upbeat Panglossian style, he managed to put a positive spin on the army's overdose of pestilence, putting it in the light of useful background research, from which mankind would reap the benefit, and for which he would be personally responsible: 'I had to intervene in order to preserve the results of this vast and novel observation for the purpose of further study, and perhaps for the improvement of the art of medicine [*le perfectionnement de l'art de guérir*], and therefore for the well-being of a considerable part of the human species' [*le bien-être d'une partie considérable de l'espèce humaine*]. With the evacuation of Egypt looming, everyone was intent on getting out their story first.

The Egyptian expedition began with the formation of a library. And it ended with the destruction of one. One might almost say that the whole point of the expedition was to re-enact the annihilation of the library of Alexandria. Certainly this was the scenario that the Institut had in mind as they were finally forced out of Egypt (where they had been sketching ancient monuments and making a detailed copy of the zodiac) and back to France: You're setting fire to another Alexandria! was the stinging denunciation Geoffroy Saint-Hilaire lashed at the philistine British navy as they went about appropriating French trophies (notably the Rosetta Stone). They were, after all, only sailors, not savants, insufficiently versed in the arts and sciences, and therefore had no right to Egypt. The Institut's last meeting applauded a paper on the crocodiles of the Nile.

Napoleon did not forget the army he had left behind, even after becoming First Consul. Back in Paris he went almost immediately to the Institut, where Laplace gave him a copy of his *Celestial Mechanics*. Napoleon promised to read it 'as soon as I have six months free', invited him to dinner and commissioned him (on 15 November 1799) to ship over a troop of actors and dancing girls to entertain the troops in Egypt. And he was determined that his men would never complain of a lack of reading material:

> The First Consul charges me, Citizen Minister, to beg you to assemble tomorrow the best magazines of recent times, the most interesting pamphlets and books, including some copies of the military work published in Hamburg concerning the recent campaign. All these objects will be gathered together and sent to Toulon, divided into three parcels, to be transported to Egypt on separate ships.

And to General Kléber, who had been left to hold the fort in Cairo (and would die in November 1800 with a knife in his back), he personally sent a bundle of books that he thought 'would be agreeable to you to receive'. These included copies of:

1 The French Constitution
2 The Song of Battle, with music
3 Memoir on Egypt
4 Tableau of 18 Brumaire
5 Possible Result of 18 Brumaire
6 Journey to Finisterre, 1794–5
7 Memoir on the Insurrections in the West
8 Decimal Arithmetic, by Lewal
9 Universal Alphabet, by Montigny
10 Minutes of the Institute for Year VIII
11 The Philosophical Weekly, two issues
12 The Encyclopedic Magazine
13 Chemistry Papers
14 Contemporary Knowledge, Year X
15 On Modern Philosophy, by Roederer
16 On the Condition of Women in the Republics
17 The Cosmopolitan Englishman
18 On Man, a fragment.

Many years later, as his ship approached Saint Helena, his final destination, Napoleon turned to General Gourgaud and said, 'I should never have left Egypt.' Certainly it never left him.

4
Mentioned in Dispatches

Napoléon décore un soldat de sa garde.

Camaret Bay, east of Toulon, in the shadow of French batteries, should have been a safe haven for the *Chevrette*, a 20-gun corvette. But, on 20 July 1801, the rampant, almost reckless British navy, in the form of the frigates *Beaulieu* and *Doris*, decided otherwise and set about 'cutting out' the French ship. The *Chevrette* sailed a mile closer to shore right under the guns and, to be on the safe side, embarked a supplementary party of soldiers, bringing her total crew up to 339 men. Her cannon were primed and loaded to the muzzle with grape-shot. Mockingly, contemptuously, but overconfidently, the *Chevrette* raised the French ensign over the top of the English one. It was intended and understood as an insult. The provocation was too great. On the night of 21 July, the British, 280 of them in fifteen rowing boats, took up the gauntlet and stormed her, defying grape and musket. After vicious hand-to-hand fighting (involving cutlasses, pikes and – an American influence – tomahawks) that left (conservatively) a grand total, on both sides, of 223 men killed or wounded (the vast majority killed), the British swarmed up the rigging, let down the sails, and overran the helm. By the 22nd, the *Chevrette* had been captured and was being triumphantly steered away from the coast and out of range of the French guns that were now trying to blow their own vessel out of the water. The 'Kid' had been kidnapped.

This was one of a whole series of similar exploits of the period (as cheerfully recorded in the annals of the British navy). It was far from being another Aboukir (although it was in some sense a supplement to Aboukir, a reminiscence, inspired by the earlier mass encounter of British and French navies). Nevertheless, Napoleon singled the Kid and its hapless crew out for exemplary attention and fired off a series of percussive letters. On 19 September, officers and crew-members Levasseur, Jaumont, Tourneur, Laura, Dupont, Catherine, Eugène, Dubure, Loyer, Dort, Scelle and Roppart were all 'charged with cowardice in the defence of the *Chevrette*' [*prévenus de lâcheté dans la défense de la corvette la Chevrette*]. Presumably they were among those who either jumped overboard or fled below and surrendered. Napoleon personally handed down orders to have them brought before a court-martial and an almost certain firing-squad. He reasserted the principle that 'cowards will be punished with death' [*les lâches seront punis de mort*]. On the same day, he commended Gabriel-Joseph Baron, from Seurre, 'for the zeal, courage and devotion he showed in combat'; promoted Guillaume Steetz, 'who received four wounds'; awarded a 'badge of honour' [*grenade d'honneur*] to mark the nation's gratitude to Jean Gaillardie, a sergeant who had received no less than 'six serious wounds in fighting with the greatest bravery' and announced an extra month's pay for all those injured in the cause of 'courageously defending the honour of the flag of the Republic' [*défendant courageusement l'honneur du pavillon de la République*].

With so many wounded, so much bravery and the tricolour stoutly defended, honour had been preserved. But there was no denying that the *Chevrette* was a deeply symbolic loss to France. The isles that the French typically referred to as *Angleterre* stood geographically and ideologically in opposition (to just about everything). The lands on the far side of the Channel were proving resistant to the appeal of becoming a piece of the Continent. In Napoleon's early Corsica-centric writings, the island had represented a refuge against (largely French) tyranny. But, in the evolution from pro-insular to pro-Continental thinking, it now appeared that all the tyrants had taken refuge on this particular island. England was perceived by Napoleon as the major offshore threat to the Continent, a permanent outsider lurking on the other side of the waters, a large and unscrupulous pirate vessel ready to waylay unwary Continentals going about their lawful and idealistic business. But a mere island could not stand, Napoleon argued. It was surely too isolated and angst-ridden: 'Abandoned by the whole of Europe, in a state of open war with Russia, which is today one of our firmest friends, the Englishman finds himself encompassed by fears.' (*Abandonné* and *environné*, the epithets Napoleon once automatically used to describe himself, recur applied to another islander.) But, for these same reasons, it could be dangerous: it was a wolf waiting to pounce on all peacefully grazing Kids. In one aspect, the *Chevrette* was a model of the ship of state, sailing majestically (but perilously) towards the world-historical horizon. It was a temporarily detached piece of the continent. But its main *raison d'être* was to keep messages circulating between France and its overseas outposts.

The previous December Napoleon had initiated the system of regular 'post ships', sailing every ten days (or *décade*) from Toulon to Egypt. And it was with an eye on the kind of hazards encountered by the Kid that he warned the maritime prefect of Toulon that he should not only convey 'the freshest news' to the general-in-chief of the Army of the Orient, but that he should 'put all government dispatches and his own in a lead mailbox, which will be jettisoned into the sea in case of the ship being taken by the enemy'. England stood squarely in the way, in other words, of the Napoleonic postal system. The passage between France and Egypt was probably the most difficult single route to defend (Napoleon had been lucky not to run head-on into a *Beaulieu* or *Doris* himself on his *aller-et-retour* across the Mediterranean). And lead mailboxes were, at best, a blunt instrument for outwitting the ubiquitous Admiral Nelson. Perhaps the Kid's men had simply failed to fling the box, built like a safe, safely overboard. In any case, for Napoleon's mail, the safe was no longer safe. Whether on land or sea.

On 2 February 1800 Napoleon wrote to General Lefebvre ordering him to round up the usual suspects in Sainte-Gauburge, a small market town in Normandy. But absolutely everyone was, in principle, a suspect. The crime that had been committed by a party or parties unknown was, in the First Consul's view, a particularly heinous one: a lieutenant of the 9th company of dragoons had been slain while passing through Sainte-Gauburge. Napoleon might have been willing to overlook this misdemeanour except for one small but crucial detail. The victim, in this case, was a *porteur de dépêches*, a military mail-man, ferrying dispatches to and from Paris. The Sainte-Gauburgeois had made the capital error of killing the messenger. The First Consul retaliated with extreme severity. All on account of one dead postman, some 460 men, 60 of them mounted, were drafted in to 'disarm the inhabitants', to arrest 'the most guilty' [*les plus coupables*] and then to carry out 'further errands' [*quelques courses*] in the locality, such as 'annihilating the remainder of the rebels in this area and disarming ill-intentioned communes' [*parvenir à anéantir le reste des chouans de ce département et à désarmer les communes malintentionnés*].

The struggle against the rebels in the West (ironically echoing, in rhetoric and rigour, the expedition to the East) was part of a many-pronged campaign to quell internal and external opposition that engaged Napoleon's attention for the duration of his tenure as First Consul and beyond. The *Chouans* are generally understood to have been pro-monarchy or, at least, anti-Republic (and therefore anti-Napoleon). But for Napoleon's purposes they were simply and most sinisterly people who stopped the mail getting through. They were not so much royalist counter-revolutionaries, to his way of thinking, as mailbag thieves, mad-dog bushwhackers who set traps for the postman and ran off with or destroyed his precious cargo. This attack was not an isolated incident in the period, nor were the reprisals:

> Dear Citizen Minister, please prepare for me a report on the way in which it would be possible to overturn the sentence of a mere six years in irons for the three assassins of the courier in Nantes, who were caught red-handed.

These gangs of marauding mail-snatchers (and courier-killers) were the number one public enemies of the day.

Conversely, the definition of a loyal servant and defender of the Republic was one who assisted in transmitting and delivering Napoleon's messages or those addressed to him. The messenger had become the unsung hero of the French Empire, the forgotten protagonist in that muscular drama of national expansion and contraction. On 6 September 1800 Napoleon commanded his Minister of the Navy and the Colonies to make a special ex-gratia payment of 15,000 francs to the captain of the *Osiris*, 'who delivered the most recent dispatches from Egypt'. A rather unremarkable achievement, one might have thought, except that Nelson's navy, which at least since Aboukir ruled the waves, was notorious not just for cutting out ships but for intercepting mail and combing through it for embarrassing letters which would quickly appear in print in translation. This popular genre consisted largely of subversive letters about Napoleon or depressive ones about Egypt, the heat, sickness, sex, death, etc.; but Napoleon himself also gave vent to disenchantment: 'Oh, Jean-Jacques [Rousseau], if only he could see these men [Bedouins] that he called "men of nature"! He would shudder with shame and horror at ever having admired them.' England was home to some of Napoleon's most impatient and enthusiastic readers. The captain of the *Osiris* had outwitted the might of the British navy and London publishers to get the correspondence from one side of the Mediterranean to the other, unintercepted, intact and unread.

Napoleon was not being disingenuous or paradoxical when he wrote to General Kléber in Cairo, in December 1799, that 'I don't dare write to you, even in code, for in Paris and London there are men who can decipher everything.' [*Je n'ose rien vous écrire, même en chiffres, parce qu'à Paris et à Londres on a des hommes qui déchiffrent tout.*] His fear of code-crackers was genuine, but his fear of the code-hackers, the text-terrorists, was greater. Napoleon saw the French as fighting to keep the channels of global communication open and uncompromised, knight errants whose holy grail was the free passage of information. The English, on the other hand, were a nation of *paparazzi*, salaciously snuffling after the latest scandal and sensation.

Napoleon engaged in a constant battle of wits to out-manoeuvre these would-be post-pirates. On 5 November 1800 he devised a cunning scheme for getting a letter through to

Toussaint-Louverture, the black leader of Saint Domingo (which Napoleon determined should remain French). The ship carrying the mail should pretend to leave port in the direction of Ile de France; indeed even the captain should believe that Ile de France was its true destination. Only when he was at sea should he open his own sealed orders: 'he will then find his instructions to proceed to Saint-Domingo' [*il y trouvera alors ses instructions pour Saint-Domingue*] and thus duly change course. 'If a few passengers wish to embark for Ile de France, this will not be a disadvantage: on the contrary, everything must be sacrificed to the secrecy of the expedition' [*il faut tout sacrifier au secret de l'expédition*]. Travellers and merchants, Ile de France-bound, would provide a handy cover. Feints and ploys and deceptions were the norm. But ultimately this intellectual game was liable to be aborted or suspended by combat. Battles were fought and (as per the Kid) sometimes lost over the mail. The business of getting dispatches and provisions (actors and dancing girls and edifying periodicals) to and fro across the water, hooking up the fatherland and its colony, or even from one point in France to another, came to seem like the defining imperial act.

Napoleon had one further stratagem to deploy, a less leaden mailbox, a hypertextual device which circumvented the perils of transporting written documents over land or sea: the telegraph. Napoleon's ideal was simple (if impossible): transmission without interference. Conflict arose purely out of the imperfections of the mailing system, it was a by-product of sub-optimal communication. Sending messages – as the men of the Kid had discovered – was a virtual red flag to John Bull. The telegraph, on the other hand, promised to transcend war. The *Encyclopaedia Britannica* of 1797 suggested that 'The capitals of distant nations might be united by chains of [telegraph] posts and the settling of those disputes which at present take up years or months might then be accomplished in as many hours.' Napoleon shared this techno-utopianism. The Empire was nothing if not a mirror of this perfect system of communication: maximum transmission and zero interference.

Telegraphy, 'far-writing', had long been a myth and a dream; under Napoleon it was embryonic but real. In 1774, Le Sage in Geneva had proposed a system of electrical communication involving a separate wire for each letter of the alphabet. Morse's more practical 'electro-magnetic recording telegraph' would not be tested until the 1830s. Wedged between the theory and the practice, Napoleon had access to a fully functioning, if non-electrical, telegraphic system, the prototype internet of the age, devised by Claude Chappe and his brothers. Napoleon's main problem, as he saw it, was not being everywhere at once. 'Why is it that I cannot have men like you in more than one place at a time?' [*Pourquoi faut-il que des hommes comme vous ne puissent pas se trouver à la fois en plusieurs lieux.*] He was writing to Kléber in Cairo but it could have been (like all his writing) addressed to himself. The telegraph offered to fulfil his desire for instantaneity and ubiquity. The new invention claimed to condense time and space and thus enable the government, according to Claude Chappe, to 'bestride huge distances and be present, so to speak, at the very extremities [of the empire]'.

Napoleon was notoriously impatient. He bolted his food, complained table companions (when Roederer persuaded him to slow down and extend meal-times, Napoleon commented: 'This is the beginning of the corruption of power'); he rushed, objected lovers ('Bonaparte est bon à rien'). Speed (coupled with surprise) was the defining mark of his military strategy: 'Soldiers! Inside a fortnight, you have won ten victories, taken twenty-one flags, fifty-five artillery pieces, fifteen thousand prisoners, and killed or injured another ten thousand.' Similarly, his letters are forever straining against the bit of time and his privileged adverbs – '*à l'instant*', '*de suite*' – struggle to overcome temporal constraints. 'I cannot stress enough the just impatience of the First Consul' [*Je ne puis trop vous exprimer la juste impatience du Premier Consul*] wrote one of his secretaries in a letter (to the maritime prefect in Brest, about sluggardly shipbuilders) that was repeated, with small variations, a thousandfold. 'He orders you to coerce, pursue, arrest and imprison any workers and carpenters who are slowing down the work.' Slackers were on a par with deserters and deserved to be shot. Sheer work-rate went up dramatically under Napoleon. But there were limits.

As it was with shipbuilding in Brest, so too with the mail: it could never be fast enough for Napoleon's taste. Hitherto, even with the constant *courier extraordinaire* (which soon became *ordinaire*), the fastest communication could be no faster than a mounted rider or a sail before the wind. The telegraph, in contrast, crystallized the dream of synchronicity. It was only fitting that the rapidly unfolding events of the 18th Brumaire should first be announced, concisely, by telegraph: 'The legislative body has designated a Consulate consisting of three members to take the place of the Directory. The members of the Consulate are citizens Sieyes, Roger Ducos and general Bonaparte. . . . Paris is satisfied.' General Bonaparte's coup, tilting away from the nostalgia for the future of the Egyptian period, was articulated around the theory of pure presence, a massively weighty neo-realism (which many historians have fallen for):

> Let us not seek historical models which might stand in the way of progress. Nothing, in history, resembles the end of the eighteenth century; nothing, at the end of the eighteenth century, resembles the present moment.

And just as Napoleon now shied away from history, so too he had taken against the future tense: he hated to say (or, worse, as he obsessively scoured the press, find others saying) what he would be doing, he wanted to be doing it already:

> I read in the newspapers that I have written to my mother a letter in which I am supposed to say that 'I will be in Milan in a month.' That would be completely out of character. [*Cela ne peut pas être dans mon caractère.*] Frequently, I admit, I do not say what I know, but I scrupulously avoid saying what *will* be. I want you to insert a humorous note to this effect [*sur le ton de la plaisanterie*] in *Le Moniteur*.

By the same token, he resented having to write to this or that general, 'You, General X, *will* do Y', because he knew that, to the extent that the empire depended on an imperative which hung on a prediction, it would always be tinged with the unpredictable: there was a possibility that General X would not do Y. He therefore sought to confine himself (and others) rigorously to the present tense. Claude Chappe's messages to Napoleon formulated an offer the incipient Emperor could hardly refuse:

The immense extent of your majesty's empire must prevent your government from exercising, over a great number of your provinces, this continuity of surveillance which maintains both the strength of princes and the security and prosperity of their subjects. Many of your peoples are so distant from one another that you are obliged to waste whole months getting your orders through, and still further months in ensuring that they are carried out. The distance between them is so great that they seem foreign to one another. Well, I am going to contract space by abbreviating time; I am going to give you the means of communicating every day with each of your states, as if they were right next door. You will be able to give orders, and receive information and advice, as promptly as if this correspondence were taking place within the walls of your palace.

By the same token, France would become invulnerable to sneak attacks:

And if, in this period of peace, tyrants among the foreign coalition should attempt to invade our territory, on the day that the war cry, 'To arms!' first goes up, then it will be heard up and down the land, all citizens will abandon what they are doing to take up arms, and vast armies of men will suddenly spring up to present an insurmountable barrier to the astonished enemy.

Claude Chappe, like Raynal, had begun as an 'abbé', but, perhaps inspired by the confessional or prayer, dedicated himself to the cause of sending unwritten messages. His first revolutionary but cumbersome signalling system depended on clocks and frying pans, clanging noises and numbers. Chappe's more streamlined Mark 2 optical (or 'aerial') telegraph, consisted of 14-foot high towers with whirling black arms (and hands) and pulleys and a pair of telescopes pointing in opposite directions. In 1791 the first experimental *tachygraphe* (as it was then called) in Paris either fell or was pushed off its perch at the Etoile and smashed; the following year, the apparatus was destroyed again, this time by a raging Jacobin mob who thought that Chappe and his four-strong team of brothers were conspiring with royalists and sending secret communications to the King (who was shut up in the Tuileries) and that 'this ingenious means of writing in the air' was the invention of Chouans. 'This new line of inquiry was a source of manifold perils to the experimenters', noted one of the brothers. The Jacobins – 'in a moment of effervescence' – not only set fire to the telegraph but came within an ace of throwing the telegraphers on top. 'My life', wrote Chappe, 'is, at this moment, under threat' [*Ils menacent dans ce moment mes jours*]. There was a theory that the Tower of Babel was an early shot at telegraphy and a similar fate seemed to lie in store for the Chappe towers with all their potential for anti-Republican blasphemy.

But the Convention saw the possible application of Chappe's ninety-eight potential signals to the cause of virtue and appointed Pierre Daunou in 1793 to head up a committee to evaluate the device. This was the very same Daunou, the historian, who had bested Napoleon a few years earlier on the subject of happiness. As Napoleon had anticipated, the Lyon essay had indeed become the springboard to fame and fortune and, specifically, the task of testing out new scientific inventions.

The first official message sent by Morse between Washington and Baltimore in 1844 was: 'What God hath wrought!' On 12 July 1793, at a time when such biblical rhetoric would have struck a false note, the first officially sanctioned message sent by means of the Chappe telegraph, taking a mere nine minutes to travel the 20 miles from Saint-Fargeau to Saint-Martin-du-Tertre ('almost the speed of light' trumpeted one enthusiast) was: 'Daunou has arrived here. He announces that the National Convention has just authorized his Committee of General Security to put seals on the papers of the deputies.' [*Daunou est arrivé ici, il annonce que la Convention nationale vient d'autoriser son Comité de sûreté générale à apposer les scelles sur les papiers des députés.*] It was no coincidence that Chappe should have sent a meta-message, a message about messages, specifically concerned with the matter of secrecy. The whole point about the telegraph was that it was supposed to eliminate the risk of interception and espionage. The installation of the Paris–Lille line was celebrated, in 1794, by the sending of a message from the front to Paris that Condé had been retaken from the Austrians, less than an hour after the end of the battle, arousing 'an indescribable enthusiasm' in the Convention. A reply immediately changed the name of the town to 'Nord-Libre'. By the time Napoleon came to power a further line linked Paris with Strasbourg in the east, another with Brest to the west, and the Lille line had been extended (in 1798) as far as Dunkirk.

It was by no means far enough, in Napoleon's view. The 'Free-North' had to be extrapolated remorselessly and repeated on all the points of the compass. In the south, the Mediterranean put up resistance to his dispatches; in the north, the English Channel. The telegraph could, perhaps, vault over these obstacles. Napoleon increased Chappe's salary to 10,000 francs. In return he asked that, henceforth, all telegraphic messages – not excluding weather forecasts and news of that week's lottery winners – should necessarily pass through him:

> Citizen Chappe, the telegraph-engineer [his official title from 1794 onwards], will not, under any pretext, make any further telegraphic transmission, no matter how seemingly insignificant, without a signed order from the First Consul.

Henceforth, the Tuileries (specifically the roof of the Tuileries) – where Napoleon had watched the Swiss Guard being chopped to pieces – would be the unassailable centre of the telegraphic network.

With a view to incorporating England into his optical system, Napoleon proceeded to have a line laid connecting Paris and Boulogne, the nearest point on the French coast to the rogue island that confronted it, and commissioned another of the Chappes, Abraham, to design an advanced signalling system (with 30-foot towers) capable of bridging the English Channel (perhaps he was already speculating about 300-foot towers and extremely powerful telescopes for the purpose of spanning the Mediterranean). He was at the same time attracted to the project of a submarine, diving under Nelson's fleet, but the aerial message, escaping the need for immersion altogether, and passing right over the heads of the waterlogged Englishmen, seemed to him immeasurably superior. The new device was successfully tested over a Channel-sized distance, but without waves, from Belleville to Saint-Martin-du-Tertre ('Napoleon has arrived,' the telegram might have read). Preparations for the grand invasion were complete. Now only twenty-odd miles of water (and thousands of kamikaze English sailors) stood in Napoleon's way.

But the typically piratical English had already intercepted and stolen Chappe's ideas and set up a rival string of telegraph stations in 1795 hooking up London and the ports along the south coast, plotting no doubt to plant their towers on the French side of the Channel. Soon, Napoleon realized, all the great powers would be acquiring their own telegraphs. It was therefore more timely than ever to forge a larger, definitive network from which nothing and nowhere would be excluded and all islands would at last be fused into a limitless telegraphic continent. Mountains being easier than oceans to cross, Napoleon echoed his own earlier passage south by setting up the first trans-Alpine line into Italy in 1805, hooking up Paris with Dijon, Lyon, Milan and Turin, and integrating Venice in 1810. The invention and spread of the telegraph, and the proportionate decline in exercise, accounts for the gradual transformation of Napoleon from anorexic kid into over-ample adulthood. He became, increasingly – to use the word which identified the keepers (inevitably, underpaid – or unpaid – and overworked) of the telegraph network – a *stationnaire*.

Napoleon hated to be out of touch. Napoleon's letters to his family in Corsica from Brienne and Paris are heavy with the pathos of the complaint that no one ever writes: (this to brother Joseph) 'Everyone has abandoned me, nobody writes to me. I am all alone, unsheltered from fears and misfortunes. And even you, you don't write to me either.' [*Tout le monde m'a abandonné, personne ne m'écrit. Je suis seul, livré à mes craintes, à mes malheurs. Toi non plus, tu ne m'écris pas.*] Similarly, much later, on 18 January 1800, he would write to General Gardanne in Caen, where he was supposed to be pursuing 'brigands' and sowing terror and death in their ranks: 'It is eight days since you left, and yet I have heard nothing about you . . . Will you be the only one to send me no news? Will you alone tell me nothing?' The reply could never be fast enough: 'Write back to me as soon as possible, by return of post, and let me know what you think.' 'Wait, wait a minute, Mr Postman,' Napoleon might have sung along with the Beatles, like any epistolary lover desperately awaiting the next delivery, 'look and see, is there a letter, a letter for me?' Any breakdown in communication was potentially fatal. Conversely, the best army was the one with the optimal postal service. Thus, during the fatal Russian campaign, Napoleon hoped to avert disaster by recruiting Abraham Chappe to bring in a team of mobile telegraph towers capable of bridging the immensities of the steppes. But they were lost in the maelstrom of Beresina. Had they been available at Waterloo, the outcome – the result of a breakdown in communication – could have been very different. Napoleon was prophetically conscious that when communications fail, the Empire falls.

But the English (the Germans and the Russians et al.) were not the only source of interference. The French were often their own worst enemy, or so it seemed to Napoleon. Although he sidelined his novel-writing plans, and his historical projects, until he reached Saint Helena in 1815, he remained among the most prolific writers of the Consulate and Empire period. Technically, he had now become a dictator, since he was able to walk up and down, discoursing as he went, and rely on a team of secretaries to take down his words and encode them or send them to Chappe for telegraphing. His strategy was not a subtle one: it was simply to overwhelm the opposition by sheer weight of numbers.

The old texts were dead and buried: 'Those who speak of the Constitution know full well that, constantly violated as it has been, and its every page torn to pieces, the Constitution no longer exists.' Napoleon would become the total author of the age: all messages would pass through him. And, in some measure, he attained this end, since he became the inescapable addressee (whether explicit or implicit) or subject of all other discourse. Alternative genres tended to merge into the epistolary form, so that the entire mass of texts in French (and other languages, especially English) over more than a decade constitute a body of postcards to Napoleon. In the middle of 1801, the First Consul wrote to his personal librarian, Ripault, demanding instant interpretations of all theatrical productions (and newspapers similarly, even down to posters and advertisements, and especially songs and sermons) with an eye to secret messages addressed to him: 'This analysis must be carried out, at the latest, within 48 hours of the first performance of these plays.' In Egypt Napoleon had proclaimed that he was able – through mystical means – to 'know everything'. Back in Paris he would try to put esoteric theory into practice.

Chateaubriand and Madame de Staël were two of his most persistent correspondents; together they reinvented the writer as heroic leader of the resistance. They were the liberation theologians of their day. Their story was that it was war between Napoleon and writers. Certainly the Marquis de Sade spent most of the Consulate and Empire locked up in Charenton on the orders of Napoleon. Madame de Staël's favourite story is of how, in 1810, General Savary and his troops went round all the bookstores of Paris, rounding up copies of her new book, *De l'Allemagne*, and massacring them. This was probably the first (if not the last) time that a work of literary criticism had been subjected to full-scale military suppression. Staël's books were guilty of holding up the mail, of interfering with the transmission of information around the imperial network. She was an interceptor on a par with the Chouans and the English pirates (her book was ultimately published in London in 1813 and Wellington would quote from it when entering Paris in 1814) and therefore faced similar treatment. *'Dix ans d'exil'* (the title of her autobiography) were a minimum retaliation. Chateaubriand, in turn, died at Napoleon's hands, and had his revenge, many times over, via surrogates and symbols and the ample use of the conditional tense. 'If he would gladly have had me shot, I would similarly have killed him without too much grief.' [*S'il m'eût fait fusiller volontiers, en le tuant je n'aurais pas senti beaucoup de peine.*] But in each case the relationship with Napoleon was less a simple case of insurrection than a love affair of which we tend only to remember the split. The bitter recriminations have not just coloured but virtually occluded our sense of the initial liaison.

Like a literary Beethoven, tearing up his dedication of the Eroica, Chateaubriand's take on Napoleon is that he starts well, but deteriorates. Chateaubriand was one of the first to acknowledge Napoleon's literary origins. 'Napoleon discovered the novel in his cradle', Chateaubriand wrote in the *Mémoires d'outre-tombe* [*Napoléon trouva le roman dans son berceau*]. 'The years 1784 to 1793 embrace Napoleon's literary career, a brief but extremely productive period.' [*Entre 1784 et 1793 s'étend la carrière littéraire de Napoléon, courte par l'espace, longue par les travaux.*] He shrewdly observes that Napoleon was an intellectual by inclination, '[whose] thought was in the world before he manifested himself in person'. Chateaubriand presents Napoleon as a tormented poet-figure, with whom he can readily identify ('the sight of these precocious works reminds me of my own jumbled juvenilia'). If only he had gone through with his original plan to skip the country after his initial success at blasting the British out of Toulon, 'I would have had an enormous comrade, a giant bent by my side in exile' [*j'aurais eu un énorme camarade, géant courbé à mes côtes dans l'exil*].

They first met in Paris at a soirée hosted by Lucien Bonaparte in late April or May 1802. Chateaubriand (according to Chateaubriand) was reticent and hid behind a crowd of people; but, at the sound of Napoleon's greeting – 'Monsieur de Chateaubriand!' – the crowd pulled back and reformed in a circle around the two of them, as if around a brace of boxers. It was their first conversation, and yet Napoleon behaved as if they were old acquaintances. 'Bonaparte approached me with simplicity; without paying me any compliments, without idle questions. He launched straight into an account of Egypt and the Arabs, as if I had been on intimate terms with him and as if he was only continuing a conversation we had already begun.' This was only natural, from Napoleon's point of view, for had not Chateaubriand written an extremely long-winded dispatch to him, in the shape of the *Génie du christianisme*, confirming his own idea of a rapprochement with Rome? Napoleon's daughter-in-law Hortense (who would become his sister-in-law when she married Louis), who shared his tastes, read the *Génie du christianisme* aloud to him in 1802, when it first came out. And the second edition of Chateaubriand's anti-Enlightenment manifesto on behalf of myth seemed to confirm Napoleon's assumption, since it now carried an explicit dedication, 'Au Premier Consul Bonaparte'.

Shortly afterward, on 4 May 1803, Napoleon nominated Chateaubriand as first secretary in Rome to the ambassador, Cardinal Fesch, Napoleon's uncle. Chateaubriand treated the offer with contempt and turned it down (he recalls), and had to be talked into accepting it (and then only on altruistic grounds). He was convinced, in any case, that Napoleon had been seduced by the quality of his prose; but perhaps Chateaubriand's apostrophe to Napoleon (along with a lot of supplementary wooing through second parties) was not irrelevant: 'One cannot help but recognize in your destiny the hand of that Providence that marked you out from the beginning for the fulfilment of its prodigious purposes.' Chateaubriand was not precisely saying that Napoleon was God or even God's right-hand man – but it came close and the interpretation was permissible. Napoleon said he had never been so lavishly praised.

Fesch sent a few 'malevolent dispatches' back to Paris from Rome, denouncing Chateaubriand as a royalist sympathizer. But it was not until the execution of the Duc d'Enghien, one of the Bourbon pretenders, in March 1804, that a bifurcating path severed Chateaubriand and Napoleon. A Napoleonic snatch squad had arrested Enghien in Germany and brought him back to France, where he was locked up in Vincennes, interrogated, found guilty by a military tribunal and shot. For Chateaubriand, this was Napoleon's original sin, the metamorphosis from 'hero' to 'murderer'. But the fate of Enghien is the making of Chateaubriand, who admits that if Napoleon hadn't had him killed, 'my literary career would have been over' [*ma carrière littéraire était finie*]. Enghien enables Chateaubriand to live out his death-wish. At the same time, Chateaubriand sees, in Enghien's end, Napoleon taking a sideways shot at him, Chateaubriand, and missing. The dead aristocrat is an allegory and alter ego for the writer on the run who is actually top of Napoleon's hit-list. And Chateaubriand is thus given a *raison d'être*: to write a protracted *J'accuse*.

The crux of Chateaubriand's complaint is revealing: that this pseudo-judicial execution is all carried out with undue haste, in typically Napoleonic fashion: everything happens too fast – the kidnapping, the interrogation, the sentencing, the firing squad. Too fast and in darkness, moreover, the mark of benightedness. There is no time for second thoughts, nor for Enghien to speak directly to Napoleon. Chateaubriand draws attention to the use of the Napoleonic adverb, *de suite*, in the formula according to which the sentence was mandated to be carried out. Enghien is depicted as a martyr to speed, a man who is 'dispatched', like a telegram, military-style.

There is an anecdote that may or may not be authentic, but is vouchsafed by Chateaubriand, and which he considers exemplary of the whole episode. On the night of 21 March, Pierre François Réal, state councillor at the ministry of police,

is on his way to Vincennes with orders from Napoleon to conduct further questioning of the prisoner. But at a checkpoint
coming out of Paris he runs smack into General Savary, going
back in the opposite direction, who is aware that Enghien has
already been not only questioned, but sentenced and executed.
It seems, therefore, that there must have been another set of
orders emanating from Napoleon's office, travelling faster than
Réal, which have been put more promptly and brutally into
effect.

Chateaubriand denounced the lack of a written order. What
elicits his ire, in short, is the hypertextual telegraphic culture
for which Napoleon is responsible, taking shortcuts around the
classical text, and transmitting orders mysteriously through the
air, at express speed, leaving mounted messengers behind. 'Let
us beware', he writes, 'of falling into a technological inhumanity
which would weaken the hatred which evil should always inspire in us.' [*Donnons-nous garde de tomber dans une impassibilité
machinale et d'affaiblir la haine que le mal doit toujours inspirer.*]
The speed of communications, in Chateaubriand's mind, had
reduced men to machinery, to the status of things or robots. If
only Réal had been present at the interrogation, he speculates,
the fate of the duke might have been different. 'But these
are secrets which are only written in the book which contains
everything.' Napoleon, in short, had gone wrong by forgetting
and betraying the sacred text, the book of truth, which guided
him at the beginning.

There are moments when, semi-incomunicado and certainly
cut off from the Chappe brothers' equipment on Saint Helena,
Napoleon seemed to concur with Chateaubriand's critique of
telegraphicity, expressing fears that he had become a virtual
man, locked out from reality. Las Cases reports from the depths
of the South Atlantic that, 'When he was alone with me, the
Emperor admitted that the inherent flaw [in the whole Enghien
affair] could be attributed to an excess of zeal around him . . .
He said that he had been suddenly pressured into acting, that
others had, so to speak, anticipated his ideas, rushed through
his measures, and inferred conclusions.'

And yet, even in the Enghien case, he suspected that it was
only a lack of all the necessary information, yet another glitch
in the system of communication, that was at the root of the

'error': 'if only I had been informed at the right time of certain specific details' [*si j'eusse été instruit à temps de certaines particularités*] then Enghien would probably have been pardoned. In the end, Napoleon's defence is not so much that he was too fast but that everyone else was too slow or incompetent in conveying crucial data (for example, the 'letter' or request from Enghien to have a personal interview with him never reached him, he maintains, until after the execution). It was more that messages arrived too late than too soon.

Chateaubriand waited until the Bourbons had marched back into Paris before publishing his most damning indictment of Napoleon and all his works in *De Buonaparté et des Bourbons* (and he scuttled out of town again when Napoleon unexpectedly returned from Elba). He claimed that Louis XVIII had said to him that his pamphlet was worth more to him than an army of 100,000 men. But the crux of his criticism is curiously non-strategic, and not even political except in the most general terms. In this work Chateaubriand returned to the idea that Napoleon had turned against literature. He takes the Emperor to task for his shaky command of languages, especially French. The fact that he was insufficiently instructed in Latin and Greek automatically disqualified him from leading the nation. Moreover, he had an established 'intemperance of language, a taste for popular literature, and a passion for journalism' [*intempérance de langage, goût de la basse littérature, passion d'écrire dans les journaux*]. He was, in short, a product and embodiment of telegraphic culture; he was the Anti-Text, the precise antithesis of Chateaubriand himself, champion and apostle of scripture.

But the affinity, a sense of reciprocity, between Chateaubriand and Napoleon, was never entirely lost. Napoleon supported Chateaubriand's election to the Institut in 1811. And Chateaubriand's *Itinéraire de Paris à Jérusalem* is almost nothing but a recapitulation of Napoleonic themes. In the *Mémoires d'outre-tombe* Chateaubriand argues that, in the light of his post-Enghien act of resignation, 'in daring to desert Napoleon, I had placed myself at his level' [*en osant quitter Bonaparte, je m'étais placé à son niveau*]. But he gives this line a further egocentric twist in the Orient. Napoleon left Egypt, never to return, before the end of the eighteenth century; Chateaubriand did not begin his journey East until 1806 and his account did not appear until 1811. But in the longer perspective, 'Napoleon takes the path I followed' [*Napoléon prend la route que j'ai suivie*] twisting around tense and time, following in Chateaubriand's footsteps. This inversion is not quite the raving self-promotion that it might appear at first sight.

Chateaubriand may not, after the death of Enghien, have supported Napoleon, but he was the source – one of the sources – of the imperial logic. Rousseau's iconic 'Legislator', from the *Contrat social*, the freewheeling and self-sufficient mouthpiece of the General Will, is the obvious model of Napoleon's political style. But it took Chateaubriand to deify the author. In *Génie du christianisme* he comes up with an ingenious solution to the problem of fossils. Recently uncovered palaeontological evidence seemed to imply a degree of antiquity incompatible with the Book of Genesis. Chateaubriand, a hyper-creationist, therefore resorts to a theory of 'originary old-age' [*vieillesse originaire*] according to which 'God must have created, and undoubtedly did create, the world with all the marks of dilapidation and complementarity that we see in it today.' God planted fossils to make the world appear older than it really was, thus creating a reef-filled ocean, the first man – already aged around thirty, and mother-birds with chicks already in the nest, in short, a mature universe, already fully evolved, furnished with innocence and corruption and well-advanced ruins. Chateaubriand, who loved ruins, could not imagine a decently designed universe without them.

Chateaubriand's 'author of nature' [*auteur de la nature*] is Napoleon's primordial precursor. He provides the first and most exemplary instantaneity that would come to define the telegraphic effect. God was the first telegrapher, although it has taken a while to interpret his messages. And the deity, *à la* Chateaubriand, was also the first total author, who omits nothing and controls everything, leaving nothing to chance or to random human interceptions. Everything there is always has been, from the very beginning, nothing has been added or subtracted. And thus there is no more resistance or conflict between word and thing, command and execution. Chateaubriand admitted that his metaphysics was a political allegory, but maintained that he had Louis XVIII the king-in-waiting rather than Napoleon in mind when writing about God.

But if Napoleon learned from Chateaubriand, it is certain that Chateaubriand stole directly from Napoleon. The liberationist rhetoric of *De Buonaparté et des Bourbons* and Staël's *Dix ans* is taken from the early Napoleon (who takes it from Raynal and Rousseau). The demand to be liberated from Napoleon is only a transposition of the liberating gestures of Napoleon: 'Italian people! The French army has come to smash your chains. The French people are the friends of all people. We are only against the tyrants who enslave you.' [*Peuples d'Italie! L'armée française vient rompre vos chaînes; le peuple français est l'amie de tous les peuples. Nous n'en voulons qu'aux tyrans qui vous asservissent.*]

Chateaubriand thought of himself as the Napoleon of literature, while Napoleon, conversely, saw himself as the Chateaubriand of political art. Chateaubriand made self-mythification, the hyperinflation of the ego, the grandiloquent gesture, respectable, almost obligatory. He brought back the God who had been put in doubt by the *philosophes*, but made over in the image of the author. Napoleon adapted it to fit the vacuum left by the French Revolution. Royalist plots were a variation on attempts to intercept Napoleon's mail by conspiring at the death of the author. The elevation from First Consul to Emperor, in 1804, was nothing less than an attempt to immortalize him. Only the unsurpassable author was on a par with the Emperor: only Chateaubriand could write 'if Napoleon had finished with kings, he had not yet finished with me' [*si Napoléon avait fini avec les rois, il n'en avait pas fini avec moi*]. *Génie du christianisme* was a blueprint for the Empire. Chateaubriand's strong author theory mapped out the concept of a singularity at the centre of a system of signs and coincided miraculously with Chappe's thinking about another force that could condense time and space: 'In a sense, the telegraph . . . condensed an immense population into a single point' [*Le télégraphe . . . réunit en quelque sorte une immense population en un seul point*]. Small wonder, then, that Napoleon should have heaped such contempt on the old idea of the 'idle king' [*roi fainéant*] – a 'roi de théâtre' – who would do nothing but 'inscribe his signature on the work of others and do nothing by himself' [*apposer sa signature sur l'oeuvre des autres, et ne rien faire par soi-même!*].

The Restoration not only dispatched Napoleon to the outer darkness of Saint Helena, but at the same time cut back radically on the telegraphic network that was the work of revolutionaries and regicides and Corsicans. Chateaubriand began by supporting the Bourbons on the grounds that, in contrast to the overly precipitate, excessively creative Napoleon ('an extraordinary adventurer, endlessly generating new plans, dreaming up new laws, only feeling fully in charge when he is labouring to disrupt the established order, overturning, destroying in the evening what he created in the morning') they were slow, ponderous, lumbering, unimaginative ('a prince who would only have in his head two or three commonplace but useful ideas'). Perhaps it is not so surprising that, as the Restoration went on, Chateaubriand – like so many others, Stendhal among them – became nostalgic about the Napoleonic golden age and the *ogre de Corse* was once again the *géant* and the writer who virtually single-handedly brought him down began to have second thoughts.

While he was serving in the embassy in Rome once more, in 1829, this time under Charles X, the Pope (Leo XII) was in the throes of a mortal illness. Chateaubriand was determined to be the first to get the news of his death back to Paris. Having stationed a collaborator inside the Vatican, on the night of 9–10 February, beside the dying Pope, like an angel poised to carry off the pontiff's immortal soul, he was perfectly positioned to send off a dispatch almost at the very moment of death, in the early hours of the 10th (or, indeed, before, arranging for horses 'avant la mort du pape'). But, to his chagrin, there was a roadblock cordoning off the Vatican City, and riders could not get through. Bitterly frustrated, Chateaubriand was forced to wait until the evening before the dispatch could effectively be dispatched. His urgent message did not reach Lyon for a further four days. From there it could be telegraphed to Paris within a matter of hours.

In his revisionist period, Chateaubriand finally swung around to the advantages of speed and regretted that the direct line over the Alps into Italy had been lost. 'Forced to wait in Rome, which has become a kind of prison, locked and bolted, I still hope that the news will reach you, by means of the telegraph, some hours before it is known to other governments beyond the Alps.' It was at this time that he stressed that there was no necessary incompatibility between God and the telegraph and that Christianity was pro-speed. 'In vain have the impious claimed that Christianity encouraged oppression and held back progress . . . The sciences, which remained almost stationary in Antiquity, have received an injection of rapidity from the apostolic spirit of renewal . . . The Christian religion grows with civilization and moves with the times.' All Chateaubriand's writings, like Napoleon's, converge on a grand synthesis of text, technology and theology.

One of the first experimental messages sent by one Chappe brother to another (from on top of the dome over the main staircase of the Louvre on 2 March 1791) went as follows: 'If you succeed you will soon be covered with glory' [*Si vous réussissez vous serez bientôt couvert de gloire*]. That Napoleonic confidence wasn't entirely misplaced. In 1844, before being eclipsed by the electric telegraph, Chappe's semaphoric network had grown to over 4,000 kilometres and boasted a total of 556 stations and 29 cities linked with Paris. Chappe telegraph towers sprang up in Algeria and Egypt and were last seen in the Crimea, in 1855, boasting of victory at Sebastopol. Napoleon's vision had, in some sense, been realized, even if not all messages would pass through the office of the Emperor.

In the nineteenth century, writers contrived to corner the market in heroic resistance. But the truth is that the quest for the perfect telegraph line was just as fraught with peril, as Chappe the Elder says:

> How much in the way of blood, sweat and tears we expended to overcome unforeseen obstacles which were always multi-plying in this hitherto unknown sphere, and how much we suffered from the fear of failure: in those days death hung over all our heads.

In fact, telegraphers were more heroic, since, like the mailman whom they supplanted, they really died in the performance of their duty rather than just fantasizing about it.

Claude Chappe, like Napoleon, felt his achievements to be inadequate and precarious. His fate provided an anticipatory telegraph of Napoleon's own. He knew that the existing system was 'still incomplete'. Ironically, given that speed was its selling-point, the Chappes felt that they had been forced to rush, working 'with a precipitation that prevented us from giving the telegraphic lines the perfection of which they were cap-able' [*une précipitation qui a empêché de donner aux lignes télégraphiques la perfection dont elles sont suspectibles*]. And, like all empires, it was under attack by rivals. Other inventors claimed to have priority: the Chappes, they argued, were merely imitating, plagiarizing, stealing (while they blatantly stole from and plagiarized the Chappes).

The pressure – overworked and underfunded, accused of theft and being robbed at the same time – began to tell on Claude Chappe. The unfortunate inventor fell prey to 'an over-excitement of the brain', wrote his biographer, a brain which was already immoderately excitable. 'His nature became more anxious, irritable, already manifesting the symptoms of hypo-chondria, that sickness characteristic of great but weary intel-lects.' Chappe, haunted by paranoid anxieties, feared that calumnies about him were being telegraphed behind his back. In Lyon, while working on improving the line from Paris, he was either poisoned or thought that he was. Either way, he hurried back to Paris, stricken with 'a crushing melancholia'. It had become clear to him – whether in the light of the Napoleonic wars or his own personal battles – that the telegraph was unable to deliver on its sacred promise to bring peace, or even optimal communication. The idea of suicide presented itself to his mind, as it had to Napoleon's. But he could not die with-out leaving a message. On the other hand he had transcended the text and preferred to write on the air. So, to provide an unambiguous optical sign of his deep depression, and the cause of it, he flung himself, on 23 January 1805, down the well out-side the Telegraph Administration building, the Hôtel Villeroy, in Paris. He died, wrote his brother Abraham, 'a victim of his zeal for science and his country'.

In place of a gravestone, a telegraph tower was built over Chappe's grave. The whirling arms were fixed for all time to signify 'At rest'.

5
The Third Man

Mariage de Napoléon avec Marie Louise.

The year is 1808. It is autumn, the beginning of October, to be precise, with winter ('General Winter' Napoleon half-jokingly called it) massing on the horizon. The triumphant if corpse-strewn battlefields of Austerlitz and Jena (and, more ambiguously still, Eylau) lie behind Napoleon, the humiliations of Spain have already begun, and the catastrophes of Russia are in the making. Napoleon is in Erfurt (formerly in Thüringen, now nominally a piece of France) together with Talma, his favourite actor, and other members of the Comédie-Française. There is a brief cessation in the exchange of cannon-fire sounding across all the borders of Europe, long enough at any rate to ask the question: what is Napoleon doing here? There is a simple technical answer: attending yet another European peace conference (and, therefore, manoeuvring for another shot at England). Napoleon himself reinforces this interpretation by putting on a show of emotion during Voltaire's *Mahomet* in response to the lines: 'To the name of conqueror and hero, he wishes to add the name of peace-maker.'

Napoleon is negotiating with Czar Alexander while his ex-foreign minister Talleyrand (still, however, officially of the Emperor's party) is going about behind his back unravelling any deals he is trying to stitch together. There are balls, concerts, exhibitions, banquets, a full-on assault by French culture on the assembled kings and dukes and princes. There is dancing: Napoleon wrote to Josephine: 'Emperor Alexander danced but I didn't. After all, forty years old is forty years old.' There are performances of Corneille and Racine and Voltaire (Napoleon thought the Germans would not appreciate Molière) and visits to historic sites (Napoleon escorted Alexander around the battlefield of Jena, with a running commentary on his most skilful manoeuvres). It is a classic exercise in power politics.

But beyond the immediate occasion of Napoleon's presence in Erfurt, there are other more far-reaching answers as to what he is doing here, concerning the logic of his expansionist policies. The first (the idealist answer), virtually contemporaneous, comes from the philosopher of history, Hegel. The second (the anatomical answer), from Napoleon's pathologist and probable castrator, Antommarchi. And there is still one more, the third answer, involving the third man.

Napoleon himself always claimed Austerlitz and Jena as among his finest hours, his most rocklike achievements: 'In my career people will doubtless find fault. But Arcola, Rivoli, the Pyramids, Marengo, Austerlitz, Jena, Friedland: this is all granite and immune to the tooth of envy.' And Hegel at least was prepared to agree with him. Hegel was Napoleon's almost exact contemporary (born in 1770) and welcomed the French Revolution and Napoleon alike. He wrote his *Phenomenology of Mind* like a man possessed, in a desperate rush, completing it – in its admittedly chaotic form – in October 1806 on the very eve of Napoleon's victory at Jena, one of the oldest university cities in Europe, and the centre of German Romanticism, where Hegel was a professor. The book and the battle not only coincided but concurred, standing together to constitute a moment of high historical optimism. It seemed to Hegel that Napoleon had sent his troops in to surround him and the academy and the dregs of an old empire. 'The composition of the book was concluded at midnight before the battle of Jena', Hegel wrote to Schelling. Hegel's commentator, Baillie, registers a sceptical note: 'This sounds a little hollow and melodramatic. For one naturally asks what the roar of Napoleon's cannon had to do with the philosophical delineation of the Absolute. The

Absolute, as well as his expositor, could surely afford to wait till the smoke of such temporalities had cleared.' He assumes that the rush to finish the book had more to do with a 'pitiless publisher' than the 'roll of war in his ears'.

But the fact is that Hegel and Napoleon were linked, almost twinned, at least in the mind of Hegel. It was not just the book that was completed in 1806, at Jena, but similarly, by a strange coincidence, universal history. But for Hegel there were no coincidences, everything was part of the unfolding and flowering of the Absolute, nothing – least of all the roar of cannon – was irrelevant to its relentless forward movement. 'The self-realization of the Absolute Spirit', otherwise obscure and intangible, seemed to find empirical demonstration in the global itinerary mapped out by Napoleon. So much so that the *Phenomenology* reads like a commentary on the growth of empire, with the small difference that Hegel tilted the evolution of the dialectic towards the crystallization of the German state. Hegel saw the defeat of Prussia and the Holy Roman Empire as paving the way for the consolidation of a modern republic. Thus he celebrated Napoleon's victories and praised him as a 'world-historical individual': 'This extraordinary man, who brought order out of the anarchy of France, has the greatness of soul that is needed to rise above being merely the benefactor of a single nation to become the benefactor of mankind.'

Bertrand Russell was no doubt over-simplifying when he wrote that Hegel's entire philosophy comprised 'only minds and mental events', but his book was probably the most purely metaphysical work since Bishop Berkeley. And it is clear that Hegel greeted the advent of Napoleon as essentially an intellectual event – the final one – doing away with certain old ideas, breaking an outmoded philosophical mould, revitalizing the academy and ushering in the era of truth. The whole of human history was the complex working out of an Idea, according to which all conflict and contradiction would be resolved in a perfect synthesis, and Napoleon was the personification of that Idea. 'The purpose of the phenomenology is to show that *nothing can be left out*', wrote another of Hegel's exegetists; so too it can be said, Napoleon was determined to leave no one and nothing out of his holistic scheme of things. This is why Hegel was so enthusiastic: 'The Emperor – this world-soul – riding through the city . . . It is indeed a wonderful feeling to see such an individual who . . . sitting on a horse, reaches out over the world and dominates it.'

There are many times when Napoleon himself appears to explicitly echo Hegelian thinking. His whole ambition, he told Las Cases, had been

> the grandest and the most high-minded that perhaps ever was: to establish the empire of reason and to consolidate, finally, the full exercise, the entire enjoyment of all the human faculties! And here the historian will perhaps find himself compelled to regret that such an ambition should not have been accomplished and satisfied . . . In a few short words, there is my history.

But, in contradistinction to Hegel, Napoleon allows that his universalizing tendency was never fully achieved. And the hard fact is that Napoleon had not come to Erfurt to see Hegel. So far as we know he was oblivious to the existence of Hegel. The other answer – the anatomical answer, the sexualist theory – as to why he was in Erfurt is: he was there to see a woman.

Napoleon died on Saint Helena in 1821, but his remains were exhumed and finally laid to rest with full honours at Les Invalides in Paris in 1840. Some part of Napoleon now lies entombed within six embedded coffins, mounted on a massive plinth. But another smaller part floats in a solution of formaldehyde in a test-tube in New York. This is his penis. Antommarchi, the surgeon attending Napoleon, who carried out his post-mortem, was almost certainly also responsible for carrying out an improvisatory castration. There is some uncertainty as to his motives. One theory holds that he was a simple trophy hunter cashing in on Napoleon mania; another that it was an act of vengeance for some derogatory remarks Napoleon had allegedly made about his manhood. In some sense he was only re-enacting Waterloo, where Napoleon had already to all intents and purposes been militarily and politically castrated. But this obscure pathologist was also driven by a pervasive phallocentric fixation. (An alternative theory holds that it was the British surgeon, Arnott, who carried off various body parts, ostensibly to put a stop to fetishistic collecting.)

The early nineteenth century was not immune to the idea that power and sexuality hang together, that great power produces a sexual charge or that a highly charged sexuality generates a desire for power. Rather, it was a commonplace of the age that Napoleon, perhaps unwittingly, did much to inflate. This popular psychology – which we can broadly call the sexualist view of history – was all of a piece with the mythology of empire. The French Empire was constructed on the premise of *dissemination*: the object of the *mission civilisatrice* was to spread enlightenment and republican ideas among benighted, typically monarchical, nations. And the model for this process was *insemination*: France was construed as a male propagating itself through coition with the female of the foreign. The contemporary debate concerned whether it was, as France maintained, a genuine seduction of a willing partner, or, on the other hand, a plain case of rape.

Napoleon's rise to power was founded on an allied metaphor. He was the outsider bringing a fresh genetic injection to France. In one aspect, he claims to father a reborn nation; in another, he is the midwife bringing to an end the labour pains of the Revolution and the Terror. By the same token, he can be projected, by his opponents, as an unwanted invader thrusting himself upon pure French innocence. Napoleon himself, following his elevation to Emperor, became obsessed with fatherhood and the task of founding a dynasty and placing a relative in every capital of Europe. And this narrative of cultural transmission and regeneration is passed on, through the nineteenth century, via Victor Hugo and Napoleon III (among others).

But there is a larger historical complex at work, which we could call Napoleon's-penis envy. The passage of the missing penis from hand to hand, from the South Atlantic to Europe, thence (via Christie's auctioneers) to the United States, is mirrored in the expansion of the sexualist view: that history is essentially penis-driven, that Napoleon was only ever following the dictates of his biology and scattering his genetic seed as widely as possible. Napoleon is the hard man of history. In the phallocentric imagination, his penis has been perceived as the hardest part of him, a microcosm of the man, the fragment out of which, as with Cuvier's heelbone, the whole entity, and thus History itself, can be reconstructed. That test-tube in New

York contains an archaeology. (Ironically, rival pretenders to the title have sprung up. The classic asylum condition, the claim to be Napoleon, is repeated in miniature as other penises have laid claim to being Napoleon's. The phallus has been going forth and multiplying, if only *in vitro*.)

Among Napoleon's contemporaries, the sexualist case was taken up most passionately by Charles Fourier, the utopian thinker who would be mocked by Marx and Engels for being wildly optimistic and who looked forward to a sexual revolution. In 1803 Fourier wrote a letter intended for Napoleon ('the High Judge') in which he set out the way he thought France should be going and sketched his theory of the 'four movements'. Rooted in seventeenth-century science, born out of eighteenth-century rationalism, but drawing on the vocabulary of Romanticism, Fourier saw himself as the Newton of 'passional attraction'. Whereas Newton had only discovered the laws of material attraction, Fourier was in the process of setting out the laws of gravitation as they drew human beings towards one another. The universe is governed by the laws of attraction: material, organic, animal, social. By the same token there is a form of gravity that attracts human beings to certain things or other humans: desire. 'Civilization' (the fifth out of 32 possible societies) was predicated on the erroneous attempt to suppress this natural passion. The point was to surrender to it, immediately, systematically, totally.

In his ideal society, the 'phalanstery', all desires would be automatically satisfied, thus producing the state he refers to as Harmony or the Harmonian age. To take account notably of what Fourier calls the 'butterfly passion', he foresees the repressive regime of marriage giving way to a *nouveau monde amoureux* of endless multiple liaisons, public orgies and a sexual AA call-out service in case of emergencies. All in the cause of providing what he calls the 'sexual minimum'. This was anathema to Hegel, who wrote that 'What is anti-human, the condition of mere animals, consists in keeping within the sphere of feeling pure and simple, and in being able to communicate only by way of feeling-states.'

Stendhal called Fourier a 'sublime dreamer'. And his claim that all the seas would turn to lemonade under Harmony has not increased his credibility. Certainly there is no evidence that Napoleon ever read Fourier's letter (perhaps the victim of another interception and carried off in triumph to London?) or even acknowledged his existence. And yet not only does Fourier provide a more carnal counterpart to Hegel's idealist system, and a 'radical eudemonism' (in Roland Barthes's phrase – a systematic theory of happiness), but there is a strong Fourierist tendency in all our subsequent thinking about Napoleon. Nietzsche, for one, was seduced by this concept: he imagined Napoleon ruthlessly accumulating conquests between battles. We like to suppose that he was living out the Fourier dream, constantly going about satisfying every flutter of his butterfly passion. Frédéric Masson, his late nineteenth-century chronicler, states this line quite plainly in *Napoléon et les femmes*: 'Nature has attached to the perpetuation of the species – the essential function of the male – a whole series of sensations which compel him, force him, subjugate him, to which the greater part of the deeds of his existence are subordinated.'

This is the orgasmic approach to human history, which upgrades Napoleon's desire for happiness into a demand for perpetual ecstasy. According to Masson, 'We manage to find in Napoleon a faculty of love as large as his faculty of thought and action, and which demonstrates a lover and a husband as astonishing as the warrior and the statesman . . . he is the lover par excellence.' And it is true that, between battles, Napoleon took it upon himself to construct his own personal phalanstery. In his oriental mood, Napoleon saw himself as a sultan surrounded by his harem. Contemporary accounts vied to chalk up his score. The hit-list is limitless: La Grassini, the Italian diva; Pauline Fourès, the Cleopatra of his Egyptian expedition; Madame *** in the Tuileries, and on and on to the point of satiation.

The British navy certainly took a serious view of Napoleon's sexual powers and did their best to stymie him. When Nelson was not sinking the French fleet he was trying to scuttle Napoleon's romances. The British were of the counter-Fourierist tendency: their strategy was to cause maximum frustration. Marguerite-Pauline Bellisle (Madame Fourès) was one of the few women to accompany the French troops and the Commission des Arts et des Sciences to Egypt. She was initially disguised as a man, but her body – reports the lubricious Masson – was 'delicate and appetizing'. Only her husband, Lieutenant Fourès, stood in the way of Napoleon possessing it. So the commander-in-chief found him an urgent mission to attend to, delivering dispatches to Italy and France, and gave him a warship, *Le Chasseur*, to speed him on his way, at the same time installing his wife in a house close to his own palace. But the British, thanks to an efficient intelligence network in Egypt, had wind of Napoleon's erotic plans and sent in the Royal Navy vessel *Lion* to intercept *Le Chasseur* within a day of it leaving Alexandria. The letters were sent to London for publication while Fourès was put ashore again (under oath not to fight against them for the remainder of the war) and urged to return to Cairo, specifically with a view to interrupting the Napoleonic coitus. There was a violent showdown between husband and wife in her bathroom *chez* Bonaparte, but the commander-in-chief soon had him trekking across the desert to Syria – 'try intercepting him this time!' he seemed to say to Nelson.

The obsession with the imperial phallus may explain why it was that the British army surgeons on Saint Helena declared, in their post-mortem, that Napoleon had under-sized genitalia ('The private parts were seen to be remarkably small, like a boy's', wrote Walter Henry.) The collective unconscious had so enlarged his sexual powers that the real thing was bound to seem inadequate by comparison. The diagnosis of 'hypogonadism', in short, may have come of a certain hyper-gonadic spirit. Or of sheer vengeance. Another unreliable witness, Josephine put it about that '*Bon-a-parte est bon-à-rien*', implying that he was impotent as well as unsatisfactory as a lover. But that apprehension of physical inadequacy was certainly (if intermittently) shared by Napoleon himself: 'What is love?' he once wrote. 'The sense of his own weakness, which quickly possesses the solitary or isolated man.'

On the Fourierist view of Erfurt, and even that of the British navy, it is not implausible that Napoleon could be passing through on his way to a date with Marie Walewska. In Poland, Masson records in Napoleon's romantic CV the experience that – transposed to Paris – would later be immortalized in Baudelaire's poem, 'A une passante': a woman passing in the crowd, an exchange of glances that say, 'I love you', and then she is lost forever. This particular chance encounter was supposed to have occurred at Bronie, near Warsaw, on New Year's Day, 1807. Some days before Napoleon had written to Josephine, chiding her for a jealous dream: 'The winter nights are long, all alone.' Now, as he returned to his winter quarters in Warsaw, pausing to change horses, snow was falling on Napoleon's carriage and a blizzard of cheers and hurrahs from enthusiastic Poles, who credited him with achieving the liberation of Poland from its oppressors. One of Napoleon's fans among the adoring peasant throng at the post-house was a young girl with flowing blonde tresses and blue eyes and pink cheeks (so says Masson) who came up to his carriage – assisted by Duroc, his aide-de-camp – and thanked him fervently (in excellent French) for being Poland's messiah and repelling the Austrian and the Russian and the Prussian. In return he gave her one of the bouquets that had landed at his feet before the carriage drove off again, leaving his heart behind and his mind full of the mysterious stranger. In an immensely more epic vein, it is Baudelaire's story.

But Napoleon, being Napoleon, was not content with that frustrating ending. He wanted to satisfy his passing passion. Back in Warsaw he commissioned Duroc to find out who the *passante* was and to track her down. Within days, Countess Marie Walewska, the pious and nationalist wife of an ageing Polish aristocrat, was being invited (or ordered) to a ball given in Napoleon's honour. All that winter he lay siege to Marie Walewska's virtue and ultimately brought down the citadel. The coercive letters and declarations verge on blackmail: surrender to me or your country is doomed: 'Come to me; all your desires will be fulfilled. Your country will be dearer to me when you take pity on my poor heart . . .' [*Tous vos désirs seront remplis. Votre patrie me sera plus chère quand vous aurez pitié de mon coeur*]. Even then she might have held out against the charm offensive, except that other Polish patriots, and even her own husband, joined in on Napoleon's side. French officers (such as Bertrand and Périgord) who showed a flicker of interest in her were promptly dispatched to far-flung outposts of the Empire.

This appears as one of Napoleon's purest conquests, a love affair which was an extension of war. 'I want to force you, yes, *force* you to love me. Marie, I have brought back to life your country's name. It only exists because of me. I will do much more.' When she showed signs of resistance he flung his watch to the floor and ground it furiously under his boot: 'If you persist in refusing me I'll grind your people into dust, like this watch under my heel.' It was more like rape than seduction, sheer power mustered to back up desire. She succumbed, according to her own account, thinking of Poland. And Josephine, who is desperate to come and join him in Poland, must be kept at bay: 'There is too much ground to cover between Mayence and Warsaw' [*Il y a trop de pays à traverser entre Mayence jusqu' à Varsovie*]. Or, 'the weather is too bad, the roads are unsafe and atrocious, the distance too great for me to allow you to come all the way here, where I am detained by affairs of state.' Affairs of state became a euphemism for affairs *tout court*.

Although there is no doubt Napoleon really had a long-term on-off affair with Marie Walewska, the story as a whole, and notably the overture, has been massively enhanced. More plausible than the whole Cinderella scenario of coaches and bouquets in the snow (for which there is no corroboration from Walewska) is Christine Sutherland's hypothesis that Talleyrand (who was already well acquainted with Walewska) coolly set up the whole affair with a view to sweetening Napoleon towards Poland. Even in the more legendary version it is still Duroc who is responsible for singling out the mysterious stranger and bringing her forward and presenting her to Napoleon's attention ('Sire, look, here is a woman who has braved all the dangers of the crowd to see you') before – almost miraculously – identifying and delivering her into Napoleon's arms. It is as if Napoleon has to be maneouvred into position, as if he has to be 'forced' to love her. Many of Napoleon's love affairs are undoubtedly invented ('they make me out to be a Hercules!' he joked on Saint Helena.) But even when not, they have to be stage-managed and propped up in the public interest, deliberately engineered to counter the widespread rumour that Napoleon was impotent or under-sexed and incapable of producing children (Josephine blamed him just as he blamed her). 'I refused to listen to the cry of my own impotence', Napoleon wrote in his *Lettres sur la Corse* [*je n'écoutais pas le cri de mon impuissance*]. 'What is needed is a soul which is not shaken by the fear of potent men who must be unmasked' [*il faut une âme qui ne soit pas ébranlée par la crainte des hommes puissants qu'il faudra démasquer*]. But the fear of the potent man (who 'rapes' Corsica, for example) was never completely overcome.

The problem of the third man, the other (more powerful) phallus, the supplementary, alternative lover who invariably blows apart the perfect circle of romantic oneness, was central to Napoleon's thinking from the beginning. He entertained doubts about his mother's fidelity (Carlo? Paoli? Marbeuf?), which may have inspired his passion for symbolic idealized father figures. The formative novel of Napoleon's youth, the one he came back to again and again (he read it seven times in all, he claimed), and took with him on the Egyptian expedition, was Goethe's *The Sorrows of Young Werther* (even though he was reportedly furious when he found all his officers poring over it on the Mediterranean voyage – 'reading for chambermaids!' – and commanded them all to read some more masculine and uplifting works of history). Goethe's novel of 1774, partly based on his own experiences, pitched its protagonist into a doomed love for the unattainable woman, Lotte, who is betrothed to and eventually marries Albert, thus precipitating Werther's suicide, leaving behind a diary and letters full of the void of unsatisfied yearning. Albert and Lotte actually give the rejected Werther the pistols he uses to blow his brains out. The third-man narrative of the tragic triangle – Werther/Lotte/Albert – was the point of departure for Napoleon's own early experiments in fiction, notably his would-be novel, *Clisson et Eugénie*. 'I began to read novels,' Napoleon said, 'and they interested me deeply. I even tried my hand at writing some.' Napoleon's own efforts in turn inspired a family of novelists: Louis Bonaparte wrote *Marie or the Trials of Love* (and a memoir on versification), Joseph a pastoral idyll, *Moina or the Village Lass of Mount Cenis*, while Lucien dreamed up the exotic and escapist tale, *The Indian Tribe* (1799). On Saint Helena, Napoleon condemned them as 'boring'.

The date of Napoleon's unfinished sketch of a novel is uncertain: Masson places it in 1789, seeing in it analogies with the *Corsican Novella*, written around this time, and the more Rousseauist period. Jean Tulard pushes the date forward to

1795, when Napoleon is twenty-six years old, the same age as his hero Clisson. The later date also coincides with the affair with Desirée Clary, whom Napoleon always called by the name Eugénie. Perhaps both hypotheses are correct given that the text is a palimpsest of drafts. In any case, the love story is a variation on the theme of the *Discourse*: a shot at happiness that misses its target. Again there is a rejection and thoughts of suicide. And, as in the *Discourse*, there seems to be a close connection between writing and happiness. What exactly prompts suicide? In *Werther*, it was the loss to matrimony of Lotte. In *Clisson et Eugénie*, it occurs when the beloved's letters dry up. When she stops writing she stops loving. 'Eugénie no longer writes to him. Eugénie no longer loves him' [*Eugénie ne lui écrit plus. Eugénie ne l'aime plus*]. It is as if the act of writing itself is the sign of love.

On the title page of the manuscript Napoleon has crossed out the name *Eugénie*, leaving *Clisson* in place. This erasure betrays a certain anxiety or hesitation in Napoleon, even in terms of his commitment to a woman character. At the beginning of the story, Clisson is already a successful warrior figure. 'However his soul was not satisfied.' [*Cependant son âme n'était pas satisfaite.*] Still happiness eludes him: 'Like all men he was still looking for happiness and all he had found was glory.' [*Comme tous les hommes il avait encore le désir du bonheur et n'en avait encore trouvé que la gloire.*] In Napoleon's writing, glorious deeds are commonplace, the patrimony of all men, whereas happiness is rare to the point of non-existence. There is a brief moment in the narrative where it seems as if the two can be exchanged, and Clisson settles down to domestic bliss, and obscurely returns to the 'circle of nature' [*le cercle de la nature*] (the image is perhaps that of an island), but in the end he is called off to battle once more, is injured and sends his aide-de-camp Berville back to report the news to Eugénie that he will be delayed. As soon as she stops writing he goes out to seek death in combat – inferring that she has run off with Berville – and 'expired, shot through with a thousand wounds' [*expira, percé de mille coups*].

If this story is a response to his affair with Desirée (or Eugénie) Clary, then it is an exact inversion of the facts, since it is Napoleon who, having won her affection, decamped to Paris, took up with another and failed to write. 'You are married then!' Clary wrote to Napoleon when the news of his marriage reached her in Marseille. 'Poor Eugénie is no longer permitted to love you, or even think of you . . . At present the only consolation remaining to me is to know that you are persuaded of my constancy, beyond which all I desire is death.'

The anxiety of betrayal, or the expectation of betrayal, or, as seems likely, the desire for betrayal, may explain why Napoleon sought the company of prostitutes. One of the works he wrote while on another of his sabbaticals from the army, *Rencontre au Palais-Royal* ('A Meeting at the Palais-Royal'), is a detailed account of one of his encounters. Napoleon scrupulously dated the manuscript (Thursday, 22 November, 1787) and even spelt out his address (Hôtel de Cherbourg, rue du Four-Saint-Honoré), as if to give the text yet more authenticity. But this also squares with his overall approach, which is anthropological and scholarly. Masson argues that the *Rencontre* is, in fact, the record of Napoleon's loss of virginity, the moment at which, on the loose in the capital, his senses are overwhelmed by the perfume and touch of femininity: 'in this Paris, where she reigns, woman surrounds him, besieges him, takes hold of him.' But this text has the flavour less of eros than of a dry sexological experiment: it is the record of an exercise in advanced research. The eighteen-year-old is going about chatting up women, but only, the *Rencontre* implies, in a spirit of detached scientific inquiry. The phrase that he uses to describe a woman, 'une personne du sexe', suggests that only women are sexual, while he at least is sexless.

It is a freezing cold night, but Napoleon is striding restlessly about the streets of Paris, rehearsing for his own personal revolution. In the arcades of the Palais-Royal – once the base of Cardinal Richelieu and now the Soho of Paris – Napoleon comes across a woman just as it appears that he is about to beat down the doors: 'I was standing on the threshold of these iron gates when my gaze was distracted by a woman.' [*J'étais sur le seuil de ces portes de fer quand mes regards errèrent sur une personne du sexe.*] She is shy, pale, slight, softly spoken. He realizes that she is 'a person who will be useful to me for the purpose of making certain observations' [*une personne qui me sera utile à l'observation que je veux faire*] while he, on the other hand, is no longer the naive youth who feared he would be 'soiled by the mere gaze [of a prostitute]'. This is obviously not the first time Napoleon has had this kind of 'meeting', but this is his first cordial conversation: 'I was delighted for I saw that she replied to me at least, a success which had not always crowned the attempts I had previously made' [*succès qui n'avait pas couronné toutes les tentatives que j'avais faites*]. He has clearly been touring around the red-light district asking questions and regularly getting the brush-off. We have to assume that he has been asking some pretty odd questions. In this case, he inter-rogates the woman about her erotic history:

Napoleon: How did you lose your virginity?
Woman: An officer took it from me.

It turns out that the woman, a Breton, has had a string of liaisons with soldiers, each of whom in turn has abandoned her. Napoleon looks a likely candidate to take their place when she adds, 'Let us go to your place' [*Allons chez vous*]. But his next question demonstrates how unlikely this is after all: 'But what will we do there?' [*Mais qu'y ferons-nous?*] In his fervent quest for truth, he has completely forgotten that he might have some role other than doctoral researcher and note-taker.

When she replies, 'Come along, we will warm ourselves and you will satisfy your pleasure' [*Allons, nous nous chaufferons et vous assouvirez votre plaisir*], he is shaken out of his semi-trancelike state like a lepidopterist surprised at seeing a butter-fly he has pinned under a microscope take wing. But he is too embarrassed to make an excuse and leave, thereby repeating the army's habit of leaving her in the lurch – and putting his manhood in doubt. His strategy at this point is one of denial: he never intended to be so coolly detached ('*scrupuleux*'), he was only counterfeiting '*honnêteté*' – 'an innocence that I wanted to prove to her I did not have' [*que je voulais lui prouver ne pas avoir*]. In other words, he has to fake desire and pretend to have been faking the passionless analyst. He is polite enough to eschew politeness. Talleyrand shrewdly remarked that Napoleon's 'true feelings escape us, for he still finds a way to feign them even when they really exist' [*ses passions nous échappent; car il trouve encore le moyen de les feindre – quoiqu'elles existent réellement*]. There is certainly a large question-mark over Napoleon's sex-drive here. Nothing actually happens in the text: Napoleon is thinking and talking but not doing. One thing that is clear from the story is that he could not resist the whore's tale: of alliance followed by desertion, repeated over and over. The betrayal even acquires a certain political dimension in the case of one of her partners: 'Although French, his business [or his affairs?] called him to London and he remains there.' [*Quoique Français, ses affaires l'ont appelé à Londres et il y est.*]

Paris, sexuality and power are inseparable. Such is Napoleon's perception when he returns to the capital under the Thermidorian Convention, with Robespierre dead, the theatres overflowing (in Michelet's account) and a more sexually permissive mood abroad. 'Everywhere in Paris,' he wrote to brother Joseph in 1795, 'you see beautiful women. Here alone of all places on earth they appear to hold the reins of government, and the men are crazy about them, thinking of nothing else and living only for and through them . . . A woman needs to come to Paris for six months to learn what is her due, and to understand her own power. Here only, they deserve to have such influence.' [*Une femme a besoin de six mois de Paris pour connaître ce qui lui est dû et quel est son empire.*] There is a sense in which Napoleon allowed himself to be seduced by a certain *idea* of women – a 'sensuality of the mind', as Masson says. But even here he is careful to draw a line around the 'empire' of the woman, who is allowed to hold sway only in Paris.

One of Napoleon's literary precursors was the pseudo-Scottish storm-and-stress poetry of Ossian (as conjured up by Macpherson). And although he came to prefer the novel and history, he never entirely gave up his attachment to verse. It was natural that he should try his hand at the genre. A love poem dating roughly from the same period as the letter to Joseph, dedicated to a diva singing the part of Dido, has been attributed to Napoleon although, as Chateaubriand argues, its form indicates the collaboration of a more accomplished versifier ('*si le fond peut appartenir à l'Empereur, la forme est d'une main plus savante que la sienne*').

Romans, though you boast of an illustrious origin,
Consider how lucky was the birth of your empire!
Dido's considerable charms were powerless
To prevent the hurried departure of her lover.
But if our Dido, the ornament of this city,
Had been queen of Carthage,
Aeneas would have sold his soul for her,
And your beautiful country would still be untamed.

[*Romains, qui vous vantez d'une illustre origine,*
Voyez d'où dépendait votre empire naissant!
Didon n'a pas d'attrait assez puissant
Pour retarder la fuite où son amant s'obstine.
Mais si l'autre Didon, ornament de ces lieux,
Eût été reine de Carthage,
Il eût, pour la servir, abandonné ses dieux,
Et votre beau pays serait encor sauvage.]

Masson casts doubt on the authenticity of this 'madrigal', but
its Virgilian theme of the choice – between love and empire
– becomes the fulcrum of Napoleon's *Dialogue on Love*,
dating from 1791 and his garrison period in Valence. This is a
satire on the destructive effects of love, in which 'Bonaparte'
ridicules 'Des Mazis' (his friend from Ecole Militaire days)
for an infatuation which clouds his commitment to society
and state. Sexuality is linked with depravity, delirium, malady.
But Des Mazis has a good case to argue and often scores off
Bonaparte. His question, 'Are you not made the same as other
men?' [*Eh quoi! n'êtes-vous donc pas composé comme les autres
hommes?*] reflects a genuine (possibly hypogonadic) self-doubt in
Napoleon, coupled to a fear of domination by women, whom he
associates with moisture, stickiness, swampiness: 'love sinks you
in the mire at every step' [[*l'amour*] *vous immétrigue à chaque
pas*]. The dialogue is in one aspect a footnote to the *Discourse
on Happiness*: love is declared to be 'harmful to the happiness of society and individuals'. In opposition to the perils of
feminine viscosity, he sets a yearning for monastic purity and
immortality: 'it would be an act of beneficence by a kindly
divinity to redeem us from love and to deliver the world from
it' [*ce serait un bienfait d'une divinité protectrice que de nous en
défaire et d'en délivrer le monde*].

But Bonaparte changes tack in this dialogue and argues that in fact this salvation has already come to pass in part, as we have passed (reverting to Rousseauisms) from the state of nature to the social contract: 'The cry of nature has been superseded of necessity by the realm of beliefs.' [*Il a donc fallu substituer au cri de notre sentiment, celui des préjugés. Voilà la base de toutes les institutions sociales.*] There is no longer pure desire but only the fantasy of desire. Bewitchment is still an option, but you have to consciously choose to be bewitched. This evolutionary framework is hinted at in *Clisson et Eugénie*, where once you – 'wretched man!' – have left the magic 'circle of nature', 'your soul is prey to illusion, effervescence, and apprehension' and you start playing 'language-games' (*'jeux de mots'*).

This apparent privileging of discourse over intercourse is echoed by Caulaincourt, Napoleon's Russian ambassador, in his *Mémoires*:

> It is a mistake to think that he had many mistresses. He lost his head sometimes, it is true, but it was rarely that he felt any need of love, or indeed any pleasure in it. The Emperor was so eager to recount his amorous successes that one might almost have imagined that he only engaged in them for the sake of talking about them.

Nietzsche said marriage is a long conversation and certainly Napoleon's relationship with Josephine has to be seen as another dialogue on love (although, as before, he virtually had to write both parts himself). On Saint Helena, Napoleon freely admitted that although Marie-Louise was honest and affectionate and capable of producing a son for him, he was always more attached to Josephine, precisely because she was false, because she was always what she was not. And it is this uncertainty (or rather, certainty that she was faithless and unreliable) which is the spring of his correspondence to her, which is among the best known of all Napoleon's texts and the least trustworthy.

In his writing about Italy, Stendhal contended that love set Napoleon apart from the crowd: 'Quite distinct from the majority of conquerors, who were grosser beings [*êtres grossiers*], we see that Napoleon was madly in love during the 1796 campaign.' Stendhal's theory only makes sense if understood as opposing 'love' to 'sex': a mental or metaphysical event rather than a physical one. Napoleon confirms Stendhal's line: 'I never ran after women . . . what would have become of a twenty-five-year-old general if he had been a skirt-chaser?' [*Je n'ai jamais couru après les femmes . . . que serait devenu un général de vingt-cinq ans s'il avait couru après le sexe?*] Napoleon precisely took little or no sexual advantage of his victories – unlike other '*êtres grossiers*' – because of his prior attachment to Josephine. Napoleon uses Josephine as an alibi, to avoid other entanglements. When Germaine de Staël once asked him point blank if it was true that he did not love women, he replied, 'Madame, I love my wife.' He comes up with the idea of love, in other words, in order to avoid sex, or with an idea of infinite passion to avoid mere love: 'My heart never felt anything mediocre . . . it defended itself against love, but you have inspired in it a limitless passion, a drunkenness which is dragging it down.' [*Mon coeur ne sentit jamais rien de médiocre . . . il s'était défendu de l'amour; tu lui as inspiré une passion sans bornes, une ivresse qui le dégrade.*] And since Josephine is typically unavailable he is able to invest all his desire in his letters, where he is bewitched above all by his own language.

Napoleon's probable model, in these letters, is Rousseau's epistolary novel, *La Nouvelle Héloïse* (1761), where linguistic excess depends on being deprived, one way or another, of the 'sexual minimum'. Just as Goethe (rather more concisely) set up Werther/Lotte/Albert as a trap that ends by closing shut, so too Rousseau explores the ramifications of another tragic triangle, Saint-Preux/Julie/Wolmar. Later in life Napoleon would come back to the text (an edition of 1806), editing it as he went, scribbling in cuts, boldly crossing out words, sentences, whole paragraphs, and adding some judicious rewriting in his own style (while one line receives the damning judgement in the margin, *phrase fausse*). On Saint Helena Napoleon told Las Cases that just about every work in the canon, with the possible exception of Montesquieu, stood in need of radical abbreviation (a work to be carried out '*avec goût et discernement*'). Always something of a structuralist and a geometer, he saw the triangle as enough in itself. But at this stage Napoleon is prolific and unabbreviated in his own passionate correspondence.

'I cannot put my pen down' [*Je ne puis laisser la plume*],
he writes in a phrase which could be echoed by any of his
epistolary heroes.

At his height, Napoleon was dashing off several letters a
day, all the way through France and down into Italy back to
Paris, and complaining as usual that Josephine didn't write
to him often enough. And even then, when she did write, he
complained about her style, which was insufficiently lyrical for
his taste: 'When you write to me, there are too few words, and
your style never smacks of profound feeling.' [*Quand tu m'écris,
le peu de mots, le style n'est jamais d'un sentiment profond.*]
To his mind, both quantity and quality are lacking. Thus he
is obliged to dictate what she ought to be writing in her letters
but never does: 'In your letter, my dearest, take care to say
to me that you are convinced that I love you to an extent
beyond imagining.' And again, as usual, even though garlanded
with victories, happiness eludes him: 'Your husband could be
happy,' he writes from Arcola, 'except that he lacks the love
of Josephine.' The whole *raison d'être* of Josephine is to be
unattainable or undependable or, quite simply, elsewhere.

The major drama – the erotic thrill – of Napoleon's letters
resides in absence and the distance separating the lovers (as
it will be, in other circumstances, when he is enjoying his
Polish idyll). Even though he had already left, his privileged
word is 'Adieu!'. 'Every moment takes me further away from
you' [*Chaque instant m'éloigne de toi, adorable amie*] (14 March
1796). 'How much space, how many countries separate us!
How much time before you read these words, feeble tokens
of a tormented soul over which you reign!' [*Que de pays, que
de contrées nous séparent! Que de temps, avant que tu lise
ces caractères, faibles expressions d'une âme émue où tu règne!*]
(23 April).

Josephine is synonymous, in these letters, with the loss of
transparency, the tragic wilderness of beliefs that lies beyond
the circle of nature. Whereas the impersonal empire will be
predicated on perfect knowledge and the transmission of knowledge, the realm of intimacy opens up a huge gulf of ignorance:
'What is the future? What is the past? What are we? What
magic fluid encompasses us and conceals from us the very
things which it is most important to us to know?' [*Qu'est-ce*

que l'avenir? Qu'est-ce que le passé? Qu'est-ce que nous? Quelle fluide magique nous environne et nous cache les choses qu'il nous importe le plus de connaître?] Love is the source of all this foggy fluidity: 'There is a magic fluid between people who love one another.' [*Il est un fluide magique entre les personnes qui s'aiment.*] Thus Napoleon's plea – 'I ask of you . . . only truth, a limitless candour.' [*Je ne te demande ni amour éternel, ni fidélité, mais seulement . . . vérité, franchise sans bornes.*] – is fruitless: truth is not a woman. If knowledge is impossible, then we are at the mercy of deceivers:

> We pass by, we exist, we die in the midst of mysteriousness. Is it surprising that priests, astrologers, and charlatans should have taken advantage of this propensity of ours, this singular circumstance, to take our ideas for a walk and lead them wherever they please?

'Taking ideas for a walk' might sum up the whole of the French Empire.

Napoleon is a lucid dupe of his own fabrications. He is quite self-conscious about the role he has cast himself in, of willing victim to a *femme fatale*. 'But I am inventing trouble for myself. As if there was not enough real trouble already! Do I have to go about making still more!!!' [*Mais je me forge des peines. Il en est tant de réel! Faut-il encore s'en fabriquer!!!*] Josephine remains remorselessly in Paris while Napoleon marches ever further south, beyond the Alps, down towards Rome. Her letters are a string of pretexts: business, illness, pregnancy (non-existent). Most commentators refer to a notional 'turning-point' in Egypt when (Bourrienne dates it as 3 June 1799) on a ride around the Pyramids, an aide (Junot) takes Napoleon on one side and reveals all about Josephine's affairs and Napoleon is furious, then despondent and remarks that 'the veil has been entirely torn away' (this in a letter to Joseph, intercepted by the British). But the less melodramatic truth is that all this is anticipated from the very beginning: 'Farewell, Josephine, to me you are a monster that I cannot explain.' [*Adieu, Joséphine, tu es pour moi un monstre que je ne puis expliquer.*] Napoleon expected and even seemed to relish the prospect of betrayal: 'Go on, mock me, stay in Paris, take lovers, let everybody know, never write, what do I care? I will love you ten times more.' [*Enfin, moque-toi de moi, reste à Paris, aie des amants, que tout le monde le sache, n'écris jamais, eh bien! je t'en aimerai 10 fois davantage.*] He knows, as Clisson knew, that if she is not writing it must be because she is too busy having an affair.

It was inevitable that he should start to quote his own novel: 'fate . . . overwhelms me with glory in order to make me feel my unhappiness with greater bitterness.' [*Je respecte la volonté et la loi immuable du sort. Il m'accable de gloire pour me faire sentir mon malheur avec plus d'amertume.*] Napoleon becomes Clisson even to the point of looking forward to some autoerotic death-scene: 'If glory does not suffice to ensure happiness, at least it will furnish me with the opportunity of death and immortality.' [*Si la gloire ne suffit pas à mon bonheur, elle fournit l'élément de la mort et de l'immortalité.*] In fact, so pervasive, so popular, did this lonely-heart suicidal tendency become that Napoleon actually had to issue orders in 1802 against his men blowing their brains out for love ('To surrender to grief without resisting, to kill oneself to escape it, is to abandon the field of battle before achieving victory'). The empire existed in order, if not to furnish death, much less to ensure happiness, then at least to escape from women, even if Napoleon kept coming back to them – and then running away again. It was a fantasy fortress, a monastic island proof against invasion, a perfect geometry immune to seismic shudders.

> 'Farewell, woman, torment, happiness, hope and soul of my life, that I love, that I fear, who inspires in me tender feelings that call me back to Nature and impetuous impulses as volcanic as thunder.
>
> [*Adieu, femme, tourment, bonheur, espérance et âme de ma vie, que j'aime, que je crains, qui m'inspire des sentiments tendres et qui m'appellent à la Nature, et des mouvements impétueux aussi volcaniques que le tonnerre.*]

The Empire, as the *Dialogue on Love* asserted, was supposed to have the clarity and closure that is absent from the 'empire' (or domination) of women.

I love power (he admitted), but I love it the way an artist would . . . I love it as a musician loves his violin. I love to be able to draw from it sounds, chords, harmony; I love it as an artist.

[*J'aime le pouvoir, moi; mais c'est en artiste que je l'aime . . . je l'aime comme un musicien aime son violon. Je l'aime pour en tirer des sons, des accords, de l'harmonie; je l'aime en artiste.*]

The Empire was part art-form, part male-bonding ritual, in which no one would have to listen to the cry of their own impotence. It is no coincidence that the Code Napoléon should have sought to tie women up in every conceivable legal knot. The Code constituted a kind of revenge on womanhood. Or as Napoleon put it, more lyrically, in a letter to his uncle: 'Women everywhere are royalists. This is not surprising. Liberty is a lovelier woman who eclipses them.'

Just as Rousseau went on a walk with his head in a book, so too Napoleon (beyond the usual conventional compliments) never really took to Nature. It would be truer to say he had an aversion to it. His first military-style campaign was aimed against all the goats on Corsica, which he planned to massacre, thus eliminating the goat problem at a stroke (his uncle held him back from this final solution, accusing him of '*nouvelles idées*'). Perhaps they represented goatishness in general. He was fond of organizing great hunts, in which the corpses of hundreds of assorted quadrupeds would be piled up (he joked to Josephine that every animal in the park was 'prolific' except for her). The idea of nothingness held a permanent appeal for him: 'The rest of the world,' he wrote to Josephine, 'has no more reality for me than if it were completely annihilated.' [*Le reste du monde n'existe pas plus pour moi que s'il était anéanti*]. The 'circle of nature' that he had in mind was an empty circle, a pure lifeless geometry.

But despite all the annihilation, Napoleon could never entirely quell the fear of 'potent men' (especially ones from across the sea), of the third man, even in affairs of state. What Napoleon came to realize, in Erfurt if he did not realize it before, is that empire is also a narrative of failure and betrayal which repeats all the platitudes of marriage. 'I am pleased with [Czar]

Alexander,' he wrote to Josephine in 1808, in the early optimistic stages of the peace conference, 'so must he be with me.
If he was a woman, I believe I would take him for a lover.' [*Je
suis content d'Alexandre; il doit l'être de moi; s'il était femme, je
crois que j'en ferais mon amoureuse.*] But the perfect circle which
he tried to draw around Europe in his 'continental system' was
always liable to be disrupted by a gate-crasher. All Napoleon's
strategies of shutting in and shutting out – the crux of his peace
conferences – are already neatly summarized in his attempts
to control his wife:

> I have just cause to complain of Monsieur T . . . I have sent him
> back home, to Burgundy; I don't want to hear of him again. . . .
> I desire that you should only ever dine with those who dine
> with me . . . do not allow yourself to be surrounded by people
> that I do not know, and who would not come to your house if
> I was there.

The continental blockade saw Britain in the role of scoundrel,
always trying to seduce Napoleon's latest conquest or, as in
the case of Pauline Fourès, frustrating his desires. 'At last,' he
writes hopefully to Josephine post-Austerlitz, 'a condition of
rest has been restored to the Continent; we must hope that
it will be to the world at large: the English would not dare
affront us.' [*Voilà enfin le repos rendu au continent; il faut espérer
qu'il va l'être au monde: les Anglais ne sauraient nous faire front.*]
Which means that they would.

   In *De l'amour*, Stendhal argues that the fear of fiasco is a
constant: 'If a particle of passion enters the heart, then there
also enters the particle of a possible fiasco.' *Fiasco* was his
word for impotence. He offered various practical solutions to
the problem, but the phenomenon of the fiasco pervades his
novels. Even successful coitus is followed by disappointment
and the lover typically slinks away in dismay, perhaps because
(as Camille Paglia put it so scathingly) 'men enter in triumph
but withdraw in decrepitude.' The opening of *La Chartreuse
de Parme* celebrates Napoleon's entry into Italy – billed as
the open sesame to happiness and prosperity – but in the next
chapter Stendhal fast-forwards to Waterloo. If 'the sex act
cruelly mimics history's decline and fall' (Paglia again), it is

also true that Stendhal's fumbling and confusion and collapse on the battlefield is another version of the fiasco. As quartermaster general in Napoleon's army, Stendhal only ever had three meetings with Napoleon himself, in only one of which did they have anything approaching a conversation; yet he has captured something of the Emperor's anxiety in his writing. And not just because Napoleon eventually tired of the performance of craning himself back into position for his next assault on womanhood. In contradistinction to Chateaubriand, who identified with Napoleon's rise, Stendhal stood four-square with the fall: 'I fell with Napoleon in April 1814,' he wrote in his autobiographical *Vie de Henri Brulard*.

Napoleon lived to the full the Stendhalian narrative of fiasco and failure, and he wrote about it before, during and after. His last letter to Josephine, written from Fontainebleau in 1814, prior to exile in Elba (and shortly before her death), explicitly embraces the fiasco:

> I will never repeat to you what I said: then I complained to you of my situation, but today I congratulate myself on it, my head and my mind have been relieved of an enormous weight. My fall is great, but at least it is useful, so they say.

Everything ends in betrayal: 'I have filled to overflowing the cup of thousands of scoundrels! And what have they done for me recently? I'll tell you: they have betrayed me, yes, every last one of them.' [*J'ai comblé de bienfaits des milliers de misérables! Qu'ont-ils fait dernièrement pour moi? Ils m'ont trahi, oui, tous.*] Abdication is an opportunity to concentrate on writing:

> In my retirement I shall substitute the pen for the sword. The history of my reign will be a curious one. I have only been seen in profile, now I will show myself in my entirety.

At last he can drop the mask and reveal himself as the loser, the heroic failure, a man who aimed at happiness and missed, and perhaps express regret – as he put it to Las Cases – that his ambitions 'should not have been accomplished and satisfied'. Thus Napoleon plays a broken lyre – to use Chateaubriand's image – on which he is forced to render notes of joy in a key dedicated to sighs.

This aesthetic consolation, turning life into literature, helps to explain why it was that in Erfurt, Napoleon summoned neither Hegel nor Fourier, but Goethe, author of *The Sorrows of Young Werther* and *Faust* (permeated by Napoleon, according to Nietzsche) and who was then working on his *Theory of Colours*. He seized on a truce to meet at last the writer whose novel had informed his undertaking, the novel he had read so often and flourished in the face of Nelson and in the shadow of the Sphinx.

Milan Kundera has sketched out a reconstruction of this scene in his novel *Immortality* (1991), which reflects most twentieth-century preconceptions. In this version of events, Napoleon is a manic, monstrous megalomaniac intent on exploiting Goethe for propaganda purposes and publicizing a few 'sound bites', while Goethe is a mild-mannered, wise old man, almost Buddhist in his self-effacingness. The contrast between the two could hardly be greater. In fact, Napoleon and Goethe discussed literature, the novel, the theatre, the classics and the moderns, Tacitus and Voltaire, and came back to these subjects in a second meeting. Albert Bielschowsky, more attuned to the secret affinities between the two men, suggests in his *Life of Goethe* that 'Napoleon did not speak [to the poet] as a general and statesman, but as a literary critic, an historian, a philosopher.' To Kundera's mind, the poet would only have been faking any respect towards the tyrant, out of sheer fear and trembling, apprehensive that if he said the wrong thing Weimar would be turned to dust. And yet to Cotta, his publisher, Goethe wrote that 'I will gladly confess that nothing higher and more pleasing could have happened to me in all my life than to have stood before the French Emperor on such a footing.' In 1815, after his second (and final) abdication, Goethe remarked to the collector Boisserée that Napoleon had 'the greatest understanding the world has ever seen'. The writer Christophe Wieland, who was also present at part of their conversations, recalled of the French Emperor that 'I have never seen a calmer, simpler, gentler and less assuming man' and (according to Talleyrand) said to Napoleon at the time that he saw him as a genuine 'man of letters'. None of this sounds remotely like Kundera.

When the conversation came round to *The Sorrows of Young Werther* Napoleon sang its praises, but he had objections: was there not a lack of clarity in the motivation of the suicide? Was it unrequited love or thwarted ambition? (Werther, the rejected lover, also finds himself excluded from polite society.) Was it, in short, sentimental or political? Goethe said afterwards that Napoleon was, in his critique, as penetrating as a skilled tailor who could discern the cunningly concealed seam in an apparently seamless sleeve. No doubt Napoleon recognized in Goethe his own confusion of the sentimental and the political. Having unpicked the novel, Napoleon turned to the theatre and, preferring Corneille, made some acerbic remarks about Shakespeare. He didn't like to see tragedy and comedy mixed ('the genres should remain clearcut and exclusive: any mixing-up of the two easily leads to confusion'). Perhaps this was his greatest fear: not tragedy alone, which he expected and increasingly felt himself to be living out, but rather that comedy might impinge on the heroic qualities of tragedy and turn it all to farce. 'Tragedy,' he said, 'must be the school of kings and peoples: it is the highest point to which a poet can aspire.'

The conversation between Napoleon and Goethe continued at the theatre, where they had been watching a production of Voltaire's *Death of Caesar*. Goethe had translated the same author's *Mahomet*, and Napoleon explained why (with his own experience of Islam) he thought it a bad play. Now, again, Napoleon was in a critical mood. Voltaire had omitted to show that if only Caesar had been given more time he could have brought happiness to mankind. Yet another insufficiently motivated death-scene. Another shot at happiness that goes wide. Surely Goethe could do better? There is more than detached discrimination and seam-spotting here. Napoleon earnestly begged Goethe to rewrite Voltaire. Perhaps he was hoping that Goethe could change the plot. But Goethe made no promises. He could not change history, nor even a word of Voltaire. Napoleon understood that he could not change Goethe and his doomed Werther either. But he could, perhaps, collaborate with him. It was this sense of a common spirit between them that prompted his invitation to Goethe to come to Paris: 'There you will have a broader view of the world. You will then find an over-abundance of material for your poetry.' (It should be added that, according to Talleyrand, Napoleon had already made a similar proposal to Jean de Müller in Berlin the previous year.)

Goethe was, in Napoleon's own phrase, a 'tragic poet'. And it is true that even his *Theory of Colours* describes colours as 'the exploits and sufferings of light'. The exploits and suffering – the 'material' Napoleon had in mind – derived from Napoleon's own utopian plan for producing happiness running up against resistance in the shape of some third man or other. He asked Goethe, 'Are your people happy?', to which Goethe replied: 'They have high hopes.' Napoleon had, to an extreme degree, the sense of the imminence of a revelation that does not in fact occur. This is the aesthetic attitude (as defined by Jorge Luis Borges in 'The Wall and the Books'), which will be echoed by many other writers through the nineteenth century, but by none so concisely as by the poet Mallarmé: 'Everything in the world exists in order to become a book.' Napoleon even thought that his conversation with Goethe should be the subject of another work, perhaps to be written by Goethe himself: 'you should stay here and write your impressions of the great spectacle we have provided for you.' Everything existed in order to become a book. Karl Marx would summon the ghosts of both Hegel and Fourier because he saw that the historical dialectic and the phalanstery were both versions of the perfect circle, the ideal form, that would become communism or, with a twist of Nietzschean *Übermensch*, fascism. Napoleon, in contrast, wanted to see Goethe because he, of all men, had spoken on behalf of the tragic triangle and the third man and the broken dream. When Napoleon exclaimed to Goethe, 'What need have we of fate now? Politics is fate!' it suggests that he has reverted to his sense of an overpowering narrative force at work, a text which he was powerless to rewrite: the fiasco scenario.

Napoleon half-expected the Erfurt conference to fail and it did. He had entertained hopes of marrying Czar Alexander's sister, the Grand Duchess Catherine. But in spite of his court-ing of Alexander, it came as no surprise to him when, a month later, the Czar announced that Catherine would be marrying the Prince of Oldenburg.

Goethe gave serious thought to the proposal to go to Paris, but never went. Nevertheless Napoleon did not forget Goethe. In December of 1812, stripped of his army, on the run from Cossacks, Napoleon passed through northern Germany on his sleigh-ride out of Russia. One night he and Louis de

Caulaincourt put up at a small town, not far from Erfurt. Napoleon asked where they were. 'Weimar, Sire', came the reply. 'Please convey my greetings to Monsieur Goethe', said Napoleon. In the circumstances, Caulaincourt was entitled to see this as a kind of madness. But Napoleon must have felt that Goethe would appreciate his current over-abundance of material, which he summarized for Caulaincourt like this:

> This universal empire is a dream, and I have wakened from it. If, once upon a time, I might have been carried away by this warlike passion, it would, like all passions, have misled me but for a moment.

But even in the midst of the mad dash back to Paris, the dream of happiness had not faded, if it had not been fulfilled either:

> I am touched by the woes of peoples. I want to see them happy, and the French shall be so. If I live another ten years, there will be contentment everywhere.

With the image of the third man at the back of his mind, it must have been with a certain sense of inevitability, at Waterloo, while Napoleon was on the brink of toppling Wellington from his hill-top, that he saw Blücher and the Prussian army driving a wedge through the French ranks and calling time on the dream.

6
The Death of the Author

Napoléon à Ste-Hélène.

Napoleon did not die on Saint Helena in 1821. Despite the heavy security he managed to effect a daring escape thanks to a double (an old friend from Brienne days) taking his place. By a circuitous route, intended to throw off any pursuers, he sailed back to Europe to take up the mantle of Emperor once more and rectify the humiliation of Waterloo. Saint Helena, like Elba, was not destined to be an end but only a new beginning, a springboard to fresh adventures. Napoleon landed safely in France and returned to Paris. Unfortunately, before he could declare himself openly, his surrogate, still marooned on the island, died (perhaps of natural causes, but conceivably the victim of an assassination plot). Thus, when Napoleon finally announced to his subjects that the Emperor had returned once more to lead them to further inevitable triumphs, he was carried off and locked up in a lunatic asylum, along with the hundreds of other madmen also claiming to be Napoleon.

Although strictly unfalsifiable, this legend (preserved and nuanced in *La Mort de Napoléon*, a 1986 novel by Simon Leys) does not seem any more probable than any of the other myriad myths and fictions that have been spun brightly around Napoleon's gloomy fate. Frustratingly for the imaginative novelist, when all the smoke has cleared, it appears certain that Napoleon did indeed die on Saint Helena at the age of 51.

Nevertheless, his close imprisonment did not prevent many people, including members of his own family, from supposing that he had in reality hoodwinked his cruel British gaolers and slipped away under cover of darkness and was temporarily in hiding elsewhere. It was a reasonable assumption. After all, he was on Elba for less than a year. Admittedly Saint Helena, in the South Atlantic, one of the most far-flung islands in all the world, was rather further away: 5,000 miles from France and some 1,400 from the nearest coastline. But that mere geographical inconvenience should not have proved too much of an obstacle for the great escapologist, the Houdini of his day. Had Napoleon not, after all, considered capturing the island? 'The English are in no wise expecting this expedition and it will be a simple matter to surprise them', he had written a decade earlier. With his knowledge of the terrain and his superior generalship, it would surely have been an even simpler matter to surprise them by making good his escape.

The irony of this optimistic prophecy is that, far from being self-fulfilling, it had the effect of reinforcing his captivity. The British had this scenario in mind as much as the French. So convinced were they that Napoleon would attempt to get away that they stationed upwards of 2,000 troops on the island (and two brigs on patrol around it) to keep him under constant surveillance. And, equally, on the other hand, so certain were his relatives and supporters that he must have already eluded his dull-witted captors that they involuntarily left him to rot. It was in part because everyone believed that he was already at liberty and on his way back to France that it became impossible for him to escape.

All communications from Saint Helena had to be examined with due scepticism: the English – famed as interceptors – could be faking those letters. Certainly when Napoleon wrote to his brother-in-law, Cardinal Fesch, pleading for a decent doctor (to treat his worsening illness) and a priest (for the purpose of theological discussion) to be sent, Fesch responded – a year or so later – by despatching one gibbering idiot who had already suffered a major stroke (Buonavita), a semi-illiterate peasant (Vitali) and a pathologist (Antommarchi). It was a

neat joke. Not one that Napoleon, still cooped up on Saint
Helena, was in a position to appreciate. But it would be a shrewd
trick to play on the British authorities, who blatantly were
sending out letters, in Napoleon's name, intended to persuade
the world he was still manacled to his rock when the truth was
that he was long gone. Fesch was too cunning to fall for that
transparent ploy. He had it from reliable sources (a medium)
that Napoleon was free and biding his time waiting for the
best moment to reappear in Paris. Most subsequent readers of
the Saint Helena samizdats are, like Fesch, ironic and sophisticated and over-anxious to find ploys and strategies.

In fact, contrary to all expectation, Napoleon was not especially eager to engineer his escape. Like many another artist,
Napoleon had begun to understand, long before his end, that
he would be better appreciated posthumously. Death was to
be his great escape from obscurity. He did not die of stomach
cancer (like his father before him), nor was he poisoned by
the English or the French, nor, finally, did the wallpaper, oozing
lead in the damp climate, do him down. He chose his fate
and the whole period of his exile on Saint Helena was what
Heidegger would call a 'living-towards-death'. Saint Helena
was not the grim tragedy it is usually made out to be but the
natural fulfilment of Napoleon's 'small ambition of becoming
an author'. He was too busy writing to escape.

After abdication, Napoleon was less anxious about his usual
enemy than what the French (notably the returning Bourbons)
might do to him. He rejected Marie Walewska's offer to follow
him into exile and rode west out of Paris to the coast. He
dismissed all ingenious escape plans, involving decoy ships and
the like, out of hand. Captain Maitland of the *Bellerophon* –
the British navy vessel that he boarded at Rochefort and which
carried him to England – was astonished that Napoleon seemed
to take no evasive manoeuvres whatsoever. Maitland only had to
welcome his illustrious guest on board with elaborate courtesy.
Napoleon appeared relaxed, unhurried, impassive, indifferent.
It was almost too easy. Was it (the temptation to irony again)
all part of some devious strategy? But no, the letter Napoleon
wrote to the Prince Regent, seemed genuine enough: 'I come,
like Themistocles, to throw myself on the hospitality of the
British people. I place myself under the protection of their

laws.' [*Je viens, comme Thémistocle, m'asseoir sur le foyer du peuple britannique; je me mets sous la protection de ses lois.*] There had been some talk of America, but Napoleon rather looked forward to taking up residence in England, perhaps in some comfortable country house, away from the capital, where he could devote himself to contemplation and live the life of a simple squire, with regular hunting expeditions. He saw England not so much as a place of exile, more as a refuge from the clamour of the world. Were the English not another island race, on the same wavelength as a Corsican? 'America,' he wrote, speaking of himself with detachment in the third person, 'had been his place of choice; but, on reflection, England, with its unequivocal laws, could well suit him better' [*l'Amérique était le lieu le plus convenable, le lieu de son choix; mais enfin l'Angleterre même, avec ses lois positives, pouvait lui convenir encore*]. One theory holds that he had an idea of becoming Emperor of England and launching a war against France.

The English, however, unequivocally shoved this unwanted asylum-seeker on board the *Northumberland*, sailing south, almost as far south as it was possible to sail. Even though deposited at the opposite end of the world, Napoleon still took up learning English with a view to becoming a country gentleman. By March 1816 he could report in a letter to Las Cases, written in English, that 'Since sixt wek, y learn the english and y do not any progress. Sixt week do fourty and two day. If might have learn fivty word, for day, I could know it two thousands and two hundred . . .' In English, even his mathematics, usually so reliable, is off (at 50 words a day he could have learned 2,100 in 6 weeks). He concludes – demonstrating his point – that 'you shall agree that to study a tongue is a great labour who it must do with the young aged.' Perhaps he even had some idea of passing himself off as a local on the island and fading away amongst the population, but if so he was forced to give it up. In October 1816 he conceded defeat at the hands of the English language and therefore kept his tally of languages over which he had perfect command at zero.

Perhaps it came as no surprise to Napoleon to be betrayed by the British once again and whisked away from England, just as it began to seem that his vision might be realized. It was predictable. When Barry O'Meara, the ship's doctor attached to the *Northumberland*, first caught sight of Saint Helena he thought that 'nothing can be more desolate or repulsive than the appearance of the exterior of the island.' Napoleon was more philosophical and resigned, with a dash of bitter humour. 'It is not an attractive place to live in. I should have done better to have stayed in Egypt.'

He was moved to wonder what on earth he was going to do on this barren rock. He had to be reminded of his plans, to write up the epic story of his life, by the Count of Las Cases, who would be his closest companion for the next eighteen months. Las Cases was already secretly mapping out his bestseller, *Le Mémorial de Sainte-Hélène*, even before they landed. Frédéric Masson wrote that the motives that led this career diplomat to accompany Napoleon into exile 'remain obscure'. But Las Cases was actually quite up-front about his motives. He had already enjoyed one cross-Channel success with his *Atlas historique et géographique*, written while he was in exile in London (Napoleon was, according to Las Cases, 'enchanté' when he read it, and reckoned he would have made it compulsory reading in all schools). Now, after his tenure as 'Chamberlain and Master of Requests at the Council of State' under the Empire, as a further period of enforced exile beckoned, it was high time for another. And Napoleon was an infallible subject. The disadvantage, for the writer, of Napoleon's style of existence, was its speed and 'over-abundance of material'. While his would-be biographer was writing about one battle, he was already on to fighting the next. Defeat and imprisonment had this inestimable advantage, that Napoleon would be required to slow down and reminisce and stop producing so much new data. In fact, he regarded his dialogues with the ex-Emperor as quasi-posthumous, 'conversations of definitive revelation, which seemed to belong already to the next world' [*ces conversations du dernier abandon, et qui se passaient comme étant déjà de l'autre monde*].

Las Cases was not a strong proponent of escape either: he didn't want his subject to slide away from him. He naturally favoured the contemplative life. 'We will live off the past', Las Cases assured him as they sailed for Saint Helena in the summer of 1815. 'It has enough to satisfy us. Do we not enjoy the life of Caesar and that of Alexander? We shall possess still more:

you will reread yourself, sire!' [*Nous posséderons mieux, vous vous relirez, sire!*]

Napoleon was quick to embrace this vision. 'So be it!' he replied. 'We will write our *Mémoires*. Yes, we must work, for work is the scythe of time. After all a man ought to fulfil his destinies (Napoleon insisted on the plural); this is my grand doctrine. Let mine also be accomplished.' [*On doit remplir ses destinées; c'est aussi ma grande doctrine.*] He had done enough fieldwork: here was an opportunity to present the fruit of his research. The book would virtually write itself. 'What a novel my life is!' [*Quel roman pourtant que ma vie!!!*] he remarked later to Las Cases: a classic narrative, a meteoric rise, a catastrophic fall. How could it miss? It was all already in his head (as Balzac would say), it was just a question of getting it down on the page. Napoleon embarked on the autobiography while still at sea. Immediately he was inspired, in full verbal flow (Las Cases struggled to keep up with him). His ideas were developed enough by the time the *Northumberland* paused at Madeira on the long haul south for him to dash off a list of required reading (notably the *Moniteur* from 1793 to 1807, for the purpose of verifying dates) to be delivered – at his own expense – to his final destination. (This would be in addition to the 400 or so volumes, chiefly tragedies and novels, the abdicating Emperor had been authorized by the provisional government to select from the Rambouillet library on his journey into exile.) Books were a kind of escape.

During the first phase on Saint Helena, Napoleon became once again the great dictator. 'I cannot write well because I am torn between two currents: one, the flow of ideas, the other, ink. And since my thoughts move faster than my hand, my writing becomes incomprehensible. Therefore I can only dictate, and this is convenient, it is as if one were having a conversation.' So he came to rely on a squad of secretaries and ghostwriters to take down his thoughts as he strode about discoursing. Here is the scene sketched out by Montholon:

> While the Emperor was dictating, he paced up and down, with his head bent and his hands behind his back. His brow was creased in concentration, the mouth slightly contracted. The speed at which he walked and dictated was determined by the

thoughts that occupied his mind. He never waited until what he had already dictated was taken down; he seemed not to notice that anyone was writing, and when he paused, it was only to ask us to read out what we had written. If, unfortunately, one did not read fluently, he manifested his impatience; it was the same when the text of the dictation did not satisfy him: he would then claim that we had distorted his thought and that we did not know how to write. He would not sit down until he was exhausted.

He was ruthless, obsessive, happy to follow a single train of thought for up to ten or twelve hours at a stretch (according to Bertrand). Even towards the end, less than a month before his death, he was still at it, night after night. An insomniac, he marshalled his memories from midnight till four, then dictated from four till seven. 'At my best,' he recalled, speaking to one of his last doctors, Arnott, 'I could dictate to four secretaries and keep them all busy. I am a real workhorse.' [*Dans mon beau temps, je pouvais dicter à quatre secrétaires et leur donner beaucoup de travail. Je suis un cheval pour le travail.*]

Saint Helena was half court-in-exile (with all the scheming and conflict that entailed), half writers' colony (no less fraught and conflictual). Napoleon had a plan, to start with, that would keep his troops in line. He assigned a different period, a time and a place, to each of Las Cases, Gourgaud, Bertrand and Montholon, from Italy and Egypt, through the glimpse of total European domination that was Austerlitz and the conversation with Goethe, through to the cataclysm of Russia and beyond. It was motion – rather than emotion – recollected in tranquillity. Another literary empire took shape at Napoleon's hands, as he strove relentlessly towards a mighty synthesis which would cover everything, encyclopedically, irrefutably, magisterially. A proto-structuralist systematizer, Napoleon dreamed of pulling together into one consecutive narrative all the campaigns of Alexander, Hannibal, Caesar, Gustavus Adolphus, Turenne, Prince Eugene, Frederick the Great – and, of course, Napoleon himself. He had invented nothing, all his battles were simply permutations on a few simple principles. He had learned nothing, he argued, that he didn't already know at the beginning.

But his new system, like the old one, even as it expanded, so it progressively fell apart and fragmented. Napoleon found it hard to switch at will from one period and place to another, and all the neat chapter headings and labour demarcations dissolved into chaos. Disputes soon broke out among the various members of the team. Gourgaud drew the short straw in the shape of Waterloo and Russia and developed an enmity towards Las Cases, who seemed to be getting all the lollipops, such as Corsica and Italy. Still, there was a period – or it would be truer to say there were periods – when something like a small literary utopia was achieved. Napoleon said that, if he could live his life over again, he would be happy to live in the Latin quarter, like a permanent student, going to the theatre, attending salons and exchanging bons mots about the latest books with other literati. And, just as the Institut d'Egypte had been an extension of the Institut back in Paris, so he strove to make Saint Helena a remote outpost of the Left Bank. As Hudson Lowe, the governor, acutely remarked to Bertrand: 'He creates an imaginary Spain, an imaginary Poland. Now he wants to make an imaginary Saint Helena.'

Sainte-Beuve called Napoleon 'a great critic in his spare time' – and he had an awful lot of spare time on Saint Helena. Napoleon staged readings of Corneille and Voltaire (Mme de Montholon and General Gourgaud plotted to get rid of his copy of *Zaïre*, so often was it repeated), and pronounced judgement on works from the Bible (beautiful parables, not enough facts) to Bernardin de Saint-Pierre's *Paul et Virginie* (great novel, author a scoundrel). While praising Homer's exactitude in martial matters, he dismissed any serious claim Virgil might have had to sing of arms and the man. It seemed to be the collapse of Troy he most strongly objected to, as if he were trying to rewrite the ending (or in the case of the *Aeneid*, the beginning): the Trojan horse story was implausible and, even in the event of a surprise attack, 'the Palace of Priam alone should have been able to soak up a siege of several days . . . It would have taken a good fortnight to burn down a city like Troy.' [*Le palais seul de Priam aurait dû soutenir un siège de plusieurs jours. . . . Il fallait quinze jours pour brûler une ville comme Troie.*] Likewise, he too expected to hold out for a good deal longer. And he admired, with a degree of critical detachment, elements of his own *oeuvre*:

He read his Egyptian correspondence, the third volume. There are certain letters to Dugua, for example, in which he adds considerably to our enlightenment. 'Moreover,' he said, 'this is beautiful writing, and posterity will be able to reread this correspondence and cite from it whole pages of history.'

On another occasion he shut the lid on a box-load of the *Moniteur* (carrying many of his own articles) with the comment: 'And they dared to say that I couldn't write!' There are moments, at least, on Saint Helena where Napoleon felt well content with his situation and at peace with the world: 'after all, considering the alternatives, Saint Helena was perhaps still the best place' [*après tout, exil pour exil, Sainte-Hélène était peut-être encore la meilleure place*].

Las Cases, more in tune with this writerly ethos than any of his fellow exiles, other than Napoleon himself, recalls this idyllic, contemplative side of life in Saint Helena, tinged as always with majestic melancholy. Here is part of his entry for Tuesday 14 November 1815:

> In the evening, in his chamber, after our post-prandial stroll, the Emperor read to me the chapter on 'Provisional Consuls', which he had dictated to M. de Montholon. Having finished reading, the Emperor took a ribbon and started to bundle together the loose sheets of paper. It was late: the silence of night reigned around us; I gazed at the Emperor as he continued with his work. My thoughts, on that day, were predisposed towards melancholia. I looked upon the hands that had wielded so many sceptres and which were now tranquilly, and not perhaps without a degree of pleasure, occupied in the humble task of tying together some sheets of paper. He had stamped those pages, it is true, with certain events that will never be forgotten.

Attacks of depression and Gourgaud's temper notwithstanding, Las Cases was tempted to see his own Saint Helena experience as the culmination of his life and art: 'And the Emperor reads to me all he has written, he speaks to me on intimate terms, he sometimes asks me what I think, and I dare to offer my opinion! Ah! Am I not rather to be envied than pitied in my exile on Saint Helena?' [*Ah! je ne suis point à plaindre d'être venu à Sainte-Hélène*.] In any case, the worse things get the better, in the terms of a classic aesthetic (and stoic) consolation. Las Cases had seen this from the beginning (of the end): without Saint Helena, Napoleon was merely a warrior; it needed Saint Helena to transform him into a tragic hero, a Romantic figurehead. The rise cried out for a symmetrical fall: 'the political fall of Napoleon has immensely increased his moral stature' [*la chute politique de Napoléon a accru de beaucoup sa domination morale*]. Aesthetically speaking, Napoleon had to become a loser. So Waterloo becomes already in Las Cases, as it would be in Victor Hugo, a kind of moral (and artistic) victory. 'No one, today, can be in any doubt that his glory, the renown of his character, have gained infinitely from his misfortunes!!!' [*Qui doute aujourd'hui que sa gloire, l'illustration de son caractère, ne gagnent infiniment par ses malheurs!!!*] This is one of those rare occasions on which the normally placid Las Cases resorts to a trio of exclamation marks. The idea of a contrast between past splendour and present squalor – thus looking forward to a future regeneration – was, after all, a recurrent Napoleonic theme that went back to Egypt and beyond. It would have been a dereliction of duty to pass it up this time around.

Their first topic of conversation, while still *en route* to Saint Helena, was the Corsican childhood. Rather as if his life was flashing before his eyes, Napoleon rewound to the point of birth, where – according to this highly mythologized version – his mother delivered him on a rug illustrated with some heroic scene from the *Iliad* (had it been the *Aeneid*, he implies, the course of history could have been changed). There was a chronological logic at work. But – and this he remarked on – there was also a strong sense of continuum between his beginnings on Corsica and his ending on Saint Helena. Having acquired and squandered an empire, he had changed little from the young would-be writer intent on shaking, if not shaping, the world with his words. Still he pondered the inevitably unfinished *Discourse on Happiness*, even if he allowed himself to entertain the notion that it had carried off the gold medal after all – or that, if not, his whole life had been spent in trying to capture first prize for putting that theory into practice and going about the world inculcating the ideas and feelings that would produce happiness. Still he thought of completing the biography of Paoli and the history of Corsica. Still he was writing off to people far away to send him books. His greatest excitement was when another crateload arrived: Napoleon would spend the night cracking it open with a hammer and chisel and devouring the contents (his island library swelled to around 1,500 volumes, but in the circumstances, he said, could have done with 60,000). Still he quarrelled with Desgenettes (from afar, in the margins of recent publications) over the course of events in Egypt. One of his later conversations with Las Cases returned precisely to his point of departure: 'The emperor . . . entered into a long and most interesting review of Rousseau, of his talents, his influence, his eccentricities, his immoralities.' Napoleon's final words to Las Cases were: 'Be happy!'

And still he pondered the transgressive seduction of suicide. 'What is it after all? Only a desire to return to Him a little faster.' [*Qu'est-ce après tout? Vouloir lui revenir (à Dieu) un peu plus vite.*] Sometimes it seemed as if his whole life had been one prolonged suicide attempt, in the manner of his hero Clisson. He recalled how he was on the brink of ending it all post-Toulon and only a chance encounter with his old school friend Des Mazis pulled him back. He revealed that ever since the retreat from Russia, after being pursued by bloodthirsty Cossacks, he had carried a lethal concoction in a flask around his neck. Moreover, he once actually drank it, in a fit of black depression. 'I drank it with a sort of happiness.' Still, it appears, the only happiness lay in going down to the grave in peace. But the potency of the potion had by that stage faded and he survived. In Fontainebleau, in 1815, his thoughts turned to suicide again, along with some idea of sparing France civil war. But 'Saint Helena was in my destiny': Saint Helena came to seem a suitable substitute for the suicide that he had long been tempted by but had failed to commit.

Perhaps this explains why, in part, Napoleon ultimately shied away from outings and freedom of movement. Saint Helena offered a finite space to move about in, and there were restrictions imposed by the British, but it was as if there could never be enough constraints for Napoleon: he had to pile on still more. Faced with enclosure on an island, he retaliated by immuring himself within Longwood, rarely venturing out. 'Every day he shrinks the circle – already so narrow – of his movement and his activities', Las Cases recorded in 1816. So unusual did it become for him to take exercise that it is possible to provide a rapid résumé of the highlights:

1819   He takes up gardening for a spell, and gets everyone up at the crack of dawn to build fountains; but he soon gives up again.

1820   He goes to a party.

1821   In a last desperate throw, he designs, builds and installs a see-saw in the salon of Longwood, and bounces up and down on it with Bertrand and Montholon. It lasts only a few days before the salon is restored to its state of funereal calm.

And that is it. Almost. Some writers have liked to fantasize about Saint Helena as a seraglio, with the Emperor being serviced by every other woman, be she wife or slave. But Napoleon's monastic mood is airily detached: 'I never was one for chasing after women', he recalled, and now even less so. 'The machine', he said, 'is breaking down.' But it would be truer to say that he broke it down, by self-imposed paralysis.

Vincent Cronin has called the Saint Helena period 'the creative years'. And this judgement is surely justified by the prolific output of the Saint Helenians. It would not be an exaggeration to speak of a Saint Helena 'industry', with a certain quality of mass production. But from the beginning there were signs of dissatisfaction with the almost obsessive regime, driven by an obscure sense of imminent deadlines ('he was desperate to finish the 1800 volume in 20 days'). Gourgaud, always ultra-touchy, seems to have had genuine cause for complaint. He could never get it right. 'I am scolded and sent away to collect the fragments of my work.' 'I read my chapter on Waterloo. Napoleon reacted moodily.' [*Je lis mon chapitre sur Waterloo. Maussaderies.*] There appears to have been some dispute over matters of style, but in truth Waterloo was always going to be a difficult not to say impossible chapter to write. 'The 18 June [1820] brought him back to the memory of Waterloo. He chose to revise what he had dictated to General Gourgaud, and spent eight days reworking the narrative of this short but decisive campaign.'

Napoleon kept going over it again and again, as if it might be possible to get it to end differently. But Gourgaud went back to the drawing board in vain, it would always come out the same: the scent of victory over Wellington, the surprise (or was it?) arrival of Blücher instead of Grouchy ('Blücher! Blücher!'), the frantic retreat that turned into a rout, the return to Paris, abdication, Saint Helena, memories, Waterloo: endless, circular, as tautological as a mathematical equation. Russia, similarly, was a problem. Despite encouragement from Bertrand, Napoleon remained reluctant: 'I could only write a few comments on this fatal campaign.' [*Je ne pourrais écrire que quelques remarques sur cette fatale campagne.*]

Other sections took shape – Italy, the Egyptian campaign– but Napoleon recognized, as he read them out, despite all the polite approbation of his audience, that something was missing. As early as June 1816, 'His dictations . . . seem to have lost their charms for him' [*il abandonne même son travail régulier; ses dictées, auxquelles jusque-là il avait semble trouver quelques charmes, ne vont plus*]. They had gravitas, they had grandeur, but these third-person military memoirs were too impersonal and remote, they were anything but confessions. (Las Cases made a virtue of this detachment: 'He speaks of his personal history as if it was three hundred years old . . . He often speaks about himself as of a third person.' [*Il parle de son histoire passée comme si elle avait trois cents ans de date . . . Il s'exprime souvent sur lui-même comme sur une tierce personne.*]) Politically, they were sound, but aesthetically, they suffered from a certain hollowness. A glance at volumes twenty-nine and thirty of Napoleon's collected correspondence suffices to demonstrate that his campaign memoirs are impoverished by the absence – to use the terms of the Lyon examiners – not of truths but of feelings. Contrary to the familiar critique – that everything Napoleon wrote smacks of propaganda – there is an excess here of objectivity, there is too much of reportage, dating and quantifying, and over-reliance on the premise of the omniscient author. What is omitted – oddly for a man who devoted himself so explicitly to its pursuit and propagation – is any mention of happiness or, for that matter, unhappiness. Whereas this is the chief preoccupation of the Saint Helenians. No wonder then that Napoleon had drastic measures in mind: 'He hadn't yet made up his mind about his manuscripts: if he was in danger, he would probably incinerate all his papers.' Or, as a last resort, bring in a ghost-writer: 'Arnault would have to be given the job of reviewing all the flaws of his Memoirs.' Decidedly, he was not happy with the first drafts – the 'rushes' – of his South Atlantic period. Something was missing, a vital spark.

Napoleon's original Saint Helena plan was military in conception, it was strategic, predicated on total control and maximum information. Nothing was to be left to chance, everything was mapped out and smoothly manoeuvred into position, men and machinery and mathematics. Napoleon saw himself as the maestro, orchestrating, commanding, scripting entrances and exits and feeding lines to his players. They were not supposed to improvise and invent. There was a certain monastic simplicity to this streamlined scheme of things, almost Trappist (with the clear exception of one man) in its rigour. In his dark tower, far from everywhere, Napoleon would carry on his lifelong project of inculcating thoughts and feelings.

But the 'almost conversation' of dictating yielded ground progressively, but from the very beginning, to full-on conversation. Monologic was displaced (as Bakhtin, the Russian formalist, would say) by a dialogic. The author was dying by degrees, not so much by a thousand cuts as by a thousand interpolations, qualifications and refutations. Far from following his orders, and confining themselves to taking down his memories, Napoleon's 'secretaries' had ideas and impressions of their own, which they insisted on interjecting. It was as if his whole life was being replayed in front of his eyes, as secret rebellions, open insurrections and the mere plurality of voices wreaked havoc on his grand monolithic designs. Napoleon had difficulty coming to terms with the failure of his exercise in total authorship. The tragedy built into a comparison of the past with the present and the sense of an inevitable decline is re-enacted on Saint Helena, so that it is sometimes hard to tell if Napoleon is speaking of the loss of an empire or, more recently, his diminution of control over his immediate circumstances: 'Do you think, if I wake in the night, that I don't have some bad moments, when I think back on what I was and consider what I am at present?' [*Croyez-vous lorsque je m'éveille la nuit, je n'aie pas de mauvais moments, quand je me rappelle ce que j'étais et où je suis à présent?*].

Escape became just another of the recurrent topics of conversation, another of the narratives on offer, a way of passing the time. When the question arose, Napoleon would often amiably play along with the game and fantasize about alternative scenarios. He envisaged himself in the United States, or forging a new empire in South America, or holding back the tide of Cossacks overrunning Europe, even masquerading as a simple citizen back in France. Perhaps he could be king of Corsica? But these hypothetical narratives were on a par with his frequent 'if only' excursions (if only Acre had fallen, for example, he would have been Emperor of the Orient). Any serious offers and suggestions, any practical plans, were instantly dismissed. Disappointed sea-captains sailed away without an escaped convict – *the* prisoner – secreted on board. The alternative submarine scheme, similarly, sank without trace. 'All I can see in America is assassination or oblivion. I prefer Saint Helena.' [*Je ne vois en Amérique qu'assassinat ou oubli. J'aime mieux Sainte-Hélène.*]

Escape, if anything, was more of a problem for Napoleon than a solution. It was his fellow exiles, his regiment of writers, who were escaping, either fleeing the island forever or evading Napoleon's command. 'Here we are on a battlefield,' he told Gourgaud, 'and anyone who deserted, in the midst of combat . . . would be a coward.' Napoleon was conscious that his battles had to be fought out without access to artillery. 'Once everyone was afraid of rape, slaughter, pillage. That is war. Whereas, now, in the modern campaigns, there is a distinct whiff of rosewater.' [*C'est qu'alors tout le monde avait peur pour soi d'être violé, égorgé, pillé. C'est faire la guerre, tandis que, dans les campagnes modernes, tout se passe à l'eau de rose.*] He was capable of putting this case more enthusiastically, however: one day, he said, 'victories will be won without cannon.' The Saint Helena conflict was largely verbal in character, but none the less ruthless for all that, and ultimately deadly.

The youthful, hot-headed, irascible, paranoid Gaspard Gourgaud, who owned to slaking his sexual desire among the whores of Jamestown, was the first to object to the rosewater craze for literature, which he saw embodied in the person of Las Cases. He, Gourgaud, a graduate of the Polytechnique, was a soldier not a writer: had he not served the Emperor bravely, swum the Beresina, been injured three times and shot dead a marauding Cossack who was bearing down on Napoleon, thus saving his life? (Napoleon claimed, to Gourgaud's fury, not to recall the incident.) Las Cases, on the other hand, the 'little Jesuit', was never anything but a mere scribe. Gourgaud was the first to spot Las Cases's ulterior motive: 'He was nothing but a writer whose plan was to collect anecdotes in order to put them into a book and gain himself a reputation.' But he was honest enough to concede that Napoleon, on the other hand, found nothing shameful in this writerly motivation and saw a straight parallel with his most devoted soldiers: 'Hah! Do you think Drouot, who was always pushing his way up to the most forward cannon, was doing it out of affection for me? He too wanted his name on everyone's lips.'

Gourgaud found Napoleon's fondness (preference, in his eyes) for Las Cases incomprehensible. Perhaps he thought Las Cases should be writing up his, Gourgaud's, story: 'Bertrand assures me that the Emperor is the most tragic of us all. Personally, I believe that I am even more so. I would gladly exchange my fate for his.' [*Bertrand . . . m'assure que l'Empereur est le plus malheureux de nous tous. Je trouve moi, que je le suis encore plus: je changerais bien mon sort contre le sien.*] Gourgaud, more than anyone else, incited Las Cases to – in all probability – engineer a melodrama (smuggling out secret letters through his servant) which ended in his enforced departure in December 1816. But it appears there was a rapprochement between Gourgaud and Las Cases towards the end. 'Even though his enemy,' Gourgaud wrote, 'I was deeply affected by the misfortune he had suffered.' [*Quoique son ennemi, j'étais bien affecté du malheur qu'il éprouvait.*] And, as Las Cases was finally evicted, at the end of December 1816: 'All in all, he and his son behave very well towards me. I forgot all my hatred and I see them depart with regret.' [*Enfin, lui et son fils se conduisent fort bien envers moi. J'oublie toute ma haine et les vois partir avec peine.*] It seems likely that their reconciliation was due to a growing sense, on Gourgaud's part, that he too had potential as a writer. 'I work all morning . . . We must complete this narrative of Waterloo. The Emperor has found a way of sending it to England. It will be published in French and English, and will surely bring me fame and fortune.'

Gourgaud became increasingly jealous of access to Napoleon. He automatically resented anyone else playing chess with him or having a seat at the table closer to him. One theory (resting largely on Gourgaud's use of 'Elle' for Napoleon, the feminine pronoun taking the place of 'Sa Majesté') maintains that Gourgaud was a homosexual suffering from frustrated desire for Napoleon. Napoleon himself remarked that Gourgaud 'was in love with me' and they had passionate quarrels:

> Napoleon: 'I prefer Montholon to you!'
> Gourgaud: 'All I ask is not to be humiliated!'

Although tough enough to have a tooth removed by O'Meara without anaesthetic and without uttering a cry, Gourgaud was often to be found sobbing into the pages of his journal over some imagined slight. Bereft of Napoleon's company, he makes journal entries reminiscent of Baudelaire or perhaps of Sartre's *Nausea*: 'Ennui' is probably his favourite word. On Wednesday, 9 July 1816, he writes: 'Ennui'. The following day consists of 'Grand ennui'. The 11th, in contrast, is 'Ennui, mélancolie'. Elsewhere it is 'rain and ennui', 'sadness and ennui', and 'beaucoup d'ennui'. All in all, Gourgaud is probably the most self-revealing, and certainly the most depressive, of all the memorialists. But, like Las Cases, he found consolation for his strife in the form of the best-seller-to-come.

With Las Cases gone, Gourgaud turned his capacity for wrath and resentment on Montholon. Montholon became – in Gourgaud's now explicitly literary metaphors – 'the author of all my misfortunes'. He challenged him to a duel, but Montholon managed to back away from it, and this time it was Gourgaud who took his leave and found himself excluded from Napoleon's will. There is a view (held by the sympathetic editor of his journal) that Gourgaud was secretly engaged on a mission, conferred upon him by the Emperor, to make his case in Europe. But to win over new believers he had to appear to be a sceptic. To defend Napoleon, he had to attack him. But if so, Gourgaud was too successful, materially worsening the conditions of Napoleon's captivity as he went about asserting to anyone who would listen that – contrary to the plaintive case Las Cases was making in correspondence and petitions – Napoleon was only faking his illness and, moreover, could escape at any time he chose. Masson condemns all this as 'temporary delirious ravings'. But Gourgaud himself had explicitly signed up to the view that it was war between them, or rather 'war between our pamphlets – and Napoleon has a great talent in this genre' [*je serais alors en guerre de pamphlets avec Elle et Elle a un grand talent en ce genre*].

Again, as at Waterloo, Napoleon was outnumbered: there was always a Blücher sneaking up behind. He undoubtedly fantasized about the lot of them dropping dead and leaving him in sole possession of the terrain: 'In the army I frequently saw the people I was talking with drop dead on the spot.' And he harked back repeatedly to the total author model: 'all these works, all these prodigies, were authored by one man.' Hence his astronomical metaphor of the sun versus the planets: 'No one can have dominion over me,' he growled at Gourgaud. 'You want to be the centre of everything here, like the sun with the planets revolving around it. But that is my position: I must be the centre.' [*Personne ne peut prendre d'empire sur moi. Vous voudriez être le centre de tout ici, comme le soleil au milieu des planètes. C'est moi qui dois être le centre.*]

But the death of the author was not quite so cataclysmic as this image suggests. Saint Helena was Napoleon's second Waterloo. But in defeat, as Las Cases would say, lay a kind of victory. Napoleon was resigned to giving up the model of total authorship he had found in Rousseau, Chateaubriand, Staël, and being a non-authorial type of author. In this frame of mind, he came round to seeing his *oeuvre* as collaborative: intertextual and collective rather than ruthlessly singular and dominant. He was content to delegate and facilitate and disseminate, in short to generate a multiplicity of texts, united by a common topos and rhetoric, even if not uniformly sympathetic. He knew that the 'Memoirs' were doomed to be eclipsed by 'Memorials', all those texts that reproduce Napoleon under another name. He knew, for example, that Las Cases was keeping a journal. 'He asked me one day to read him a few pages.' And

the reaction? 'He was not displeased' [*il n'en fut pas mécontent*].
Las Cases submits to being edited by Napoleon (*au contraire,*
my men never fought better than at Waterloo, he insisted).
Napoleon participated actively in the project and was attached
to the fate of the *Mémorial*. 'The Emperor was secretly very
angry about the confiscation of the *Journal*' [i.e. the *Mémorial*],
Gourgaud reported after Las Cases's arrest.

Napoleon linked Saint Helena and the idea of authorial
pluralism. Conversely, when he thought of authoring his own
work, he located it elsewhere. The novel and escape became
synonymous. Thus he remarked to Las Cases in June 1816:
'[when he got to America] he would be truly free . . . and he
would at last write his novel.' Even in England, he thought,
he would be able to settle down to the novel, finally. He did
not reveal what would go into the novel, perhaps the kind of
'material' he recommended to Goethe, or a sequel to *Clisson
et Eugénie*. But giving up on the idea of escape was another
way of renouncing the novel and surrendering to the Saint
Helenian intertext. Someone else – almost everyone else –
would effectively write the novel for him in which he would
be a character.

Las Cases cursed himself for failing to record certain sparkling conversations that would therefore be lost for all time.
In fact, they were all sparkling, in his view. In a spirit of
documentary exhaustiveness, Napoleon therefore insisted
that Bertrand omit nothing ('he recommended to the Grand
Marshal that he write down the conversation that had taken
place between them at his bedside'). General Bertrand, perceived by Gourgaud as a cold fish ('glacial'), became, rather
against his will, the master of the post-imperial post-authorial
dialogue. Self-effacingly writing in the third person (he is
always 'le Grand Maréchal'), Bertrand was the most faithful
of all Napoleon's interlocutors on Saint Helena: firstly, in
the sense of being constant and uncomplaining (even if his
English wife may have kept her distance from the Emperor);
but secondly, even more so, in the sense that he doggedly
recorded the conversations that he had with Napoleon, no
matter how dismal and unsparkling, with the maximum precision and persistence. Having served under him from Italy

and Egypt through to Elba and Saint Helena, Bertrand's final service to Napoleon was to become the punctilious witness of his every enema and *vomissement*. His Saint Helena 'tapes' omit no embarrassing breakdowns, not even those obscene episodes where Napoleon was accusing Bertrand's wife of being a whore who willingly screwed every passing sailor. Whereas Napoleon remains, in Las Cases, a witty, aphoristic, incisive speechmaker, a master of self-vindication, he has become, in Bertrand's involuntary hands, a genuine victim, a man at the end of his tether, on the brink of total collapse. Perhaps for the first time, he is to be heard using 'foutre' and 'con' freely.

It is as if Bertrand is acting under orders to include every last scrap of discourse in his Journal. But Bertrand entertained doubts about his own ability to do the job. 'What the Emperor needed,' he reflected in a state of high anxiety, 'was a real man of letters beside him, Arnault or Denon for instance, who were serious professional writers, who saw writing as the way to glory.' Others may have had a hand in undermining his confidence: 'Not one of you can write!' [*Vous autres, ne savez pas écrire!*] Mme de Montholon announced in a scathing judgement that embraced all the scribblers of Saint Helena (except possibly her husband).

It seems as if Napoleon may, in certain moods, have expressed the same opinion. 'The Emperor considers that I do not appreciate the ellipses in his language.' Gourgaud, to Napoleon's way of thinking, made the mistake of papering over gaps and contradictions and producing a smooth metonymic narrative. Whereas Bertrand is all cracks and fissures. It is hardly surprising that Bertrand's work was not published until 1949 or that Bertrand himself should have been so nervous about what he was writing: there is nothing else like these dialogues in the nineteenth-century canon.

In Bertrand, absence becomes a recurrent theme of Napoleon's conversation, perhaps *the* theme, in connection not just with his wife and child but, more often, with those who have occupied Saint Helena. Napoleon was preoccupied, towards the end, with the sense of others slipping away and escaping his grasp:

- Is he here?
- No.
- So he has gone?
- Yes.
- To England?
- Yes.
- Why?
- Because he was recalled by his government.
- So he will not be coming back?
- No.
- So we will no longer have any contact with him?
- No.

The tragedy, as perceived dimly by Napoleon, seems to lie in the end of conversation as, one by one, his interlocutors desert their general.

- Is O'Meara here?
- He has left.
- Ah! I didn't see him. Did you see him?
- Yes.
- He took his leave of you?
- Yes.
- Who made him leave?
- The governor.
- Why? Because he was too attached to us?
- Yes.
- So, he will not return?
- No.
- Is Montchenu here?

And so it went on, twenty or thirty times, the same or similar, going round and round, as Napoleon tried desperately to keep track and retain an exact inventory of the occupants of the island. Bertrand managed to keep track of the conversation, at least, and produced a text the like of which would not be seen again for more than a century, in certain short stories of Kafka, of Hemingway, and especially, in the plays of Beckett. These quasi-posthumous, semi-apocalyptic, absurdist conversations present as bleak a picture of the human mind confronted by a profound sense of the void as anything in modernism. If one phrase could summarize all of them, with Napoleon struggling against the dissolution of his mind and personality, it would be the line given to Hal the computer, as his brain is systematically unplugged, in Clarke and Kubrick's *2001: A Space Odyssey*: 'I can feel it going . . .'

- Was this boat carrying lemons?
- No.
- Almonds?
- No.
- Pomegranates?
- No.
- Grapes?
- No.
- Wine?
- No.
- So it has brought nothing?
- Animals.
- How many oxen?
- Forty.
- How many sheep?
- Two hundred.
- How many goats?
- None.
- And hens?
- None.
- So it has brought nothing? Was it carrying walnuts?
- No.
- Walnuts come, I believe, from cold countries, almonds from warm countries. Are lemons good here?
- Yes.
- And pomegranates?
- I have seen some good ones.
- Was this boat carrying any lemons, pomegranates, almonds?

As on Corsica, so on Saint Helena: the man and the island are one. Napoleon struggled heroically to keep a tally of everything coming in and going out, as if it were identical with the contents of his consciousness. Progressively the island was being emptied of all those Napoleon was attached to, whether through departure or death. There is a sense in these dialogues that when the island is finally evacuated, it will be time to die.

Saint Helena and the Napoleonic ego become inseparable. Man, after all, Napoleon remarked to Gourgaud, was nothing but a mutation of mud heated by the sun [*je crois que l'homme a été formé par la chaleur du soleil sur la boue.*]

Napoleon certainly expected to be out-generalled, in the end, by his own language. Gourgaud and he would talk grammar long into the night and Gourgaud typically turned their disagreements about rules into an opportunity to score over Napoleon. 'His Majesty asserts that when two substantives are in agreement with an adjective, then the adjective must take the gender of the second noun. I assert the contrary, citing the case of *Un homme et une femme bons.*' Napoleon was forced to concede and to pull back. But it had to be the language itself that was at fault. 'Why not allow that *naval* becomes *navaux* in the plural?' He regretted not having attended to the reform of French, in the direction of making it more orderly and methodical and eliminating exceptions. 'The French language is not a well-made language. I should really have fixed it while I had the chance.' Now it was too late and language had spun anarchically out of control and beyond any possibility of fixing it and bringing it under his power.

By the same token, he fully expected to be betrayed by others. No longer was he the writer but rather he who was written, and therefore subject to reconstruction. A lot of the Saint Helena years were spent in reading about himself, sometimes – as in the popular and plausible *Manuscrit venu de Sainte-Hélène d'une manière inconnue* (variously attributed to Talleyrand and Staël, actually written by a Swiss, Lulin de Chateauvieux) – in works purportedly by him. A cloud of literary apocrypha and misinformation gathered about him during the years of captivity. He laughed out loud at the exaggerations and inventions of the *Secret Amours of Bonaparte,* unacquainted as he was with most of the women he was supposed to have bedded ('They make me out to be some kind of Hercules!') He admired and considered adopting some of the equally imaginary *Maximes et pensées du prisonnier de Sainte-Hélène.* Occasionally he would be pleasantly surprised by the atypical appreciative acknowledgement, as in Parke and Hornemann's *Travels in Africa*: 'The polite and handsome manner in which these facts were mentioned was very gratifying to the

Emperor, who had been long accustomed to find his name connected with insulting epithets.' From time to time he would be driven to marginalia and corrections (as in the memoirs of General Bernadotte) and stiff letters of complaint, but by and large he remained genially resigned to misrepresentation. It was all part of the great game.

The work of Dr William Warden – *Letters written on board His Majesty's Ship the Northumberland and at St Helena* – amused him, even though as Gourgaud furiously pointed out none of the notional dialogues could have taken place, since 'Warden does not speak a word of French and his Majesty does not speak a word of English' (and must therefore have been borrowed from the libellous Las Cases). 'He is a writer,' Napoleon observed sympathetically of Constant, 'he has to write and he has to apportion blame.' [*C'est un homme d'esprit. Ecrivain, il faut qu'il écrive, qu'il accuse.*] In the same spirit of detachment ('He could become the ally of his cruellest enemies', Las Cases said) Napoleon even felt sorry for Chateaubriand that he could not do a better job of his denunciations: 'This man has not enough logic to produce a serious political work. He will strew it with flowers, but flowers will not suffice, it requires logic, tight and inexorable logic!'

Similarly, the idea of being let down or sacrificed by his own companions was a given from the beginning. If he was, as he claimed, a modern Jesus Christ (to Lord Amherst, visiting British ambassador: 'You have made me another Jesus Christ by placing a crown of thorns on my head') then he must have expected a Judas among his disciples too. Napoleon, as much as anyone, was conscious that a cult required a corpse. He was the first to articulate the theory of poisoning (that Sven Forshufvud would take up in the 1960s), so much so that it seeped into the thematics of his discourse. He would regularly accuse one or other of his attendants or the governor, Hudson Lowe, of 'poisoning' the atmosphere at Longwood. Sickness became the governing trope, so that utterances were understood as involuntary expulsions and emissions, vomited forth. Napoleon, complaining to Montholon that not everyone loved him, held that 'the poison of the soul has far more potency over me than a dose of arsenic.' Gourgaud may well have had Montholon in mind when he blurted out that 'Poison is the weapon of cowards!'

Montholon has subsequently been seen as the shadiest of all the inmates of Longwood, the most likely agent in any plot to assassinate Napoleon. According to Masson, he was at best a rogue and a fortune-hunter, selling off his memoirs to the highest bidder. He was certainly the greatest plagiarist among them, stitching together the shreds and patches of everyone else's conversations. And certainly he was fond of anticipating the death of Napoleon: 'I fear that it is already too late to fight the illness which is undermining him internally.' [*Je crains bien qu'il ne soit déjà trop tard pour combattre la maladie qui le mine intérieurement.*] But his essential ambiguity was transparent even at the time. Montholon scarcely bothered to conceal it: he may even have boasted of it. 'We must wait and dissemble,' he blithely remarked to Gourgaud [*il faut dissimuler et patienter*]. He openly admitted manipulating Napoleon's will in his favour: 'Montholon says that the Emperor was not in his right mind, that one could say that it was not the Emperor who made out this will, but rather Montholon who had dictated it to him.' His record – his royalist background and his eagerness to serve under the Bourbons – was not in dispute. It was this moral precariousness and inscrutability which probably endeared him to Napoleon, who tolerated treachery almost with admiration and certainly with indulgence. Gourgaud, on the other hand, was resentful both of Montholon's opacity and – perhaps even more so – of Napoleon's tolerance towards him. Napoleon's sense that he was part of a 'masked ball' was acute. No one was ever quite what they seemed – or they ought not to be. He went so far as to encourage Gourgaud to be less open, more devious: 'To succeed in this world you have to be a charlatan' [*Dans le monde il faut être charlatan. Ce n'est que comme cela que l'on réussit*]. Napoleon automatically assumed that everyone was always plotting or 'intriguing', even if, by way of therapy, he once suggested to Gourgaud that he should try not to think about it too much – for that way madness lies [*vous deviendrez fou*]. But plotting was the normal state of affairs. The only problem was that he, Napoleon, was no longer plotter-in-chief.

Perhaps everyone, even his strongest supporters, wished Napoleon dead at some stage, with even Gourgaud asserting that he should have died at Waterloo. Whatever the cause or causes of death – climate, depression, genetic inheritance, human volition, murderous medicine – it is clear that Napoleon embraced death and acquiesced to its authority: 'do you not think that Death would be a Heaven-sent relief to me? I do not fear it, but while I shall do nothing to hasten it, I shall not grasp at a straw to live.' Like Montholon, he went on anticipating it for years. Variations on 'my end draws near' and 'I am dead/assassinated/sacrificed!' became increasingly prevalent. Almost of necessity, Napoleon had engaged his past/future mode of thought. 'Consider: at this moment, while I am speaking to you, I can float back to the Tuileries, I see them, I see Paris. . . . It is in the same way that, in past times, I used to explain my prophetic soul.' Just as he looked back towards his beginning and his middle years, so too he looked forward to his end. The sense of an ending – protracted as it was – was all-pervasive on Saint Helena.

Nietzsche's dream of 'writing posthumously' was a reality for Napoleon. The whole of the Saint Helena period reads to us now like a gigantic epitaph. The central ongoing dispute between the British government and the Napoleon team, which spanned the whole of the six years, concerned what name should go on the cover of any of the prisoner's writings (as well, conversely, as on the front of any correspondence to him). The French contingent argued for 'Napoleon' or just plain 'Emperor'. The British, on the other hand, insisted on 'General Bonaparte' or possibly 'Buonaparte': everything else was illicitly adopted and invented. In London he was only ever a general and everything else was an add-on. In Paris – and on the extension of Paris that was Saint Helena – it was the add-ons that were ineradicable, and everything else was secondary.

It was only fitting that the dispute continued beyond the death of Napoleon. An inconclusive autopsy was carried out on the body (followed by post-post-mortems). The liver and the heart were removed and (if the proliferation of these collectors' items is anything to go by) the penis and testicles too. A plaster-cast was taken of the features, which appeared curiously youthful in death. All the remaining players, on both the French and the English side, turned out to see Napoleon laid to rest, on 9 May 1821, under a grove of willows close to a spring he had been fond of. But there could be no agreement on the thorny question of the name. The Emperor's disciples argued for 'NAPOLEON', followed by the dates of birth and death; Lowe would allow only 'BUONAPARTE'. As Stendhal said, both names were appropriate and fitted alternative personae (personally, he preferred General Bonaparte). But neither side could back down, with honour. In the end it was agreed to leave the gravestone blank, unmarked. In contrast to the highly textual, iconic tomb of Les Invalides in Paris, there was no name and no epitaph on Napoleon's Saint Helena grave. It was like an open invitation – a provocation – to writers to write upon the grave.

Napoleon died anonymous. Perhaps it was with this in mind that one of his last conversations, on the eve of his death, turned precisely on the question of naming. His mind too was going blank, emptying out into the void. He was getting particularly hazy about names and who was who. Whispering into his servant Marchand's ear, he asked, desperate to remember: 'What is the name of my son?' To which the answer came: 'Napoleon'.

Napoleon I had high hopes of Napoleon II (who would die young) as a writer. 'I will soon be forgotten. Historians will have little to say about me. Perhaps, if my son comes to power, he will write up what I have done.'

Epitaphs

Entrée du corps de Napoléon
à Paris.

Napoleon may have been a great critic in his spare time, but he was in many ways a frustrating and baffling one to wrestle with. Arnault, recalling their sparring on the *Orient* over Homer and Ossian, considered that Napoleon's literary analyses were 'a form of intellectual fencing in which he was less concerned to bring out the truth than to show off his subtlety'. Napoleon went to work on a poem that Arnault knew, liked, and thought he understood. 'By the time he had finished analysing it, I could no longer make head or tail of it, and I still can't.' Napoleon's whole life had this same deconstructive quality of mystification, shedding obscurity on the plain text of history. Even Napoleon was left in the dark by Napoleon: 'I would have had extreme difficulty in affirming with any degree of veracity my unedited thoughts.' Others felt no such difficulty. The death of the failed writer opened a literary floodgate to a lot of failed Napoleons.

'After I am dead,' Napoleon observed, 'my body will be a turnip or a carrot.' In fact he felt that on Saint Helena he was already dead, having attained a quasi-vegetable state: 'I have been vegetating here for six years.' The island was the scene of heated arguments between materialists and immaterialists about the existence of the soul. Napoleon was sceptical: 'If someone hammers a nail into your head, you go mad: where is your soul then?' [*Un clou enfoncé dans votre tête vous rendra fou: où sera alors votre âme?*] Napoleon took the view that if man was nothing but mud heated by the sun then he would return to mud. Death was peace, death was oblivion.

And yet perfect nothingness, he knew, was about as hard to bring off as the perfect plenitude of the empire. He suspected his death would be instantly reclaimed by a thousand writers. 'When I am dead there will be a universal reaction in my favour.' Like the Hakem of his own *Le Masque prophète*, he expected his supporters to raise him up to heaven. It was Las Cases's paradox on the success of failure expanded into the regenerative potential of mortality. He said to Gourgaud at one point that 'one can die, and then be restored to life, that there is a certain period of time in which that is possible.' What he could not have foreseen is that a man can be restored to death. Napoleon's death produced a terrible vogue for dying. Worse still, for funerals.

The second Napoleon – Napoleon II, the 'King of Rome' or *l'Aiglon* (the Eaglet) to Edmond Rostand – was doomed to die young, but other surrogate Napoleons (and other empires) sprang up to fill the vacancy. Napoleon syndrome was rife and writers more than anyone fell victim to it, from Stendhal (who served under Napoleon) and Hugo (whose father did) and Balzac, the most explicitly Napoleonic of novelists whose *Comédie humaine* mimics the Empire, through to the unlikely figure of Henry James, who claimed to be Napoleon only on his deathbed. James signed one of his last letters 'Napoleone' (with the Italian spelling) and wrote asking to have work carried out on the Louvre and the Tuileries. The 'distinguished thing' (as James had called death) and Napoleon had become indistinguishable. 'Yes, I wanted to become Napoleon,' said Raskolnikov in Dostoyevsky's *Crime and Punishment*. 'That is why I have killed.' But it was the dying more than the killing which inspired others. The nineteenth century became a long funeral procession, an immense snuff drama, necrophile heaven. If there was a Napoleon cult, it was a cult of death.

The idea of a void within and without, a lurking emptiness or unreality beneath all the grand words and deeds, had haunted Napoleon long before he died. Language was not used to refer to anything real, it was the realm of nostalgia and the dream. Historical truth, after all, was nothing but 'a fable we have agreed upon'. The theme of absence was already securely in place while Napoleon was still present; when he absented himself, it expanded to fill the intellectual and political landscape. In dying he seemed to give enhanced credibility to his argument that there always seemed to be something missing. Napoleon, disembodied, came to embody that lack. So pervasive was the idea that it became a popular quasi-theological pastime to prove that, in fact, Napoleon had never even existed in the first place, that he was nothing but myth from the very beginning, a personification of the sun-god or an honorific military title that had acquired fictional substance. Stendhal's hero in *La Chartreuse de Parme* (1839) acts out this obsession when he goes hunting for Napoleon at Waterloo, but in vain. The disappearance of the Emperor was the mystery at the core of the nineteenth-century novel. And what the novelists celebrated was not so much an imaginary golden age as the liberating sense of loss in its passing. Tolstoy's scathingly anti-Napoleonic *War and Peace* was, in some sense, the template of even the most avowedly pro-Napoleonic fictions: getting rid of the Emperor was, aesthetically, a good thing. Even Balzac smacks of Wellington.

It became a matter of national honour to establish the reality of the myth and restore what remained of it to France. General Gourgaud, having left under a cloud, returned with some style to Saint Helena in 1840. His mission: to fulfil Napoleon's wish to be buried on the banks of the Seine. Gourgaud, together with Grand Marshal Bertrand, a couple of Napoleon's servants and the Prince de Joinville, looked on as whatever was left of his body (the surgeons had made more of an impact than twenty years in the ground) was laboriously dug up and shipped back to Paris. On 15 December, a day of sun and snow showers, Gourgaud and Bertrand – amidst the remnants of the Grande Armée – escorted the coffin to Les Invalides. Bertrand placed the sword of the Emperor on the lid of the coffin and Gourgaud the hat. Las Cases was still alive, but blind (his son had taken his place on the return to Saint Helena and had challenged Hudson Lowe, the cruel gaoler of Saint Helena, to a duel). But the poet Victor Hugo would serve as the eyes of a generation. 'Now the swordsmen have finished, it is the turn of the thinkers,' he wrote.

Hugo had kept alive the idea of the *Géant* in his poems ('Ode à la colonne', 'Lui,' 'Bounaberdi') and tried to rewrite Waterloo in *Les Misérables*. 'We will make you a beautiful funeral' (or possibly 'beautiful funerals') he had predicted. Now he followed in the wake of the cortège through the streets of Paris and under the Arc de Triomphe (completed in 1836). He was disappointed by the over-emphasis on the military and felt that Napoleon had been betrayed yet again. There were too many generals and marshals for his taste, too many sailors and sabres. Drums and cannon salvoes were a mistake (farcically, the legs of a national guardsman were taken off by the first blast, as nobody had bothered to unload). Sixteen horses to pull one hearse! Eight would have been enough. The 'gold' on the coffin was fake. Only a humpback dwarf and ragamuffins cried out 'Vive l'Empereur'. It was either overdone or underdone, too magnificent or too cheap.

Napoleon did not belong to politicians: he was too big and they were too small. The gravest fault was that the purple cloth, embroidered with the motif of the imperial bees, concealed too much: 'It hides what everyone wants to see, what France demands, what the people expect, what all eyes seek: the coffin of Napoleon.' The coffin had become a national treasure. It was up to writers and intellectuals – to Hugo above all – to save Napoleon from soldiers and senators and become Napoleon's true pall-bearers and inheritors. The civilizing mission was more than ever necessary. 'It is up to us to illuminate the world', he said. Something had been missing even from Napoleon's funeral, and Hugo saw it as his life's work – his death's work, it would be truer to say – to rectify that omission.

Faced with the inevitably dismal reality of a surrogate Napoleon – *Napoléon le petit* – in power, Hugo fled and took himself off to another island, this time Guernsey. As if escaping from Elba, he eventually returned to Paris in triumph and died there at the end of May 1885. Immediately, a street was named after him. Avenue Eylau, already renamed after one of Napoleon's victories, became avenue Victor-Hugo, to consecrate the genealogy. At dawn on Sunday 31 May, Hugo's mortal remains were borne along that street in a pauper's hearse (a detail he had insisted on in the script for his own funeral) followed by his family and the twenty mayors of Paris, 652 generals and roughly another 10,000 people, and temporarily brought to rest beneath the Arc de Triomphe, there to lie in state for 24 hours.

The coffin is perched on top of an immense urn, itself raised up by a double pedestal covered in purple, so that the whole construction reaches up towards the arch itself and it can be seen from a considerable distance, like a lighthouse. A dozen young poets (including Tancrède Martel, editor of Napoleon's *Mémoires et oeuvres*) form a guard of honour beneath the sarcophagus, while around them banners are unfurled bearing the names of Hugo's greatest works emblazoned upon them: *Les Misérables, Les Orientales, Quatre-vingts treize, Les Contemplations, Notre Dame de Paris*.

The sea of mourners stretches down the Champs Elysées to the Place de la Concorde. One of them is Maurice Barrès (one of the founding fathers of the *Ligue des patriotes*) who celebrates the Hugo funeral under the heading 'The Social Virtue of a Corpse' in *Les Déracinés*. This *fin-de-siècle* novel (published in 1897) makes clear that Hugo's corpse cannot help being an allusion to the other great corpse lying in the tomb at Les Invalides, 'the crossroads of all the energies that we name audacity, will-power and desire'. All coffins recall *the* coffin. The surrounding streets – Iéna, Hoche, Friedland, Kléber, l'avenue de la Grande Armée – seem to contain a whole history. That night, as the crowds multiply, the mourning becomes still more adulatory and pagan, with the dark colossus above lit from below by the flames of the torchbearers. The cult of death turns into a Dionysiac rite, a Fourierist satisfaction of the passions. The Champs Elysées, the benches and the bushes, are the scene of a mass public orgy ('an immense debauchery', 'an enormous copulation', in the words of the Goncourt brothers). Even the police who are drafted in to control the revellers are soon joining in and flinging off their uniforms.

History was repeating itself, the first time round as tragedy, the second as sex. Barrès had his own theory to account for this 'night of madness': Parisians, having been cruelly deprived of a genius, were anxious to replace him as soon as may be and thus set about desperately, passionately, filling the void. But

Hugo, who had done everything he could to take the place of Napoleon, had arranged his ecstatic exit to fulfil another of Napoleon's wishes. At the end of the *Discourse* that Napoleon had submitted nearly a century before to the Académie de Lyon, a dying man bids those who remain behind not to despair: 'May my sepulchre not be a place of sadness [*un lieu de tristresse*], but rather the opposite, my friends: let there be merriment [*la gaîté*] and sweet pleasures [*les doux plaisirs*] going on all around it . . . If ever you leave this place, take my remains under your care and carry them away with you . . . Adieu, my blessing be upon you, and may it stand guard over your union and your happiness [*votre union et votre bonheur*].'

Sources and Bibliography

I, NAPOLEON

Napoléon à Waterloo.

Napoleon's pluralist beliefs are recalled by Pierre-Louis Roederer in his *Journal* (Daragon, Paris, 1909), p. 16. Antoine-Vincent Arnault's poem is in *Souvenirs d'un sexagénaire* (Duféy, Paris, 1833), vol. II, p. 301: 'Toi, dont la jeunesse occupée/ Aux jeux d'Apollon et de Mars,/ Comme le premier des Césars,/ Manie et la plume et l'épée;/ Qui, peut-être au milieu des camps,/ Rédiges d'immortels mémoires,/ Dérobe-leur quelques instants,/ Et trouve, s'il se peut, le temps/De me lire entre deux victoires.' Arnault also supplies the reminiscence of the Mediterranean voyage. Jean Tulard's one-volume compendium of his immense research is *Napoleon: The Myth of the Saviour* (Weidenfeld, London, 1984). His main precursor, with respect to Napoleon as a writer *manqué* is Georges Lefebvre, *Napoléon* (Presses universitaires de France, Paris, 1969, first published 1936), p. 69: 's'il n'avait passé par Brienne, il eût pu devenir homme de lettres.' For the earlier more emphatically aesthetic view, see Sainte-Beuve: 'Aujourd'hui que l'action est plus éloignée, et que la parole reste, celle-ci se montre avec ses qualités propres, et en même temps le souvenir de l'action y projette un reflet et comme un rayon.' *Causeries du lundi* (Garnier, Paris, 1868–70, 14 vols), vol. I, p. 183 ('Mémoires de Napoléon', 179–98), and *Nouveaux lundis* (Garnier, Paris, 1865–9, 13 vols), vol. VII, p. 261 for Napoleon as critic, an angle taken up again in *The Myth of Napoleon (Yale French Studies,* vol. 26). Michelet's 'comédien' is a recurrent theme of *Histoire du XIXe siècle* (Michel-Lévy, Paris, 1875). Chateaubriand's literary denunciation is in his pamphlet, *De Buonaparté et des Bourbons et de la nécéssité de se rallier à nos princes légitimes, pour le bonheur de la France et celui de l'Europe* (Mame, Paris, 1814), p. 50. Stendhal wrote two unfinished works on Napoleon, *Vie de Napoléon* and *Mémoires sur Napoléon* (and his novel, *Le Rouge et le Noir*, is a meditation on the theme). Thiers's hyperbole: 'Napoléon est le plus grand homme de son siècle, on en convient, mais il en est aussi le plus grand écrivain', in perhaps the first article on Napoleon as writer, published in *Le National*, 24 June 1830, cited in A. Périvier, *Napoléon journaliste* (Plon, Paris, 1918), pp. 4–7. Thiers would go on to write the monumental *Histoire du Consulat et de l'Empire* (1845–62). Roederer's recollection of talking semiotics with Napoleon is in his *Journal*, p. 2.

CHAPTER 1   A PRIZE FOR HAPPINESS

Rousseau's prize advertisement: I have cut the actual rather long-winded text down to its essentials and I am using the slightly modified title that Rousseau himself gives the essay. The original was: 'Si le rétablissement des sciences et des arts a contribué à épurer les moeurs', which appeared in the October 1749 number of the *Mercure*. Rousseau's account of the 'illumination de Vincennes' occurs in Book 8 of the *Confessions* (Garnier, Paris, 1964, ed. Jacques Voisine), pp. 415–16, and in the second letter of the *Lettres à Malesherbes*. Napoleon's youthful reading of *La Nouvelle Héloïse* is affirmed in Comte P.-L. Roederer, *Journal*, p. 165. '*La Nouvelle Héloïse* est pourtant un ouvrage écrit avec bien de la chaleur, il sera toujours le livre des jeunes gens. Je l'ai lu à neuf ans. Il m'a tourné la tête.' F. G. Healey, *The Literary Culture of Napoleon* (Droz, Geneva, 1959), p. 20n, has added a sceptical footnote: 'As he was not quite ten when he first came to France he did very well to read this large work in a strange tongue at that age.' Also essential on the young Napoleon's intellectual formation: the same author's *Rousseau et Napoléon* (Droz, Geneva, 1957). For the advertisement in the *Journal de Lyon*, 18 February 1790, p. 109, I have also made adaptations in the translation. The original date set for submissions was 1 April 1791 but this was put back. Napoleon's violent ambition is taken from the *Discourse on Happiness* (or 'Discours de Lyon') in *Napoléon inconnu, Papiers inédits 1769–1793*, (Ollendorf, Paris, 1895, ed. Frédéric Masson and Guido Biagi, 2 vols), vol. II, p. 327. Masson is the best source for the 'cahiers' and most of Napoleon's early writings, which are in the San Lorenzo library in Florence. Also valuable: *Napoléon, Oeuvres littéraires et écrits militaires* (Société encyclopédique française, Paris, 1967, ed. Jean Tulard, 3 vols) and Alain Coelho's edition of *Napoléon, Oeuvres littéraires* (Le Temps singulier, Nantes, 1979). The condemnations of Raynal are cited in Anatole Feugère, *Un Précurseur de la Revolution: L'Abbé Raynal* (Imprimerie ouvrière, Angoulême, 1922), pp. 267 and 278. For Raynal's maritime fantasy see the *Histoire des deux Indes* (Geneva, 1781), vol. VIII, p. 250. Even Raynal himself admits, 'Cette idée n'échappera pas au ridicule de nos esprits superficiels, mais est-ce pour eux qu'on écrit?' Napoleon's first letter to Raynal is cited in Colonel Iung, *Bonaparte et son temps* (Charpentier, Paris, 1880–1), vol. I, p. 162, who suggests that the letter was written as early as July 1786. Arthur Chuquet, *La Jeunesse de Napoléon* (Armand Colin, Paris, 1897, 3 vols), doubts its authenticity, but Feugère reaffirms it and places the first meeting between Napoleon and Raynal in September 1786, September 1787 or June 1788. Le Comte de Las Cases is in *Le Mémorial de Sainte-Hélène* (Seuil, Paris, 1968), p. 52: Las Cases remains indispensable even if euphemistic. *Horace Walpole's Correspondence* (Oxford University Press, 1974), vol. 39, pp. 167–8, letter to Lady Ailesbury, 29 December 1772. I have slightly slimmed the quotation. The 'mass of feeble athletes' judgement is cited in *Avantages et désavantages de la découverte de l'Amérique* (Université de Saint-Etienne, 1994, ed. Hans-Jürgen Lüsebrink and Alexander Mussard), p. 130. The judges add that the discourse of 1787 by the Chevalier de Castellux on this subject (which argued in favour of the advantages), had he submitted it, would 'probably' have taken the prize, p. 137. For the audacious expedition of Columbus, see *Histoire des deux Indes*, vol. IX, pp. 308–10. 'Frenchmen!', Masson, *Napoléon inconnu*, vol. II, p. 312. The same volume, p. 293 for 'Illustrious Raynal', and p. 332 for 'I am certain'. The image of the beach is in Chuquet, *La Jeunesse de Napoléon*, vol. II, p. 211. For periods of leave, see Norwood Young, *The Growth of Napoleon, A Study in Environment* (John Murray, London, 1910), p. 223. Napoleon's greed for culture, Chuquet, II, 208. The image of Napoleon living like a bear is cited in Tancrède Martel's *Mémoires et oeuvres de Napoléon* (A. Michel, Paris, 1910), p. 316, attributed to a conversation with Caulaincourt, 1810; but Masson is dubious about authenticity (*Napoléon inconnu*, vol. II, p. 202), while Chuquet considers the austerity exaggerated. Martel's introduction is a useful but hagiographic 'étude littéraire'. *Cahier* 19 is in Masson, *Napoléon inconnu*, vol. II, pp. 258–67. Victor Hugo's *Les Orientales* was first published in 1829: such poems as 'Lui' and 'Bounaberdi' pay specific homage to Napoleon. 'Sur le suicide', in Masson, *Napoléon inconnu*, vol. I, pp. 145–6. Durkheim's concept of 'anomie' is set out in his classic study, *Le Suicide* (1897). Rousseau's 'contradictions of the social system' is in the second of his *Lettres à Malesherbes*. Young's stern strictures, *The Growth of Napoleon*, p. 153. Frank McGlynn's comment is in the synoptic *Napoleon* (Jonathan Cape, London, 1997), p. 45, and Vincent Cronin's more enthusiastic line in *Napoleon* (Fontana, London, 1990, originally published 1971), p. 53. It is Masson who strenuously denies that anyone could have taken a dislike to Napoleon, *Napoléon inconnu*, vol. II, p. 213. The Baudelaire poem is 'Paysage', taken from *Les Fleurs du Mal*. Abel Gance's film, *Napoléon vu par Abel Gance*, on a similar note, depicts Napoleon hard at work in his study while the mob parades up and down the street outside. See Paul Bartel, *La Jeunesse inédite de Napoléon* (Amiot-Dumont, Paris, 1954), p. 261, for the notebooks of Alexandre des Mazis, Napoleon's college friend. Napoleon's account of 10 August 1792 is in the *Mémorial de Sainte-Hélène*, p. 392. The 'very pronounced dream' judgement by the Lyon examiners is in Masson, *Napoléon inconnu*, vol. II, p. 212, and *Histoire de l'Académie de Lyon* (J.-B. Dumas, Lyon, 1840), vol. I, p. 144. For Sainte-Beuve's confirmation of Daunou: *Causeries du lundi*, vol. I, p. 180. Las Cases, p. 53, for the more pro-Napoleon view: no doubt on Napoleon's prompting, he has substituted 'institutions' for 'feelings' in the title. Napoleon's letter is quoted in Masson, *Napoléon inconnu*, vol. II, p. 404. The fate of the Academy is recorded in Feugère, p. 350. And Feugère again, p. 364, for 'effervescence of mind'. Raynal's views on anarchy are taken from *Histoire du parlement d'Angleterre* (de la Guette, Paris, 1750), pp. 319–21, cited in Feugère, p. 35, who also gives his conception of peace, p. 54. The Abbé Georgel is cited in Feugère, p. 402. The recollection of what was said at Ermenonville is due to the respectful Baron Claude François de Méneval, *Mémoires pour servir à l'histoire de Napoléon Ier* (Dentu, Paris, 1894, 3 vols), vol. I, p. 27. Also helpful: Frédéric Masson, *Napoléon dans sa jeunesse 1769–1793* (Ollendorff, Paris, 1907); Jean Tulard, *Itinéraire de Napoléon au jour le jour 1769–1821* (Tallendier, Paris, 1992).

CHAPTER 2   ISLANDS AND CONTINENTS

Napoleon's arrival in 'the Latin Country' is in General Bertrand, *Cahiers de Sainte-Hélène* (Albin Michel, Paris, 1959, 3 vols), vol. III, p. 70. Metaphors of the desert come from the vital Egyptian campaign memoir, *Correspondance de Napoléon* (published by order of Napoleon III, Imprimerie impériale, 1858–70, 32 vols). My references are to the smaller Plon edition: here, vol. XXIX, p. 438. But this contains only 22,067 of the 30,000 items in the Archives Nationales. By way of supplement, see also the *Correspondance inédite de Napoléon*

(Charles Lavauzelle, Paris, 1912–15, 5 vols, ed. Ernest Picard and Louis Tutey). The early reference to Saint Helena: Masson, *Napoléon inconnu*, vol. II, p. 49. Napoleon always gave 15 August 1769 as his date of birth in his autobiographical works, and Dorothy Carrington's exhaustive search through the Corsican archives in *Napoleon's Parents* (London, 1988) bears this out. The 'vast abyss of the seas', and the 'melancholy of nature' are in Masson, *Napoléon inconnu*, vol. II, pp. 303–4. Napoleon's melodramatic account of his own birth is in his letter to Paoli, Masson, *Napoléon inconnu*, vol. II, p. 64. For Norwood Young's environmentalist reading, *The Growth of Napoleon*, p. 184. The titles of the chapters of Emil Ludwig's *Napoleon* (Allen and Unwin, London, 1927) are also suggestive: 'The Island', 'The Torrent', 'The River', 'The Sea', 'The Rock'. Napoleon's own line about the 'torrent', Masson, *Napoléon inconnu*, vol. II, p. 321. The 'Nouvelle Corse' is in Masson, *Napoléon inconnu*, vol. II, pp. 75–83. The letter to Wenlock is quoted in Carrington, p. 162. Napoleon's letter to his father is cited in Masson, *Napoléon inconnu*, vol. I, p. 83. For Rousseau's view of Corsica, *Du contrat social* (Garnier, Paris, 1962), p. 269. The Boswell quotations are from *Corsica* (Williams and Norgate, London, 1951, ed. Morchard Bishop), pp. 67, 92. Napoleon's letter to Paoli, Masson, *Napoléon inconnu*, vol. II, pp. 64–6. The Carrington quotation is on p. 36 of *Napoleon's Parents*. Paoli in the *Discourse on Happiness*, Masson, *Napoléon inconnu*, vol. II, pp. 299–300. The incident at Brienne is recalled by Louis-Antoine Fauvelet de Bourrienne, *Mémoires* (Garnier, Paris, 1899), vol. I, p. 7 (rejected by Joseph Bonaparte, but still plausible). It should be added that there are several volumes dedicated to refuting Bourrienne: A. D. Belliard, *Bourrienne et ses erreurs volontaires et involontaires* (Hauman, Brussels, 1830). Young provides the cartoon and its caption, p. 101. The refusal to monumentalize his father, Las Cases, *Mémorial*, p. 48. Carrington, p. 191, for the suggestion of 'relief' about his father's death. Joseph Bonaparte's recollection of his younger brother is in *Mémoires et correspondances* (Paris, 1853–4, 10 vols) vol. I, p. 32. The demand in French to write in Italian: *Revue des deux mondes*, 15 December 1931, vol. VI, 'Lettres de jeunesse de Napoléon', p. 770. Here also, the letter to his mother on the subject of pasta. The tribute to his mother can be found in Montholon, *Récits de Sainte-Hélène*, vol. I, p. 321, cited in Carrington, p. 193. For Claude Lévi-Strauss and his culinary triangle see 'Le Triangle culinaire', *L'Arc* (no. 26, pp. 19–29) and *Mythologiques I: Le Cru et le Cuit* (Gallimard, Paris, 1964). The flaming torch of truth: Masson, *Napoléon inconnu*, vol. II, p. 321. Norwood Young's comment on his compulsive falsification, *Growth*, p. 173; quasi-dyslexia, pp. 231–3. Roederer praises the dictator in his *Journal*, pp. 102–3. Sainte-Beuve's thought, *Causeries*, vol. I, p. 184. Arnault's recollection of Napoleon reading aloud is in *Souvenirs*, vol. IV, pp. 85–6. 'Ocean' is mentioned in the list of books Napoleon drew up for his portable library, mentioned by Bourrienne, *Mémoires*, vol. II, pp. 49–52. The Abbé Chardon's recollection is cited in Bourrienne, vol. I, pp. 30–1. Méneval's comment on Napoleon's handwriting is in his *Mémoires*, vol. I, p. 421. Napoleon's defence on the grounds of being hot-blooded: letter to Naudin, cited Young, p. 228. Sainte-Beuve agreed that he did a violence to French: 'Bonaparte, en s'emparant de cet idiome [French] pour rendre ses idées et ses sentiments, dut lui faire subir quelques violences et lui imprimer quelques faux plis.' Sainte-Beuve, *Causeries*, vol. VII, p. 180. Father Dupuy is in Masson, *Napoléon inconnu*, vol. II, pp. 66–70. Napoleon's reply follows. For Napoleon's analysis of his brother's style, see *Revue des deux mondes*, pp. 789–90. The acceptance letter from Massera is in Masson, *Napoléon inconnu*, vol. II, p. 125. The *Lettres sur la Corse* follow. Nadia Tomiche's book, *Napoléon écrivain* (Armand Colin, Paris, 1952), is one of the few to take Napoleon seriously as a writer, but splits his writing off from everything else. Paoli's slap in the face for Napoleon: Masson, *Napoléon inconnu*, vol. II, p. 199. Sartre's version of Jean Genet is in Sartre, *Saint-Genet, comédien et martyr* (Gallimard, Paris, 1952). Montholon's account of Napoleon on Saint Helena, *Récits*, II, p. 171. Las Cases, *Mémorial*, pp. 276–7, for the parallel of Corsica and Saint Helena.

CHAPTER 3   MIND OVER MATTER

The 'bibliothèque portative' is in Bourrienne, vol. II, pp. 49–52; also in Napoleon's *Correspondance*, IV, pp. 27–8. The story of *Le Masque prophète* is in Masson's collection, *Napoléon inconnu*, vol. II, pp. 17–19. '*Il faut aller en Orient, toutes les grandes gloires viennent de là*': Bourrienne, vol. II, p. 49. Sulkowski's article is preserved in *The Journals of Bonaparte in Egypt, 1798–1801*, ed. Saladin Boustany (Al-Arab Bookshop, Cairo, 1971, 10 vols), vol. I, pp. 19–20, which are indispensable for this period. For Tallien's leader column, see Boustany, *Journals*, vol. I, p. 5. For Monge's letters, see P.-V. Aubry, *Monge, le savant ami de Napoléon Bonaparte* (Gauthier-Villars, Paris, 1954), pp. 226–7. Napoleon's reply is in his *Correspondance*, vol. IV, p. 39. For Nicolas Turc's description of the armada, see his *Chronique d'Egypte, 1798–1804* (Cairo, 1950, ed. and trans. by Gaston Wiet), p. 9. The description of the moon and 'le sol blanchâtre de l'aride Afrique' is to be found in the *Correspondance*, vol. XXIX, pp. 431–2. Parseval-Grandmaison's lyrical warblings are in Boustany, *Journals*, vol. I, p. 225. The back numbers of the *Décade égyptienne* are contained in Boustany, *Journals*, vol. I. The self-description is on p. 6. In drawing a contrast between Ernest Gellner and Edward Said, I have in mind not just such works as Said's *Orientalism* and Gellner's *Plough, Sword, Book*, but also their quarrel in the pages of the *TLS*, dating from Gellner's review of Said's *Culture and Imperialism* (19 February 1993, pp. 3–4). My version of Jean Baudrillard's thought is taken from such works as *Simulacres et simulation* and *De la séduction*, but given that he attaches higher priority to images and film and electronic phenomena over mere texts, 'text' would have to include 'hypertext', television and cinema. Each of these three paraphrases is, of course, a gross simplification. Gellner is emphatically 1, and Baudrillard typically 3; Said, given his dialectical equation, weaves between 1, 2 and 3. For Napoleon the realist see, for example, Lefebvre: 'Tout paraît le vouer à la politique réaliste et tout, en effet, dans l'exécution est réaliste jusque dans le moindre détail' (*Napoléon*, p. 69); Tulard follows Lefebvre's lead here. Blake's view of art and empire is cited in Said, *Culture and Imperialism* (Vintage, London, 1993), pp. 12–13. Comtesse de Rémusat's unreliable *Mémoires* (Calmann Levy, Paris, 1880, 3 vols) have Napoleon harking back to Egypt, vol. I, p. 274. For the theory of the superiority of mind over matter, see *Correspondance*, vol. XXIX, pp. 475–7. Sainte-Beuve's view: 'C'est dans de telles pages qu'on sent combien Napoléon prenait au sérieux par moments sa mission de guerrier civilisateur, et qu'il n'était pas seulement une épée de plus dans cet Orient de merveilles, mais une épée lumineuse' (*Causeries*, vol. I, p. 187). The 'two systems', cited in *Ecrits de Napoléon* (Buchet/Chastel, Paris, 1969, ed. Octave Aubry), p. 236. The monumental *Description de l'Egypte* has a suitably grand subtitle: *recueil des observations et des recherches qui ont été faites en Egypte pendant l'expédition de l'armée française, publié par les ordres de sa majesté l'empereur Napoléon le grand* (1809–28, 23 vols); Fourier is on volume I, p. xxxiv. Denon on Thebes: Boustany, *Journals*, vol. III, p. 286. Napoleon's historically minded speech to the troops in front of the Pyramids: *Correspondance*, vol. IV, p. 240. Alexandrian dreams: *Correspondance*, vol. V, pp. 182–3. The toasts to the future can be found in Boustany, *Journals*, vol. IV, no. 8, p. 3 and the proclamation to 'the people of Misr' in vol. VIII, p. 87. For Napoleon's utopia, see *Correspondance*, vol. XXIX, p. 430. His point about publicity: *Correspondance*, vol. V, p. 182. Aubry, p. 260, for Monge's vision. Charles Norry's disillusionment is in his *Relation de l'expédition en Egypte* (Charles Pougens, Paris, year VII), p. 33. The theory of desertification is an extract from Arab geographer A'bd-Er-Rachyd El-Bakouy by J. J. Marcel, Boustany, *Journals*, vol. III, p. 148. For

Napoleon on Mamelukes, see Boustany, *Journals*, vol. III, p. 32. The party celebrating the rising of the Nile, as reported in the *Courier*: Boustany, *Journals*, vol. IV, no. 1, p. 2. Napoleon's omniscience is proclaimed in the same volume, IV, no. 23, p. 2 and vol. VIII, p. 33. For Abdel Rahman Al-Jabarti's scepticism, see in Boustany, *Journals*, vol. VIII, pp. 13–14. The *Correspondance*, vol. V, p. 221, gives Napoleon's exegesis of the Koran. The reply is given by Boustany, *Journals*, vol. III, p. 33. I have tried to reconstruct one of these encounter groups on the basis of printed documents. Vivant Denon's discovery: Boustany, *Journals*, vol. III, p. 286. Boustany, vol. II, p. 194 for the allegorical style. The account of the sexual proclivities of young boys is in Boustany, *Journals*, vol. I, on p. 110. The absence of onanism: in Reynati, April 1799, 'Topographie physique et médicale de Vieux-Kaire', Boustany, vol. II, p. 186. Homosexual rape in *Correspondance*, vol. XXIX, p. 433. Perrée's comment is taken from the letters intercepted by the English navy, Boustany, vol. X, p. 56. The great balloon debacle is in Boustany, *Journals*, vol. VIII, pp. 29–30. Denon's account of the uprising is in his colourfully evocative *Voyage dans la Basse et la Haute Egypte pendant les campagnes du général Bonaparte* (Institut français de l'archéologie du Caire, Paris, 1989, originally published 1802), pp. 66–9. Napoleon's continued seminars, *Correspondance*, vol. XXIX, pp. 503–4. Boustany, *Journals*, vol. II, pp. 297–8 is the source for the apologetic *Décade*. Desgenettes's account of Egyptian medicine: Boustany, *Journals*, vol. I, pp. 31–2. The late Bruant's letter is printed in Boustany, *Journals*, vol. II, p. 52. Napoleon's breezy comments on malingerers: *Correspondance*, vol. V, p. 191. The medical report roughly agreeing with him: Boustany, vol. II, pp. 261–2. The most exhaustive account of the whole episode is C. de la Jonquière's *L'Expédition en Egypte, 1798–1801* (Charles-Lavauzelle, Paris, 1899–1907, 5 vols); vol. IV, pp. 284–5 records the Desgenettes account of Napoleon in the plague-house of Jaffa. The peculiarities of the plague, according to Napoleon: *Correspondance*, vol. XXX, p. 29. Desgenettes on medical conspiracies, Boustany, *Journals*, vol. II, pp. 262–3. Napoleon's lime-pits are in the *Correspondance*, vol. V, p. 282. In the same volume, on p. 605, is the reference to plague as the enemy. For the upbeat assessment of Napoleon's achievement: *Correspondance*, vol. XXX, p. 97. The doctor metaphor is in Las Cases, *Mémorial*, p. 447. For Desgenettes's self-defence, see Boustany, vol. II, p. 263. Napoleon's letter to Laplace, back in Paris, is in *Correspondance*, vol. VI, p. 1. The same volume, pp. 88–9, is the source of the list of required reading for his troops. Napoleon's Egyptian nostalgia is recorded by the erratic, passionate but generally reliable General Baron Gourgaud, *Sainte-Hélène, journal inédit de 1815–1818* (Flammarion, Paris, 1889, 2 vols), vol. I, p. 67. A valuable overview is given by J. Christopher Herold, *Bonaparte in Egypt* (London, 1962). On the medical issues: Jean-François Lemaire, *Napoléon et la médecine* (Francis Burin, Paris, 1992).

CHAPTER 4   MENTIONED IN DISPATCHES

The adventures of the *Chevrette*, the *Beaulieu* and the *Doris* are recorded (with considerable bias) in Wm. Laird Clowes, *The Royal Navy, A History* (Sampson Low, Marston & Co., London, 1899), vol. 4, and Joseph Allen, *Battles of the British Navy* (Henry G. Bohn, London, 1852), vol. 2. Napoleon's *Correspondance*, vol. VII, pp. 259–60, gives his response to events. England abandoned by Europe: *Correspondance*, vol. VI, p. 578. The system of post ships is mentioned in *Correspondance*, vol. VI, pp. 532–3. For Napoleon's instructions to round up the usual suspects, see *Correspondance*, vol. VI, p. 113. Harsher punishment for assassins: *Correspondance*, vol. VI, p. 123, and rewards for the *Osiris*, the same volume, p. 454. 'Oh, Jean-Jacques, que ne peut-il voir ces hommes, qu'il appelle "les hommes de la nature!" Il frémirait de honte et de surprise d'avoir pu les admirer', *Lettres originales de l'armée française en Egypte*, Boustany, *Journals*, vol. X, p. 19. On the same theme: 'Je suis surtout dégoûté de Rousseau depuis que j'ai vu l'Orient. L'homme sauvage est un chien', Roederer, *Journal*, p. 165. Fears of code-breakers in *Correspondance*, vol. VI, p. 28. Cunning ploys, in the same volume, p. 498. For the letter to Kléber in Cairo, see *Correspondance*, vol. VI, p. 28. *Claude Chappe: notice biographique*, Ernest Jacquez (Alphonse Picard, Paris, 1893), p. 63, cites Chappe on bestriding distances. Food and power: Roederer, *Journal*, p. 107. 'Soldats! Vous avez remporté, en quinze jours, dix victoires, pris vingt-et-un drapeaux, cinquante-cinq pièces de canon ... quinze mille prisonniers, tué ou blessé plus de dix mille hommes', 26 April 1796, quoted in Aubry, *Ecrits*, p. 52. His secretary bullying the ship-builders: *Correspondance*, vol. VII, p. 340. The telegraph about the coup is in François Gautier, *L'Oeuvre de Claude Chappe* (Blais, Roy et cie, Paris, 1893), p. 69. 'Qu'on ne cherche pas dans le passé des exemples qui pourraient retarder votre marche! Rien, dans l'histoire, ne ressemble à la fin du XVIIIe siècle; rien, dans la fin du XVIIIe siècle, ne ressemble au moment actuel.' This Address to the 'Conseil des anciens' is in *Correspondance*, vol. VI, p. 1 and is testified to by Arnault, *Souvenirs*, vol. IV, p. 374. Napoleon reads about himself in the newspapers in *Correspondance*, vol. VI, p. 295. For Chappe's advertisement for the telegraph, see, Chappe l'Aîné, *Histoire de la télégraphie* (Chez l'auteur, Paris, 1824), pp. 177–8. (The original text,

written under the Restoration, is nominally addressed to the Czar.)
Jacquez, *Claude Chappe*, p. 59, cites the report from Rabaud Pommier
for the Committee of Public Safety, following Chappe's theories, on
rapid responses. Also Jacquez, *Claude Chappe*, p. 29, for a report by
the Committee of Public Safety describing the telegraph. The perils
of telegraphy, Jacquez, *Claude Chappe*, p. 28. 'Almost the speed of
light' is p. 59 of Jacquez, *Claude Chappe*. The message about Daunou
is on p. 13. Napoleon's warning to Chappe: 'Le citoyen Chappe,
ingénieur-télégraphe, ne pourra, sous quelque prétexte que ce soit,
même pour les détails de son service, faire aucune transmission, par
les télégraphes, que d'après l'ordre signé par le Premier Consul',
Correspondance, vol. VI, p. 465. Napoleon is feeling abandoned,
according to a letter to his brother Joseph, Masson, *Napoléon et les
femmes*, p. 45. The letter to General Gardanne is in *Correspondance*,
vol. VII, p. 190. The constitution 'torn up' in *Correspondance*, vol. VI,
p. 4. Request for textual analysis: *Correspondance*, vol. VII, p. 201.
Chateaubriand on killing Napoleon: *Mémoires d'outre-tombe* (Garnier-
Flammarion, Paris, 1964, ed. M. Levaillant), vol. I, part 2, p. 136.
The following references to Napoleon's literariness: *Mémoires d'outre-
tombe*, vol. I, part 2, pp. 302, 317, 320. Their first meeting is recorded
in *Mémoires d'outre-tombe*, vol. I, part 2, p. 81. Chateaubriand's praise
for Napoleon is cited by Jacques-Alain de Sédouy, *Chateaubriand,
un diplomate insolite* (Perrin, Paris, 1992), p. 36. Malevolent dispatches come up in *Mémoires d'outre-tombe*, vol. I, part 2, p. 124.
Chateaubriand's thoughts on his own literary career, *Mémoires d'outre-
tombe*, vol. I, part 2, p. 165. The depiction of Enghien in the same
volume, vol. I, part 2, p. 147, warning of too much technology, vol, I,
part 2, p. 175, and the sacred book, vol. I, part 2, p. 158. Napoleon's
if-onlys, Las Cases, *Mémorial*, pp. 564–5. For Chateaubriand's literary
critique, *De Buonaparté et des Bourbons et de la nécéssité de se rallier
à nos princes légitimes, pour le bonheur de la France et celui de l'Europe*,
p. 50. His comparisons of himself with Napoleon are in *Mémoires
d'outre-tombe*, vol. I, part 2, pp. 135 and 367. For his ingenious creation
theory, see *Essai sur les révolutions* and *Génie du christianisme* (Pléiade,
Paris, 1978, ed. Maurice Regard) pp. 555–6: 'Dieu a dû créer, et a
sans doute créé, le monde avec toutes les marques de vétusté et de
complément que nous lui voyons.' Chateaubriand cites Napoleon's
address to the Italian people (26 April 1796) in *Mémoires d'outre-
tombe*, vol. I, part 2, p. 328. See the same volume, p. 246, for Chateaubriand and kings. Jacquez, *Claude Chappe*, p. 30, cites Chappe's
letter about the telegraph. Napoleon criticizes idleness in *Correspondance*, vol. VI, p. 606. For Chateaubriand on the extraordinary adventurer and the boring prince, see *De Buonaparté et des Bourbons*,

pp. 61–2. His thoughts in Rome: *Mémoires d'outre-tombe*, vol. II, part 3, p. 481. Chateaubriand on Christianity and progress is cited in Sédouy, *Chateaubriand*, p. 188. The original telegraph message is in Chappe, *Histoire*, p. 20. The same text, pp. 200–1, for blood, sweat and tears ('Combien d'activités, de fatigues, de ressources il a fallu employer . . .'). Precipitation, Jacquez, *Claude Chappe*, p. 132, who also uses the phrase 'overexcitement of the brain'. The elegy for Chappe is taken from a letter to the *Journal de Paris* written by his brother, cited by Jacquez, *Claude Chappe*, pp. 72–3. The traditional Napoleon *vs* literature view is ably championed by Germaine de Staël in *Dix ans d'exil*. Also valuable: Ernest Daudet, *La police et les chouans sous le Consulat et l'Empire* (Plon, Paris, 1895) and, more recently, the special number of *Europe*, April–May 1969, 'Napoléon et la littérature'.

CHAPTER 5   THE THIRD MAN

Napoleon on dancing: *Lettres à Josephine* (Guy Le Prat, Paris, 1941, ed. Jacques Bourgeat), p. 161. His self-assessment is cited by Martel, *Mémoires*, p. 462. For *The Phenomenology of Mind*: Baillie's translation, p. xi. Hegel's comments on Napoleon, cited in Robert C. Solomon *In the Spirit of Hegel, A Study of G. W. F. Hegel's Phenomenology of Spirit* (Oxford University Press, 1983), p. 36. Russell on Hegel, *A History of Western Philosophy* (Allen and Unwin, London, 1961), pp. 701–15. Hegel's enthusiasm for Napoleon is in his letter to Niethammer, 1806, cited by Solomon, *In the Spirit of Hegel*, p. 35. Napoleon's Hegelian-sounding statement: 'mais de la plus grande et de la plus haute qui fût peut-être jamais: celle d'établir, de consacrer enfin l'empire de la raison, et le plein exercice, l'entière jouissance de toutes les facultés humaines! Et ici l'historien peut-être se trouvera réduit à devoir regretter qu'une telle ambition n'ait pas été accomplie, satisfaite! . . . En bien peu de mots voilà pourtant mon histoire', Las Cases, *Mémorial*, p. 245. For Fourier, see the *Oeuvres complètes*, especially *Le Nouveau Monde amoureux*, and Jonathan Beecher, *Charles Fourier, the Man and his World* (Berkeley and London, University of California Press, 1986) and Roland Barthes in *Sade, Fourier, Loyola*. Hegel's anti-Fourier statement, Solomon, *In the Spirit of Hegel*, p. 69. Masson's theory of 'nature' is in *Napoléon et les femmes* (Paul/Ollendorf, Paris, 1894), p. xxx. Same volume, p. 323 for the 'lover par excellence'. Nietzsche: see, for example, *The Gay Science*: 'He should receive credit some day for the fact that in Europe the *man* has again become master over the businessman and the philistine – and perhaps even over "woman" who has been pampered by Christianity and the enthusiastic spirit of the eighteenth century, and even more by "modern ideas"', Walter Kauffmann's translation (New York, Random House, 1974), p. 362. Napoleon's 'private parts', cited in Frank Richardson, *Napoleon, Bisexual Emperor* (Walter Kimber, London, 1972), p. 55. 'Bon-a-parte est bon-à-rien', see Bertrand, *Cahiers*, vol. III, p. 46. Napoleon's definition of love is given in his private *Journal*, 8 February 1791, quoted in Tomiche, p. 130. The long lonely winter nights, *Lettres à Josephine*, p. 120. Masson, *Napoléon et les femmes*, p. 208, for words to Madame Walewska. On p. 217: 'Je veux, entends-tu bien ce mot? je veux te forcer à m'aimer! J'ai fait revivre le nom de ta patrie: sa souche existe encore grace à moi. Je ferai plus encore.' Some subsequent writers, McGlynn for example, have tended to fuse Napoleon and Masson's commentary into one. The great distance to Poland, *Lettres à Josephine*, p. 124 (3 Jan 1807), the bad weather, p. 126. Christine Sutherland's hypothesis is in her *Marie Walewska, Napoleon's Greatest Love* (Weidenfeld and Nicolson, London, 1979), pp. 53–4. Napoleon's Hercules joke referred to the recent *Les amours secrètes de Bonaparte. Lettres sur la Corse*, 'Impotence': Masson, *Napoléon inconnu*, vol. II, p. 130. The anecdote about novel reading being rife on the *Orient* is Arnault's, *Souvenirs*, vol. IV, p. 81. 'Je me suis mis à lire des romans, et cette lecture m'intéressa vivement. J'essayai d'en écrire quelques-uns, cette occupation mit du vague dans mon imagination, elle se mêla aux connaissances positives que j'avais acquises, et souvent je m'amusais à rêver, pour mesurer ensuite mes rêveries au compas de mon raisonnement.' Mme de Rémusat, *Mémoires*, vol. I, p. 267. For the other Bonapartes' novels, see Gustave Davois, *Les Bonaparte littérateurs* (Edition bibliographique, Paris, 1909). Napoleon's critique is in Bertrand, *Cahiers*, vol. II, p. 216. *Clisson et Eugénie*: the full (although fragmentary) text can be found in Coelho, ed., *Oeuvres littéraires*, pp. 23–43 and 152–73. Christopher Frayling's *Napoleon Wrote Fiction* (Compton Press, Salisbury, 1972) gives a full translation. Clary's reaction to news of Napoleon's marriage: Masson, *Napoléon et les femmes*, p. 17. The 'Rencontre au Palais-Royal' is in Masson, *Napoléon inconnu*, vol. I, pp. 181–3. Talleyrand's barbed remark is in Mme de Rémusat, *Mémoires*, vol. I, pp. 117–18. Frayling (*Napoleon Wrote Fiction*, p. 35) translates the conclusion of the 'Rencontre' story as the more straightforwardly phallic, 'I did not want her to start feigning an honesty that I wished to prove she did not possess.' But Napoleon appears to be speaking of his own 'honnêteté' rather than hers. Paris and women: Masson, *Napoléon et les femmes*, p. 17. The *Dialogue on Love* is in Masson, *Napoléon inconnu*, vol. II, pp. 277–84. For Caulaincourt's reminiscence, see his *Memoirs 1812–1813* (Cassell, London, 1933, ed. Jean Hanoteau), pp. 597–8. Stendhal's *Promenades dans Rome* is cited in Martel, *Mémoires*, pp. 55–6 n. Napoleon's not running after women: Gourgaud, *Journal*, vol. II, p. 52. See Healey, *Rousseau et Napoléon* for theories of Napoleon's model. Bernardin de Saint-Pierre's *Paul et Virginie*, which Napoleon is still analysing during his last days on Saint Helena, would have been another influence. Napoleon's marginalia are in 'Napoléon, correcteur de style de Rousseau,' *Annales de la Société Jean-Jacques Rousseau*, vol. XXX, pp. 143–8. Abbreviated, but with taste: Las Cases, *Mémorial*, p. 317. Napoleon unable to put his pen down is from *Lettres à Josephine*, p. 30. The next quotations from the same source, pp. 35, 20, 25, 41, 22. 'Nous passons, nous vivons, nous mourons au milieu du merveilleux. Est-il étonnant que les prêtres, les astrologues, les charlatans aient profité de ce penchant, de cette circonstance singulière pour promener nos idées et les diriger au grai de leurs passions?' *Lettres*, p. 25. Inventing trouble for himself, *Lettres*, p. 26. Josephine as monster, *Lettres*, p. 33. 'Go on, mock', *Lettres*, p. 43. Napoleon as Clisson, *Lettres*, p. 34. The story about troops committing love-sick suicide is in Las Cases, *Mémorial*, p. 37. 'Farewell' speech: *Lettres*, p. 21. Power as a violin is from a conversation with Roederer, cited in Martel, *Mémoires*, pp. 315–16. Liberty is a woman: see the letter to Fesch, 8 February 1791, cited in Masson, *Napoléon inconnu*, vol. II, p. 196. Annihilating the rest of the world, *Lettres*, p. 40. The same volume, p. 161, for the comment on Alexander as mistress. The complaint about Monsieur T: *Lettres*, p. 140. The English at rest are on p. 104, *Lettres*. Stendhal on fiascos, *De l'amour*, chapter lx. Falling with Napoleon, *Vie de Henri Brulard* (Le Divan, Paris, ed. Henri Martineau), vol. I, p. 16. The incisive comments of Camille Paglia are taken from *Sexual Personae: Art and Decadence from Nefertiti to Emily Dickinson* (Penguin, Harmondsworth, 1990), p. 20. Napoleon's last letter to Josephine, *Lettres*, pp. 216–17. Milan Kundera's surprisingly clichéd account of the meeting between Napoleon and Goethe is in *Immortality* (Faber, London, 1991), pp. 60–3. Albert Bielschowsky's more sympathetic comments are in his *Life of Goethe* (Putnam, London, 1904), vol. II, p. 411. Talleyrand's *Mémoires 1754–1815* (Plon, Paris, 1957) have a chapter dedicated to 'l'entrevue d'Erfurt' from which I have taken many of Napoleon's lines. S. Sklower, *Entrevue de Napoléon Ier avec Goethe* (Ernest Vanackere, Lille, 1853) rectifies some of Talleyrand's omissions. For Goethe's remark on the seamless sleeve, see *Goethe: Conversations and Encounters* (Oswald Wolff, London, 1966, ed. David Luke and Robert Pick), pp. 71–2. Jorge Luis Borges' brilliant short story of the Chinese Emperor, 'The Wall and the Books', is in *Labyrinths* (Penguin, Harmondsworth, 1970). Mallarmé's aphorism, 'tout, au monde, existe pour aboutir à un livre', is in

'Quant au livre', *Poésies* (Poche, Paris, 1977), p. 223. For Napoleon's dream of universal empire, see Caulaincourt, *Memoirs*, p. 528. Same text, p. 487, for the idea of contentment everywhere. Gita May, *Stendhal and the Age of Napoleon* (Columbia, New York, 1977), usefully retraces the intersections of the two men.

CHAPTER 6   THE DEATH OF THE AUTHOR

Simon Leys, *La Mort de Napoléon* (Hermann, Paris, 1986), is a hauntingly believable fantasy. I have drawn on Vincent Cronin for the view of Fesch's behaviour. Napoleon's speech to the English people, Las Cases, *Mémorial*, p. 31. America *vs* England, also in Las Cases, p. 33. The theory about taking over in England: see Romain Rolland, 'Napoléon et la littérature', *Europe* (April–May 1969), p. 10. Napoleon's letter in atrocious English is printed on p. 178 of the *Mémorial*. Barry O'Meara's *Napoleon in Exile* (Simpkin and Marshall, London, 1822) coincides with Las Cases's on many points. The comparison with Egypt: Gourgaud, *Journal inédit*, vol. I, p. 67. Masson's idea that Las Cases's motives are obscure: *Around Saint Helena*, p. 84. Las Cases reports that Napoleon is 'enchanted', *Mémorial*, p. 45. His description of his conversations with Napoleon is in the preface to the first edition of the *Mémorial*, Las Cases, p. 20. Las Cases on rereading Napoleon, p. 37. Same source for Napoleon's life as a novel, p. 352. Why Napoleon cannot write, Gourgaud, *Journal*, vol. II, p. 110. Montholon's account of the great dictator is in his *Récits de Sainte-Hélène*, vol. I, p. 560. The image of Napoleon following an idea for ten or twelve hours: Bertrand, *Cahiers*, vol. III, p. 77. The same volume for insomniac nights, p. 133, and the real workhorse, p. 149. Howe's 'imaginary Saint Helena' crack is in Bertrand, vol. I, p. 41. Napoleon snapped back – correctly – that he had borrowed the observation from the Abbé de Pradt in *Histoire de l'ambassade dans le Grand-Duché de Varsovie*. For Napoleon on Troy, see Bertrand, *Cahiers*, vol. III, p. 67. The same volume, p. 61, for the enjoyment of his own work on Egypt. Las Cases, *Mémorial*, p. 220 for the line about daring to say he couldn't write; p. 163, for the lack of alternatives. The entry for 14 November 1815: Las Cases, pp. 97–8. Las Cases and his trio of exclamation marks, *Mémorial*, p. 65. Napoleon devouring books, Barry O'Meara, *Journal*, vol. I, p. 67. The review of Rousseau is in Las Cases, *Mémorial*, p. 429; final words, on p. 607 (the last line of Napoleon's farewell letter). Theories of suicide, Las Cases, *Mémorial*, p. 37. The suicide attempt is in Montholon, *Récits*, vol. II, p. 419. Las Cases's idea of the shrinking circle, *Mémorial*, p. 352. Cronin, *Napoleon*, p. 424, for the creative years. Gourgaud reports Napoleon's desperation to meet deadlines, *Journal*, vol. I, p. 431. Gourgaud gets scolded: vol. II, p. 289. That accursed Waterloo chapter: Gourgaud, vol. I, p. 203. Montholon on the anniversary: *Récits*, vol. II, pp. 404–5. The fatal campaign: Gourgaud, *Journal*, vol. II, p. 13. Las Cases, *Mémorial*, p. 352, for dictating's loss of charm. Napoleon's third-person style is mentioned by Las Cases, *Mémorial*, p. 99. Burning everything is in Bertrand, *Cahiers*, vol. III, p. 169. Napoleon's bad moments are recorded by Gourgaud, *Journal*, vol. I, p. 430. The fear of assassination in America: Las Cases, *Mémorial*, p. 601. Cowardice on Saint Helena: Gourgaud, *Journal*, vol. II, p. 210. The same volume, p. 266, for the new 'rosewater' war. Gourgaud's put-down of Las Cases: Gourgaud, *Journal*, vol. I, p. 313; p. 316 for Napoleon's response. Gourgaud's idea that he is the most tragic figure is in Gourgaud, *Journal*, vol. II, p. 57. Gourgaud's forgiveness: Gourgaud, *Journal*, vol. I, pp. 276 and 358. Working all morning: same volume, I, pp. 343–4. Napoleon prefers Montholon: Gourgaud, *Journal*, vol. I, pp. 533–4. The theme of ennui: Gourgaud, *Journal*, vol. I, pp. 408, 463, vol. II, p. 24. The metaphor of the author: Gourgaud, *Journal*, vol. I, p. 547. Masson's theory of Gourgaud's temporary delirium is in *Around Saint Helena*, p. 214. The fear of a war with Napoleon: Gourgaud, vol. II, p. 239. Las Cases, *Mémorial*, p. 22, has Napoleon's total author model: 'à chaque instant, notre pays se remplissait de trophées . . . exploits . . . victoires . . . l'arbitre des destinées universelles . . . Et pourtant tous ces travaux, tous ces prodiges, étaient l'ouvrage d'un seul homme.' Being the centre of everything, is in Gourgaud, *Journal*, vol. I, p. 344. Napoleon asks Las Cases to read his work: Las Cases, *Mémorial*, p. 25n. Anger at the confiscation of the Memorial: Gourgaud, *Journal*, vol. I, p. 322. Finally writing his novel: Las Cases, *Mémorial*, p. 310. Sparkling conversations: 'il n'en était aucune, sur quelque sujet que ce fût, qui n'étincelle çà et là d'expressions et de traits fort remarquables.' Cited in Tulard, *Napoléon à Sainte-Hélène* (Robert Laffont, Paris, 1981), p. 6. Tulard's book is an indispensable companion volume collecting generous selections of Las Cases, Gourgaud, Bertrand and Montholon. Napoleon's instruction to Bertrand: *Cahiers*, vol. III, p. 170. Bertrand's idea that Arnault would do a better job: vol. III, p. 69. The question of the elliptical is in Gourgaud, *Journal*, vol. II, p. 244. Bertrand, *Cahiers*, vol. III, pp. 184–5, for the poignant dialogues 'Is he here?' and 'Is O'Meara here?' The contents of the boat: Bertrand, *Cahiers*, vol. III, p. 172. Man is mud: Gourgaud, *Journal*, vol. II, p. 271. The discussion of points of grammar is in Gourgaud, *Journal*, vol. I, p. 457: 'La langue française n'est pas une langue faite. J'aurais bien dû la fixer.' For Hercules: Gourgaud, *Journal*, vol. I, p. 432. Las Cases,

Mémorial, p. 341, has the story about *Travels in Africa*. Napoleon on Constant: Bertrand, *Cahiers*, vol. III, p. 49. Sorry for Chateaubriand: Gourgaud, *Journal*, vol. I, p. 479. Gourgaud is also the source for the comparison with Jesus Christ, vol. II, pp. 226–7. The 'dose of arsenic' is in Montholon, vol. II, p. 412. The 'weapon of cowards': Gourgaud, *Journal*, vol. II, p. 218. Montholon's 'fear' that Napoleon was doomed: *Récits*, vol. II, p. 405. His theory about waiting and dissembling is in Gourgaud, *Journal*, vol. I, p. 223. Montholon writing the will is in Bertrand, *Cahiers*, vol. III, pp. 175–6. For the 'masked ball', see Gourgaud, *Journal*, vol. I, p. 79. The advice to be a charlatan: Gourgaud, *Journal*, vol. II, p. 223. For thoughts on death, see Bertrand, *Cahiers*, vol. III, p. 105. Napoleon's prophetic soul can be found in Gourgaud, *Journal*, vol. I, p. 440. Bertrand, *Cahiers*, vol. III, p. 195, gives the name of the son conversation. Napoleon speaking of his son: Gourgaud, vol. II, p. 13. Julia Blackburn, *The Emperor's Last Island* (Secker and Warburg, London, 1991), casts a novelist's eye over Saint Helena. Other useful eye-witness accounts: *In Napoleon's Shadow* (Proctor Jones Press, San Francisco, 1998) by Louis Joseph Marchand, the faithful valet. For the pathologist's view, François Antommarchi, *Les derniers moments de Napoléon* (Barrois l'Aîné, Paris, 1825). Elizabeth Balcombe Abell (the young 'Betsy'), *Recollections of the Emperor Napoleon* (John Murray, London, 1844). Among the assassination theorists, Sven Forshufvud, *Who killed Napoleon?* (Hutchinson, London, 1962) and Ben Weider and Sven Forshufvud, *Assassination at St Helena Revisited* (Wiley, New York, 1978), stand out.

EPITAPHS

Arnault: 'Après les lui avoir entendu analyser, je n'y compris plus rien, et je crois même ne plus les comprendre.' *Souvenirs*, vol. IV, pp. 100–1. Napoleon's inability to understand himself – 'moi, qui, très souvent, aurais été embarrassé d'affirmer avec vérité toute ma pleine et entière pensée' – Las Cases, *Mémorial*, p. 585. For becoming a turnip or carrot, see Gourgaud, vol. II, p. 22. The same volume for hammering a nail into your head, p. 271. Looking forward to his death: Las Cases, *Mémorial*, p. 10 (cited by Tulard). The 'fable convenue' of history is on p. 585 of the same. Examples of Napoleon-denial include Archbishop Whately, *Historic Doubts Relative to Napoleon Bonaparte* (in *The Pamphleteer*, Valpy, London, 1826, vol. XXVII, pp. 475–96) and Jean-Baptiste Pérès, *Comme quoi Napoléon n'a jamais existé ou grand erratum source d'un nombre infini d'errata à noter dans l'histoire du XIXe siècle* (L'Edition bibliographique, Paris, 1909). Hugo's idea that 'Les sabreurs ont fini, c'est le tour des penseurs',

Les Misérables (Pléiade, Paris, 1960), book 2, chapter 17, 'Faut-il trouver bon Waterloo', p. 388. The 'beautiful funeral': 'Oh, là, nous te ferons de belles funerailles' from 'Ode à la colonne'. The recollection of 1840 is in *Choses vues: souvenirs, journaux, cahiers 1830–46* (Gallimard, Paris, 1972). The Goncourt brothers' recollection of the Hugo funeral is in their *Journal*, entry for 31 May 1885. Other important works on the aftermath include Maurice Descotes, *La Légende de Napoléon et les écrivains français au XIXe siècle* (Minard, Paris, 1967) and Peter Geyl's *Napoleon: For and Against* (Penguin, Harmondsworth, 1976, originally published 1949). Lucien Regenbogen, *Napoléon a dit* (Les Belles Lettres, Paris, 1996) is a small treasure-trove, as is the classic *Vie de Napoléon* (Gallimard, Paris, 1930), probably by André Malraux.

Tombeau de Napoléon au
Invalides.

Index